COMMON CORE BASICS

Building Essential Test Readiness Skills

WRITING

Mc Graw Hill Education

Bothell, WA · Chicago, IL · Columbus, OH · New York, NY

mheonline.com

Copyright © 2014 McGraw-Hill Education

All rights reserved. No part of this publication may be
reproduced or distributed in any form or by any means, or
stored in a database or retrieval system, without the
prior written consent of McGraw-Hill Education,
including, but not limited to, network storage or
transmission, or broadcast for distance learning.

Send all inquiries to:
McGraw-Hill Education
8787 Orion Place
Columbus, OH 43240

ISBN: 978-0-07-657522-0
MHID: 0-07-657522-5

Printed in the United States of America.

6 7 8 9 RHR 18 17 16 15 14

Contents

To the Student

Common Core Basics: Building Essential Test Readiness Skills, Writing will help you learn or strengthen the skills you need when you take any Common Core State Standards-aligned writing test. To answer some questions, you will need to focus on sentence structure, grammar, and mechanics. To answer other questions, you will need to concentrate on the organization of sentences within a paragraph. These skills are also important when you are asked to write short or extended response essays.

Before beginning the lessons in this book, take the **Pretest**. This test will help you identify which skill areas you need to concentrate on most. Use the chart at the end of the Pretest to pinpoint the types of questions you have answered incorrectly and to determine which skills you need to work on. You may decide to concentrate on specific areas of study or to work through the entire book. It is highly recommended that you do work through the whole book to build a strong foundation in the core areas in which you will be tested.

Common Core Basics: Building Essential Test Readiness Skills, Writing is divided into eight chapters:

- **Chapter 1: Sentence Basics** instructs you in the fundamentals of a sentence, including the parts of a simple sentence, types of sentences, and noun and pronoun usage in sentences.

- **Chapter 2: Verbs** teaches you types of verbs, different verb tenses, and subject-verb agreement.

- **Chapter 3: Modifiers** teaches you how to distinguish between adjectives and adverbs, how to use these modifiers, and how to work with phrases as modifiers.

- **Chapter 4: Mechanics** teaches you the rules of capitalization and punctuation. You will learn how to spell possessives, contractions, homophones, and affixes. You will also learn basic spelling patterns and generalizations.

- **Chapter 5: Sentence Structure** shows you how to combine ideas in sentences. You will also learn about writing effective sentences and choosing appropriate style and diction.

- **Chapter 6: Text Structure** teaches you the basics of paragraph structure, including how to write effective topic sentences. You will learn about tone and diction and order of importance, time order, cause-and-effect order, and comparison-and-contrast order.

- **Chapter 7: The Writing Process** introduces you to prewriting, writing, and revising and editing.

- **Chapter 8: Text Types and Purposes** describe the three main types of writing. You will learn to write an effective argument, an informative/explanatory text, and a narrative.

In addition, *Common Core Basics: Building Essential Test Readiness Skills, Writing* has a number of features designed to familiarize you with and begin to prepare you for writing tests.

- The **Chapter Opener** provides an overview of the chapter content and a goal-setting activity.

- **Lesson Objectives** state what you will be able to accomplish after completing the lesson.

- **Skills** list the Core Skills and Reading Skills that are taught and applied to the lesson content.

- **Vocabulary** critical for understanding lesson content is listed at the start of every lesson. All bold words in the text can be found in the Glossary.

- The **Key Concept** summarizes the content that is the focus of the lesson.

- In the lessons, **Core Skills** and **Reading Skills** are emphasized with direct instruction and practice in the context of the lesson. The Core Skills align to the Common Core State Standards.

- In the lessons, special features presenting **21st Century Skills**, **Technology Connections**, **Workplace Connections**, and **Research It** activities will help you activate higher-level thinking skills using real-world application of these skills.

- **Think about Writing** questions check your understanding of the content throughout the lesson as you read.

- **Write to Learn** activities provide you with a chance to practice the writing skills you have learned in the lesson.

- End-of-lesson **Vocabulary Review** checks your understanding of important lesson vocabulary, while the **Skill Review** checks your understanding of the content and skills presented in the lesson.

- **Skill Practice** and **Writing Practice** exercises appear at the end of every lesson to help you apply your learning of content and skill fundamentals.

- The **Chapter Review** and end-of-chapter **Writing Practice** tests your understanding of the chapter content and provides an opportunity to strengthen your writing skills.

- **Check Your Understanding** charts allow you to check your knowledge of the skills you have practiced.

- The **Answer Key** explains the answers for questions in the book.

- The **Glossary** and **Index** contain lists of key terms found throughout the book and make it easy to review important skills and concepts.

After you have worked through the book, take the **Posttest** to see how well you have learned the skills presented in this book.

Good luck with your studies! Keep in mind that knowing how to use grammar correctly and how to write well will help you succeed on any writing test and in other future writing tasks, whether at school, at home, or in the workplace.

Writing, Part I

The Pretest is a guide to using this book. It will allow you to preview the skills and concepts you will be working on in the lessons. The Pretest will also give you a sense of what areas of writing you need the most support in. It is intended to be a check of your current level of knowledge and understanding that will serve as a starting point as you work through the lessons and develop your writing skills.

The Pretest has two parts. Part I consists of 25 multiple-choice questions that test the grammar, usage, and organization skills covered in this book. Part II contains an essay writing activity.

Directions: Choose the <u>one best answer</u> to each question. Some of the sentences contain errors in organization, sentence structure, usage, or mechanics. A few sentences, however, may be correct as written. Read the sentences carefully and then answer the questions based on them. For each question, choose the answer that would result in the most effective writing of the sentence or sentences.

When you have completed the test, check your work with the answers and explanations on page 9. Use the evaluation chart on page 10 to determine which areas you need to study the most.

Writing

1. Every four years in the summer, the presidential candidates travel East to west trying to earn support for their campaigns.

   Which correction should be made to this sentence?

   A. change summer to Summer
   B. change presidential to Presidential
   C. change East to east
   D. change west to West

2. At the yard sale, everything on the table were sold.

   Which correction should be made to this sentence?

   A. change were to was
   B. change everything to everythings
   C. change sold to selled
   D. change yard to yard's

3. The carpenter called to her apprentice "Tony, will you be able to work late tonight?"

   Which is the best way to write the underlined portion of the sentence? If the original is the best way, choose option A.

   A. to her apprentice "Tony, will you
   B. to her apprentice, "Tony, will you
   C. to her apprentice. "Tony, will you
   D. to her apprentice "Tony. Will you

4. A recent weather study of thunderstorms and tornadoes show that parts of the Midwest are frequently hit by severe storms.

   Which is the best way to write the underlined portion of the sentence? If the original is the best way, choose option A.

   A. weather study of thunderstorms and tornadoes show
   B. weather study of thunderstorms, and tornadoes show
   C. weather study of thunderstorms and tornadoes shows
   D. whether study of thunderstorms and tornadoes show

5. Either John or his sister pick up the children whenever their parents work the second shift.

   Which correction should be made to this sentence?

   A. replace his with him
   B. change pick to picks
   C. replace their with they're
   D. change parents to parents'

6. I usually listen to music, but I run around the pond.

   Which is the best way to write the underlined portion of the sentence? If the original is the best way, choose option A.

   A. music, but
   B. music although
   C. music so
   D. music while

Writing

7. Ho Kye and his wife were upset when they <u>learned that they forgot their</u> travelers' checks.

   Which is the best way to write the underlined portion of the sentence? If the original is the best way, choose option A.

   A. learned that they forgot their
   B. had learned that they forgot their
   C. learned that they had forgotten their
   D. learned that they forgetted their

8. The best mechanic in the shop really likes repairing transmissions and to tune up the largest trucks on the road.

   Which correction should be made to this sentence?

   A. change <u>likes</u> to <u>to like</u>
   B. change <u>really</u> to <u>real</u>
   C. change <u>repairing</u> to <u>repaired</u>
   D. change <u>to tune up</u> to <u>tuning up</u>

9. The managers have divided the work equally between you and she.

   Which correction should be made to this sentence?

   A. change <u>have divided</u> to <u>has divided</u>
   B. change <u>equally</u> to <u>equal</u>
   C. replace <u>between</u> with <u>among</u>
   D. replace <u>she</u> with <u>her</u>

10. Boston will have no public transportation <u>tomorrow. Because</u> bus drivers are going on strike.

    Which is the best way to write the underlined portion of the sentences? If the original is the best way, choose option A.

    A. tomorrow. Because
    B. tomorrow; because
    C. tomorrow because
    D. tomorrow, because

11. The car starts only on dry <u>days, therefore, we</u> leave it in the garage on rainy days.

    Which is the best way to write the underlined portion of the sentence? If the original is the best way, choose option A.

    A. days, therefore, we
    B. days; therefore, we
    C. days therefore, we
    D. days therefore; we

12. The speaker was <u>interesting conversational and informative.</u>

    Which is the best way to write the underlined portion of the sentence? If the original is the best way, choose option A.

    A. interesting conversational and informative.
    B. interesting conversational, and informative.
    C. interesting, conversational and informative.
    D. interesting, conversational, and informative.

Writing

Directions: Questions 13 through 20 refer to the following memo.

To: All SoftCo Employees
From: Human Resources Department
Re: Family Picnic

(A)

1   Come and join us for food, fun, and festivities. (2) As a result of the park's new water rides, this year's party promises to be the best party of all! (3) The party location is the same as in past years: Oakwood Heights Amusement Park. (4) Grown-ups and children will enjoy both the amusement rides and the musical entertainment. (5) Besides making sundaes, you will be able to toast marshmallows for a special treat.

(B)

6   He will barbecue hamburgers, hot dogs, and veggie burgers. (7) Nick Jenkins of the accounting department will be in charge of the barbecue. (8) In addition to barbecue, there will also be potato salad, coleslaw, corn on the cob, and watermelon.

(C)

9   Maria Alvarez, the company president, is making vast quantities of her special broccoli pasta. (10) There will be various ice creams and sauces so you can make your own sundaes for dessert.

(D)

11   This year we have more to celebrate than ever before. (12) SoftCo has always made a point of celebrating with our employees to show how much we appreciate them. (13) Thanks to your hard work, the company has enjoyed its biggest earnings this past year. (14) SoftCo appreciates your dedication. (15) We hope that our annual party helps us express our appreciation. (16) In order to help us plan food and activities for the barbecue, please let us know if you plan to attend. (17) Please respond to this invitation by Monday, August 19. (18) We hope to see you on Saturday, August 24!

---

13. Which sentence would be most effective if inserted at the beginning of paragraph A?

    A. Oakwood Heights Amusement Park has the biggest roller coasters in the whole state!
    B. SoftCo is hosting its annual employee party for all employees and their families on Saturday, August 24.
    C. The Hopping Hippo is the premier water ride at the park.
    D. SoftCo is a company that manufactures beds and pillows

14. Sentence 5: Besides making sundaes, you will be able to toast marshmallows for a special treat.

    Which revision should be made to the placement of sentence 5?

    A. Move sentence 5 to follow sentence 10.
    B. Begin a new paragraph with sentence 5.
    C. Move sentence 5 to the end of paragraph D.
    D. Remove sentence 5.

Writing

15. Which revision would improve the effectiveness of paragraph A?

   A. Move sentence 1 to the end of paragraph A.
   B. Move sentence 2 to follow sentence 4.
   C. Begin a new paragraph with sentence 4.
   D. Remove sentence 3.

16. Sentence 6: He will barbecue hamburgers, hot dogs, and veggie burgers.

Which revision should be made to the placement of sentence 6?

   A. Move sentence 6 to follow sentence 7.
   B. Move sentence 6 to the end of paragraph A.
   C. Move sentence 6 to the beginning of paragraph C.
   D. Remove sentence 6.

17. Which of the following sentences would be most effective if inserted at the beginning of paragraph B?

   A. Barbecue chicken is my favorite food.
   B. Many of the employees at SoftCo are vegetarians.
   C. SoftCo will provide all of the food for the barbecue.
   D. The president of SoftCo is an effective leader and a fantastic cook.

18. Which revision would improve the effectiveness of paragraph D?

   A. Move sentence 11 to the end of paragraph C.
   B. Move sentence 11 to follow sentence 12.
   C. Remove sentence 13.
   D. Remove sentence 14.

19. Which revision would improve the effectiveness of the memo?

   A. Join paragraphs A and B.
   B. Join paragraphs B and C.
   C. Move paragraph C to follow paragraph D.
   D. Move paragraph A to follow paragraph B.

20. Which additional revision would further improve the effectiveness of the memo?

Begin a new paragraph with

   A. sentence 3.
   B. sentence 8.
   C. sentence 13.
   D. sentence 16.

Writing

21. This application must be completed <u>before beginning to work here.</u>

    Which is the best way to write the underlined portion of the sentence? If the original is the best way, choose option (A).

    A. before beginning to work here
    B. before new employees begin to work here
    C. before working begins here
    D. before working at the beginning

22. Mr. Rodriguez gave the delivery boy a letter as he passed by.

    Which correction should be made to this sentence?

    A. change <u>gave</u> to <u>gives</u>
    B. replace <u>he</u> with <u>they</u>
    C. replace <u>he</u> with <u>the boy</u>
    D. replace <u>passed</u> to <u>past</u>

23. Byron went to cooking class so that <u>the meals that are cooked by him would be meals that taste much better.</u>

    Which is the best way to write the underlined portion of the sentence? If the original is the best way, choose option (A).

    A. the meals that are cooked by him would be meals that taste much better
    B. he could cook better-tasting meals
    C. the meals that he could cook would be better tasting meals
    D. he could taste meals made by better cooks

24. The frozen pizzas are for the boys that are in the freezer.

    Which is the most effective rewrite of this sentence?

    A. The pizzas, frozen for the boys; are in the freezer.
    B. The pizzas are frozen for the boys that are in the freezer.
    C. The frozen pizzas that are in the freezer are for the boys.
    D. The pizzas are frozen for the boys; that are in the freezer.

25. She would have been happier if she <u>will choose</u> a better school.

    Which is the best way to write the underlined portion of the sentence? If the original is the best way, choose option (A).

    A. will choose
    B. chosen
    C. choose
    D. had chosen

Writing, Part II

Part II of the Pretest is designed to find out how well you write.

Essay Directions:

Look at the box on the following page. In the box is your assigned topic.

Write a short essay on the assigned topic. Keep track of how long it takes you to complete your essay. You should take only 45 minutes to write your essay.

Keep in mind as you write that your essay should have the following:

- A well-focused main idea

- Clear progression of ideas and helpful transitions

- Specific development of ideas that are clearly connected to the main idea

- Control of usage, sentence structure, word choice, punctuation, and spelling

Writing

> **TOPIC**
>
> What is your favorite movie?
>
> In your essay, state your favorite movie. Explain why it is your favorite. Use your personal observations, experience, and knowledge.

Part II is a test to determine how well you can use written language to explain your ideas.

In preparing your essay, you should take the following steps:

- Read the **DIRECTIONS** and the **TOPIC** carefully.

- Plan your essay before you write. Use scratch paper to make any notes and write down any important ideas.

- After you finish writing your essay, reread what you have written and make any changes that will improve your essay.

- Make sure your essay is long enough to develop the topic adequately.

Answer Key

1. **C.** Do not capitalize names of directions when they refer to general directions.

2. **A.** *Everything* is a singular noun, so the verb form is also singular.

3. **B.** Use a comma to set off a direct quote.

4. **C.** The subject of the sentence is the singular noun *study*. Because the verb must agree in number with the subject, *shows* is correct.

5. **B.** When a compound subject is joined by *either . . . or*, the verb should agree with the closer part of the subject, in this case the singular noun *sister*.

6. **D.** The conjunction *but* is incorrect since the relationship between the two clauses is not one of contrast. Instead, the conjunction *while* correctly shows that the actions in the clauses are happening at the same time.

7. **C** In this sentence, two actions occurred in the past. To show that forgetting the travelers' checks occurred first, the past perfect tense should be used for that action and the simple past for the action that followed it.

8. **D.** To have parallel construction with *repairing*, *to tune up* must change to *tuning up*.

9. **D.** Since the pronouns are objects of the preposition *between*, the object pronoun *her* should be used instead of the subject pronoun *she*.

10. **C.** *Because bus drivers are going on strike* is not a complete sentence. C turns the fragment into a dependent clause that is written correctly.

11. **B.** *Therefore* is a conjunctive adverb between two complete thoughts. It must be preceded by a semicolon (at the end of the first complete thought) and is usually followed by a comma.

12. **D.** Commas separate the items in a series of three or more.

13. **B.** B is a good topic sentence for the paragraph because it is the main idea that all the other sentences in the paragraph tell about.

14. **A.** Sentence 5 talks about sundaes, so it should move to the paragraph that talks about ice cream and sauces and follow the sentence about sundaes.

15. **B.** Sentence 2 gives more information about the water rides that employees might enjoy at the park. It should follow sentence 4, which first talks about the rides.

16. **A** Sentence 6 gives more details about the information that is in sentence 7; therefore, sentence 6 should follow sentence 7.

17. **C.** C is a good topic sentence for the paragraph because it is the main idea that all the other sentences in the paragraph tell about.

18. **B.** Sentence 11 extends the idea of celebrating, which was introduced in sentence 12; therefore, sentence 11 should follow sentence 12.

19. **B.** Paragraph C continues to tell about the food at the company gathering and should, therefore, be joined to paragraph B.

20. **D.** Sentence 16 introduces a new main idea so it should begin a new paragraph.

21. **B.** The underlined phrase is a dangling modifier. There is no noun or pronoun in the sentence for it to refer to. It actually says that the application is beginning to work here. B adds the necessary subject, *new employees*.

22. **C.** You cannot tell whether *he* refers to the boy or to Mr. Rodriguez. C makes the pronoun reference clear.

23. **B.** The underlined phrase is wordy and repetitious. B keeps the meaning without being too wordy.

24. **C.** The phrase *that are in the freezer* is misplaced. It should be placed next to the word it modifies, *pizzas*. The original sentence implies that the boys are in the freezer.

25. **D.** This sentence contains a dependent clause beginning with the conditional word *if*. Since the verb form in the first part of the sentence is *would have been*, the *if* clause must be in the past perfect—*had chosen*.

Part 1: Evaluation Chart

Check Your Understanding

On the following chart, circle the number of any question you answered incorrectly. Next to each group of question numbers, you will see the pages you can study to learn how to answer the questions correctly. Pay particular attention to studying skill areas in which you missed half or more of the questions.

Skill Area	Item Number	Study Pages
Nouns and pronouns	9	24–37
Verb and verb tenses	7	44–59
Subject-verb agreement	2, 4, 5	60–69
Modifying phrases	24	86–91
Capitalization	1	98–107
Punctuation	3, 12	108–117
Combine ideas in sentences	6, 10, 11	136–145
Write effective sentences	7, 8, 21, 22, 25	146–155
Style and diction	23	156–165
Paragraph structure and topic sentences	13, 14, 15, 16, 17, 18, 19, 20	172–179

Writing

Part II Evaluation Guidelines

If possible, give your instructor your essay to evaluate. You will find his or her objective opinion helpful in deciding whether you are ready to begin preparing for a writing test. If this is not possible, have another student evaluate your essay. If you cannot find another student to help you, review your essay yourself. If you do this, it is usually better to let your essay sit for a few days before you evaluate it. This way you will have similar views as someone reading your essay for the first time. No matter which way you review your work, use the checklist on the next page to guide you.

After you have evaluated your essay using the checklist, look at the number you checked for each question. Pay attention to the questions where you checked a 2 or a 1—these scores indicate that you need some extra practice in certain writing skills. Studying the following sections will help you to raise your score:

1. If you had trouble answering the question that is asked in the writing prompt, pay attention to pages 172–179.

2. If you had trouble organizing your ideas, pay attention to Chapter 6.

3. If you had trouble supporting your main idea with details or examples, pay attention to pages 172–179.

4. If you had trouble writing words and sentences correctly and varying sentence structure and word choice, pay attention to Chapters 1–5.

If possible, talk to your instructor, another student, or a friend about your writing. Together you will be able to identify your current writing strengths as well as any weaknesses. Based on this combined evaluation, review the sections in this book that will help you most to improve your writing.

Writing

ESSAY SCORING CHECKLIST

A. Does your essay address the question in the writing prompt with a clear main idea and stay on topic?

☐ **1.** No, my essay does not answer the question, has a weak main idea, and does not stay on topic.

☐ **2.** My essay has a clear main idea that addresses the question, but it also includes some points that are not directly related to the main idea.

☐ **3.** Yes, my essay has a clear main idea that addresses the question, and all subtopics connect to the main idea.

☐ **4.** Yes, my essay has a strong main idea that addresses the question, and subtopics that reveal thoughtful connections to the main idea.

B. Are the ideas in your essay well organized, with enough subtopics and transitions?

☐ **1.** No, the ideas in my essay are not in any order, and there are no subtopics or transitions.

☐ **2.** My essay shows some planning, but it does not contain enough subtopics and transitions.

☐ **3.** Yes, the ideas in my essay are logically connected with more than one subtopic and a few transitions.

☐ **4.** Yes, my essay is well organized with multiple subtopics and effective transitions.

C. Do the paragraphs in your essay contain details that support the main idea, and are connections between details and the main idea stated clearly?

☐ **1.** No, many of the paragraphs in my essay contain details that don't support the main idea, or many of the paragraphs don't have any details at all.

☐ **2.** Many of the paragraphs contain sufficient supporting details, but the connections between details and the main idea are not stated.

☐ **3.** Yes, the paragraphs in my essay contain relevant and concrete details, and the connections between details and the main idea are stated but simple.

☐ **4.** Yes, the paragraphs in my essay contain excellent relevant details, and the connections between details and the main idea are fully explained.

D. Do the sentences in your essay display variety in word choice and structure as well as correct usage, punctuation, and spelling?

☐ **1.** No, the sentences in my essay are not worded correctly or varied in structure, and most of them contain errors in usage, punctuation, and spelling.

☐ **2.** The sentences in my essay contain appropriate but vague words, basic sentence structure, some errors in punctuation and spelling, and many errors in usage.

☐ **3.** Yes, the sentences in my essay vary somewhat in structure, include appropriate and specific words, and contain only a few small errors in usage, punctuation, and spelling.

☐ **4.** Yes, the sentences in my essay display excellent word choice, great variety in structure, and almost no errors in usage.

UNIT 1

Standard English Conventions

Sentence Basics

Read the following note:

Please put that over there.

The note is unclear. What is meant by *that*? Where is *over there*?

Now read these two sentences, noting the end punctuation marks:

John ran out the door!

John ran out the door?

These sentences express two very different feelings. What feeling was the writer trying to express in each sentence?

These are just two examples of why it is important to write clearly.

In this chapter you will learn about the fundamentals of a sentence. These basic skills are the building blocks that will help your writing progress. As you work through the chapter, think about how the skills and knowledge you are learning will help you become a stronger writer.

Here is what you will learn about in this chapter:

Lesson 1.1: Sentences

Can you name the four types of sentences? You will learn about them in this lesson.

Lesson 1.2: Nouns and Pronouns

What's the difference between a common noun and a proper noun? When do you use the pronouns *I* and *me*? What is an antecedent? What happens when your writing doesn't include a clear antecedent?

Answering these questions is the first step to mastering the writing process.

Goal Setting

Improving your writing skills will help you to communicate better. If you write to someone you have never met, such as a potential employer, he or she can only know who you are by the words you choose and the way you arrange them into sentences. The best way to improve your writing is by practicing. In a notebook, start a journal in which you write every day. You can write about anything that interests you: a story in the news, the weather, or your future. Think about the ways that improving your writing skills can improve your life.

What kinds of writing do you do everyday—e-mail, journal, job applications?

school writing homework.

Why do you think it is important to write clearly?

So People can understand what you writen.

What would you like to learn about writing?

To learn how to write good without makeing a misstake.

Sentences

KEY CONCEPT: A sentence is a group of words that contains a subject and a predicate and that expresses a complete thought.

Choose the complete sentence.

1. Tomás, Juan, and John.
2. Ran through the grass.
3. He slept for 10 hours.
4. The cuddly white puppy.

Lesson Objectives

You will be able to

• Identify sentences

• Identify different types of sentences

Skills

• **Core Skill:** Apply Knowledge of Language

• **Reading Skill:** Compare and Contrast

Vocabulary

determine
fragment
identify
predicate
sentence
subject

Complete Sentences

A **sentence** is a group of words that contains a subject and a predicate and that expresses a complete thought. When you write a complete sentence, your readers will understand your ideas clearly.

Subjects and Predicates

The **subject** of a sentence is whom or what the sentence is about. Evaluate the following sentence to determine whom or what it is about.

The woman bought two tickets to the concert.

This sentence is about the woman. Therefore, the subject is *the woman*.

The **predicate** of a sentence tells what the subject is or what it does. Everything in the sentence that is not part of the subject is part of the predicate. Determine the predicate in the sample sentence above.

You should have **identified**, or named, the predicate as the words *bought two tickets to the concert*.

Besides having a subject and a predicate, a sentence must also express a complete thought. After you have read a sentence you should not be asking yourself questions such as *Who did it? What happened?*

The sample sentence below has a subject and a predicate and expresses a complete thought.

| The young woman | bought two tickets to Friday's rock concert. |
| SUBJECT | PREDICATE |

COMPARE AND CONTRAST

When you think about how two or more things are alike, you are making **comparisons**. When you **contrast** two or more things, you think about how they are different. Writers often use comparison and contrast to give their writing more interest and to help readers visualize what they are reading about.

Some texts compare two subjects in one sentence. Other texts make comparisons in two adjacent sentences by describing one subject in the first sentence and the second subject in the following sentence. Still other texts use a separate paragraph to describe each subject.

To compare and contrast, ask yourself: *How are these two people (or places or things) alike? How are they different?*

Read the following paragraph about Inez and Alma. How are they alike and different?

(1) Inez and Alma are sisters. (2) Inez takes pleasure in spending her leisure time relaxing with an interesting book, talking to friends, or even taking an afternoon nap. (3) Alma prefers taking a walk, riding her bicycle, or swimming numerous laps in the local pool. (4) Both girls enjoy cooking and baking.

Sentence 1 makes a general statement that tells us that the girls are sisters. The comparison is made in the next two adjacent sentences. Sentence 2 describes what Inez enjoys doing, while sentence 3 describes how Alma likes to spend her time. We can compare the information in the two sentences to learn how the two girls are different. Sentence 4 tells how the girls are alike.

A group of words must pass three tests in order to be a complete sentence:

1. It must have a subject that tells whom or what the sentence is about.

2. It must have a predicate that tells what the subject is or does.

3. It must express a complete thought.

If you read a sentence and find yourself asking questions such as *Who did that? What happened?* or *What is this about?* it is probably not a complete sentence.

Read the following examples and **determine** [decide] if each is a complete sentence. If it is not, rewrite it as a complete sentence in a notebook.

I almost missed the train.

Going to sleep late.

That familiar song on his guitar.

I read for hours.

Simple and Compound Subjects

The simple sentence is the most basic form of the complete sentence. It has at least one subject and one predicate.

The subject of a sentence tells whom or what the sentence is about. The **simple subject** is a part of the sentence's subject. It tells what or whom the sentence is about but does not include the descriptive words that are part of the subject.

Look at the following example and identify the simple subject.

An angry, thin man	walked up the front steps.
SUBJECT	PREDICATE

The simple subject is *man*. It tells whom the sentence is about.

Sometimes the subject includes more than one word. A subject that has more than one part connected with words, such as *and* or *or*, is called a **compound subject**. In the following sentence, the compound subject is *my brother and his wife*.

My brother and his wife rented a car for the day.

Verbs and Verb Phrases

Every predicate has a **verb** that tells what the subject is or does. A verb is the most important part of the predicate. A verb does not include the descriptive words found in the predicate. Sometimes the verb shows action, as in the following sentence.

Mary Rios	walked onto the stage.
SUBJECT	PREDICATE

The verb is *walked*. It tells what the subject, Mary Rios, does.

Often a **verb phrase**, a verb made up of two or more words, is needed to express an action or state of being. This is a way of showing whether the action or state of being occurs in the past, present, or future. In the following sentence, the words *had waited* form the verb phrase.

The photographer	had waited	patiently for the bear to wake up.
SUBJECT	VERB	

THINK ABOUT WRITING

Directions: Underline the simple or compound subject once. Then underline the verb twice.

Example: The crisp, autumn <u>leaves and berries</u> <u><u>had crunched</u></u> under our feet.

1. The team's manager should win an award.
2. Everyone has ordered something different to eat.
3. Andrej searched his pockets for his car keys.
4. Mr. and Mrs. Hastings complained about the defective lamp.
5. The old run-down bus pulled slowly out of the station.

Core Skill
Apply Knowledge of Language

Complete sentences and sentence fragments both give information, but sentences give more complete information. There are time when using a sentence fragment is okay:

- spoken conversation

- informal communication such as text messages

- notes or reminders

In formal communications, it is almost always better to use complete sentences. Read the list of situations. Decide if you should use only complete sentences or if sentence fragments are okay. Write in a notebook why you made each choice.

An e-mail to your boss

An essay on a test

An online conversation with a friend

Fragments

A group of words that does not include a subject and a predicate and does not express a complete thought is called a fragment. A **fragment** is an incomplete sentence. Look at the following group of words and determine if it is a sentence or a fragment.

> The party last night.

The group of words has a subject, *party*, but it is missing a predicate. The sentence does not express a complete thought. What is it about the party last night? What happened? What was it like? If we add the predicate *was very crowded*, the sentence now expresses a complete thought.

> The party last night was very crowded.

Other fragments can result when a group of words begins with a connecting word such as *because*, *when*, or *if*, and the thought is not completed.

> If you leave on the earlier train.

This group of words does not tell what will happen if you leave on the earlier train. An easy way to fix the fragment is to combine it with another sentence.

> If you leave on the earlier train, I will drive you to the station.

Now the sentence is complete. The subject is *I* and the predicate is *will drive you to the station*.

When you compare and contrast, you think about how two or more things are alike or different.

Remember, all complete sentences are alike because they have a subject and a predicate and express a complete thought. But the type of sentences can be different. A sentence can be a command, a question, a statement, or an exclamation.

Compare and contrast the types of sentences below. How are they alike? How are they different?

That was the best movie I've ever seen!

The movie started at 8:00.

Where should we sit?

Buy some popcorn.

THINK ABOUT WRITING

Directions: Read each group of words. Write *S* if it is a sentence or *F* if it is a fragment.

Example: __*F*__ Went to St. Louis.

1. _____ You need three stamps on that envelope.
2. _____ Yesterday, Sam and his nephew fished all morning.
3. _____ When that thick magazine fell off the sofa.
4. _____ This room is a mess!
5. _____ My client in Dallas will send you the brochure.
6. _____ Rattled and chugged all the way down the street.
7. _____ My former neighbor and good friend.
8. _____ The workers walked carefully through the construction area.
9. _____ Because you and your coworkers are dependable.
10. _____ Juanita received dozens of cards during her illness.

Types of Sentences

There are four types of sentences: statements, questions, commands, and exclamations. Each type of sentence is used for a different purpose.

Statement A **statement** gives information or tells something. A statement ends with a period.

> The young woman bought two tickets to Friday's rock concert.

Question A **question** asks for or about something. Questions end with a question mark.

> Where is my math book?

> Will you go to the concert with me?

In most cases, the subject comes before a predicate in a sentence. In a question, though, this order is reversed; the predicate comes first. It can make it more difficult to find the subject. You can find the subject more easily if you change the order of the words in a question into a statement.

> Where is my math book? ⟶ | My math book | is where. |
>   SUBJECT   PREDICATE

In some questions, the subject falls between parts of the verb. To find the subject, change the order of the words to form a statement.

> Will you go to the concert? ⟶ | You | will go to the concert. |
>   SUBJECT   PREDICATE

Command A **command** states an order or a request. A command ends with a period.

> Shut the door.

> Move, please.

> Get away from there this minute.

> Don't go near the edge of the cliff.

These sentences appear to have predicates but no subjects. The subject is actually *you*. *You* is understood without being directly stated.

> You + shut the door.

> You + move, please.

> You + get away from there this minute.

> You + don't go near the edge of the cliff.

Exclamation An **exclamation** is an expression of excitement or surprise. An exclamation ends with an exclamation mark. As in a command, certain words that are understood may be left out of an exclamation. As in a question, changing the order of the words or adding words in an exclamation may help you find the subject.

> Fire! ⟶ There is a + fire.

> Wonderful! ⟶ This is + wonderful.

> Was that a great movie! ⟶ That was a great movie.

THINK ABOUT **WRITING**

Directions: Punctuate each sentence below with the correct end mark.

Example: Watch out for that other car _!_

1. Brian slowly got to his feet _____

2. Be careful with that lawn mower _____

3. Smoke is coming from the roof _____

4. Where did you find the book _____

5. Stop jumping on the bed _____

6. The train stops here every 15 minutes _____

7. Have you seen my radio _____

8. Ms. Luna left here at least 20 minutes ago _____

9. What a nightmare _____

10. Can you see her yet _____

Vocabulary Review

Directions: Match each word in column 1 with its definition in column 2.

Column 1

1. _____ determine

2. _____ fragment

3. _____ predicate

4. _____ sentence

5. _____ subject

Column 2

A. an incomplete sentence

B. the part of a sentence that tells what the subject is or does

C. whom or what a sentence is about

D. to decide something

E. a complete thought that includes a subject and predicate

Skill Review

Directions: Read each group of words below. Write *S* if it is a complete sentence and *F* if it is a fragment.

1. _____ Walking to the store.

2. _____ How far is the movie theater?

3. _____ That homemade pizza was the best I've ever eaten!

4. _____ Because I forgot my keys.

5. _____ When the alarm clock went off this morning.

6. _____ Sara made José a delicious birthday cake.

Directions: Read the paragraph below about Bart and Brad. Then use the Comparison and Contrast chart to identify which sentences tell how the young men are alike and which tell how they are different.

(1) Bart and Brad are on the swim team. (2) They both love the big pool at the community center. (3) Bart swims in short races that require a great deal of speed. (4) Brad swims in long-distance events where endurance is most important. (5) Whether they win or lose the race, at the end they always congratulate each other!

COMPARISON AND CONTRAST

Alike	Different
Sentence (1)	

Skill Practice

Directions: Choose the one best answer for each question.

1. Who would like to attend the concert.

   Which correction should be made to the sentence?

   A. replace the period with an exclamation point
   B. replace the period with a question mark
   C. insert <u>you</u> after <u>would</u>
   D. restate the sentence as a command

2. Watch out for that falling ladder?

   Which correction should be made to the sentence?

   A. insert a subject
   B. replace the question mark with a period
   C. replace the question mark with an exclamation point
   D. insert a predicate

3. Will you take this book back to the library for me.

   Which correction should be made to the sentence?

   A. replace the period with a question mark
   B. insert a subject
   C. replace the period with an exclamation point
   D. insert a verb

4. <u>Because the air pollution</u> was so bad.

   Which is the best way to write the underlined portion of the sentence? If the original is the best way, choose option (A).

   A. Because the air pollution
   B. Laws were passed because the air pollution
   C. Air pollution, which
   D. A source of air pollution that

5. During the rain, the car's <u>electric window</u>.

   Which is the best way to write the underlined portion of the sentence? If the original is the best way, choose option (A).

   A. electric window.
   B. electric window?
   C. electric window became jammed.
   D. jammed electric window.

6. <u>Migrated hundreds of miles south</u> from Canada.

   Which is the best way to write the underlined portion of the sentence? If the original is the best way, choose option (A).

   A. Migrated hundreds of miles south
   B. Migrating wolves
   C. Packs of wolves
   D. Wolves migrated hundreds of miles south

Writing Practice

Directions: Revise sentences 3 and 4 from the paragraph about Bart and Brad on page 22. Combine them into a comparison that is made in one sentence.

Nouns and Pronouns

KEY CONCEPT: Nouns name people, places, things, or ideas. Pronouns replace and refer to nouns.

Lesson Objectives

You will be able to

- Identify categories of nouns and apply correct usage

- Identify functions of pronouns and apply correct usage

- Edit to correct errors in usage of nouns and pronouns

Skills

- **Core Skill:** Demonstrate Command of Standard English Conventions

- **Core Skill:** Use Precise Language

Vocabulary

abstract
antecedent
conventions
gender
noun
possessive
pronoun
singular

You have learned that a sentence contains a subject and a predicate. You have also learned that a sentence must express a complete thought. Read the following sentences. Underline the subject once and the predicate twice. If a sentence is incomplete, rewrite it to express a complete thought. Then identify the subject and the predicate.

Maria is looking for a new job.
The perfect job.
Luis's tie with the blue stripes.

Nouns and Pronouns

Nouns make writing **precise**. They tell readers who or what is being discussed. Using too many nouns, though, can make writing repetitive or dull. Writers can improve their writing by using **pronouns**. Pronouns are words that replace and refer to nouns. However, writers must make sure that the relationships between nouns and pronouns are clear to readers.

Nouns

There are two main types of nouns: **proper** and **common**. Proper nouns name specific people, places, things, or ideas, such as *Norman Rockwell*, *Detroit*, *Newsweek*, or *Hinduism*. Common nouns name whole groups or general types of people, places, things, or ideas, such as *artist*, *city*, *magazine*, or *religion*.

Some nouns that name people, places, or things are called **concrete nouns**. You can experience concrete nouns through your five senses: seeing, hearing, touching, smelling, or tasting. Nouns that name ideas or emotions are called **abstract nouns**. Abstract nouns have no physical form, so you cannot experience them through the five senses.

Concrete Nouns	Abstract Nouns
conference room, desk, computer, supervisor, Los Angeles	accuracy, collaboration, honesty, pride, excellence

A **singular noun** names only one person, place, thing, or idea. A **plural noun** names more than one person, place, thing, or idea.

- Most nouns are made plural by adding -*s*.
  color > colors   fabric > fabrics

- Nouns ending in -*s*, -*ch*, -*sh*, or -*x* are made plural by adding -*es*.
  dress > dresses   inch > inches   ash > ashes   box > boxes

- Nouns ending in a vowel + *y* are made plural by adding -*s*. If the *y* follows a consonant, the *y* changes to *i* and -*es* is added.
  way > ways   thirty > thirties

- Many, but not all, nouns ending in -*f* or -*fe* are made plural by changing the *f* to *v* and adding -*es*.
  knife > knives   but, cuff > cuffs

- A few nouns do not change when they are made plural.
  clothing > clothing   fish > fish

- Some nouns have irregular plural forms. This chart shows some examples.

Singular	Irregular Plural
analysis	analyses
appendix	appendices
child	children
criterion	criteria
man	men
memorandum	memoranda
person	people
woman	women

To show possession or ownership, an apostrophe and sometimes an -*s* are added based on whether the noun is singular or plural. These are called **possessives**. Do not confuse possessives with plurals.

Singular Possessive	Carlita's shirt is red. James's desk is messy.
Plural Possessive	The senators' bill passed. The children's clothes are dirty.
Plural (not possessive)	The singers wear white shirts. Their lives were saved by the dog.

WORKPLACE CONNECTION

Common Nouns
You will come across many proper nouns in the workplace, such as ABC Copiers or XYZ Software. You will need to familiarize yourself with a variety of common nouns as well. Some common nouns in the workplace include the following:

charts
conference
goals
managers
performance
profit
prototype
software
teamwork

Compile a list of additional common nouns that are likely to be used in the workplace.

Language **conventions** are ways in which the language is written or spoken that are regarded as being correct. Nouns and pronouns are often joined with *and* or *or*. Sometimes it is difficult to know what kind of pronoun to use when joined with a noun. If you are unsure which type of pronoun to use, try using the pronoun by itself in the sentence. For example

- Marcus and Frank are absent today.

- *(He or Him?)* and Frank are absent today.

- <u>He</u> is absent today.

- <u>He</u> and Frank are absent today.

When two or more pronouns are joined and one of the pronouns is *me*, *me* appears last.

- The lecture was boring to her and <u>me</u>.

In a notebook, edit these sentences.

The manager asked him and I to attend the conference.

Her and Ana worked late to complete the project on time.

The supervisor gave me and Samuel awards for our work.

Pronouns

Remember that pronouns replace and refer to nouns. There are three types of pronouns, and each has a different function or job in a sentence.

A **subject pronoun** replaces a noun that is used as a subject.

- <u>Quincy</u> is my favorite uncle. (proper noun)

- <u>He</u> is my favorite uncle. (pronoun)

Singular Subject Pronouns	Plural Subject Pronouns
I	we
you	you
he, she, it	they

An **object pronoun** replaces a noun that follows a **preposition** or receives the action of a verb. A preposition connects nouns, pronouns, and phrases to other words in a sentence.

- Please give this magazine to <u>Shen</u>. (object of preposition *to*)

- Please give this magazine to <u>him</u>.

- Mr. Lopez hired <u>Lauren</u>. (receives action of verb hired)

- Mr. Lopez hired <u>her</u>.

Singular Object Pronouns	Plural Object Pronouns
me	us
you	you
him, her, it	them

A **possessive pronoun** replaces a noun that shows ownership. There are two kinds of possessive pronouns. One type is used with a noun. The other type is used by itself.

- <u>My</u> favorite pastime is fishing.
- <u>Mine</u> is bowling.

	Singular Possessive Pronouns	**Plural Possessive Pronouns**
Used with a noun	my	our
	your	your
	his, her, its	their
Stands alone	mine	ours
	yours	yours
	his, hers, its	theirs

THINK ABOUT WRITING

Directions: Rewrite the following sentences using the correct pronoun. If the pronoun used in the sentence is correct, write "Correct."

1. Last week him and Fernando installed new software on the department's computers.

   _____

2. The manager wants to begin regular meetings between himself and we.

   _____

3. The receptionist was apologetic when she spoke to us.

   _____

4. When I opened the book, I noticed that theirs binding needs to be repaired.

   _____

Pronoun–Antecedent Agreement

Pronouns must always agree with their **antecedents**. An antecedent is the noun or pronoun to which a pronoun refers. A pronoun must agree with its antecedent in number, **gender** (male or female), and person.

Number

If a pronoun refers to a singular noun (one thing or person), use a singular pronoun. If a pronoun refers to a plural noun (more than one thing or person), use a plural pronoun. Making pronouns agree with their antecedents is usually simple. However, be alert for the following situations.

Situation	Example
When a pronoun replaces two or more nouns joined by *and*, use a plural pronoun.	Aliyah and Laura went for walks on their shift breaks.
When a pronoun replaces two or more nouns joined by *or, nor, either . . . or* *neither . . . nor* *not only . . . but also* use a pronoun that agrees with the last noun in the series.	Neither Consuela nor her sisters liked their sandwiches.
When a word ends with *-one, -body, -other*, or *-thing*, use a singular pronoun.	Everyone should be careful of his or her health.
When using a collective or group noun, decide whether the noun is acting as a singular group or as plural individuals.	The jury returned its verdict. The jury took their seats.
Some singular nouns end in *-s*. Use singular pronouns with these.	Mathematics has its own set of symbols.
Some nouns have only a plural form even though they name only one thing. Use a plural pronoun with these.	I need to sharpen my scissors because they are dull.

Gender

Gender refers to whether the antecedent is male or female. If gender is not clear, use *his or her* or rephrase the sentence to avoid the problem.

Masculine Pronouns	Feminine Pronouns
he, him, his, himself	she, her, hers, herself

- The <u>actress</u> seems quite happy with <u>her</u> role.
- Every baseball <u>fan</u> brought <u>his or her</u> glove.
- All the baseball <u>fans</u> brought <u>their</u> gloves.

Person

Pronouns must show the same point of view as their antecedents. When a writer chooses who will "tell" a story, he or she is choosing a point of view. In first-person point of view, the narrator of the text refers to him or herself. In second-person point of view, the author speaks directly to the reader. Third-person point of view is told as if someone is looking at what's going on and telling the reader.

- All <u>trainees</u> should bring <u>your</u> laptops. (third and second person)
- All <u>trainees</u> should bring <u>their</u> laptops. (both third person)

	Singular	Plural
First Person	I, me, my, mine	we, us, our, ours
Second Person	you, your, yours	you, your, yours
Third Person	he, she, it, him, her, his, hers, its	they, them, their, theirs

Advertisers use compact language and sentence structure to sell their products. Often, they use visual images to clarify unclear language. For example, imagine an advertisement for a building block set. The text reads, "What it is—is beautiful." The image shows a small child holding a structure made from the blocks. Taken alone, the pronoun *it* has no clear antecedent. Yet the visual image provides readers with some clues. *It* may refer to the child, the structure, the process of building the structure, or all three. Find a print or digital advertisement that makes use of pronouns. In a notebook, analyze how the text and images work together to clarify the pronouns.

Respond to these questions:
What language clues are present to clarify the pronoun?
What visual clues are present to clarify the pronoun?
Why do you think the advertiser relies on visual images to promote his or her message?

UNCLEAR PRONOUN REFERENCE

Each pronoun must refer clearly to an antecedent. If the **reference**, or connection, to the antecedent is unclear, the reader may become confused about the meaning of the sentence.

- Before putting the <u>books</u> on the <u>shelves</u>, Lamar dusted <u>them</u>.
- Did Lamar dust the books or the shelves? In this case, there are too many antecedents.
- The pizza <u>box</u> was greasy, but <u>it</u> had a lot of flavor.
- What had a lot of flavor—the pizza box? In this case, the antecedent—pizza—is buried.
- The listener texted the radio station, but <u>they</u> didn't respond.
- Who didn't respond to the text—the station? In this case, the antecedent—disc jockeys—is missing.

To avoid this error,

- Replace the pronoun with a noun.
  Before putting the books on the shelves, Lamar dusted the shelves.

  or

- Rephrase the sentence.

Lamar dusted the shelves before he put the books on them.

THINK ABOUT WRITING

Directions: In a notebook, revise the following paragraph by substituting pronouns for some of the nouns. You may also combine or rephrase sentences as desired. Make sure that your pronoun usage is clear and correct.

Althea loves Althea's dog Baron more than anything. Baron has a lot of energy and loves to run and play. So Althea takes Baron to the park whenever Althea can. If Althea doesn't take Baron out often enough, Baron gets bored and misbehaves. Baron has chewed Althea's shoes and nibbled on the corners of Althea's old couch. Last week, Althea found a photo of Althea's grandchildren torn to shreds. When Althea went to scold Baron, Althea found Baron curled up and napping on Althea's bed. One look at Baron's sweet wrinkled face melted Althea's heart. Althea couldn't stay mad at Baron.

Relative Pronouns

Some of the most common problems in the use of pronouns involve a few specific pronouns called **relative pronouns**. These pronouns introduce relative clauses. A clause is a part of sentence with its own subject and predicate. Relative clauses are dependent clauses that tell something about a word, phrase, or idea in the main clause. This word, phrase, or idea is the antecedent.

When choosing a relative pronoun, it is helpful to remember pronoun case.

Case	Relative Pronouns	Example
Subject	who, whoever, that, which	This is the building that had a fire.
Object	whom, whomever	This is the firefighter to whom I wanted to speak.
Possession	whose	The owner whose building burned collected the insurance.

If you have trouble remembering when to use the subject or object pronouns when referring to people, try substituting *he* and *him* or *she* and *her*. If the subject pronoun *he/she* works in the sentence, then use *who* or *whoever*. If the object pronoun *him/her* fits in the sentence, use *whom* or *whomever*.

- *(Who or Whom?)* is that child?
- Him is that child. (incorrect)
- He is that child. (correct)
- Who is that child?

Rearranging the subject and verb in a question will sometimes help you.

- *(Who or Whom?)* are you calling?
- You are calling *(who or whom?)*?
- You are calling she. (incorrect)
- You are calling her. (correct)
- Whom are you calling?

If the sentence is complicated, look only at the group of words beginning with the pronoun. Rearrange the words in subject–verb order.

- I know that *(whoever or whomever?)* the coach picks will help our team.
- The coach picks *(whoever or whomever?)*.
- The coach picks he. (incorrect)
- The coach picks him. (correct)
- I know that whomever the coach picks will help our team.

There are two types of relative clauses: restrictive and nonrestrictive.

A **restrictive clause**, which does not have commas, contains information that is essential to the meaning of a sentence. The relative pronoun *that* is used only in restrictive clauses to provide information about places, things, or ideas.

- The dog <u>that</u> stole the newspaper lives next door.

A **nonrestrictive clause**, which has commas, contains information that is not essential to the meaning of a sentence. The relative pronoun *which* is generally used in nonrestrictive clauses.

- The sales contest, <u>which</u> lasted all month, was profitable.

THINK ABOUT WRITING

Directions: Write the correct relative pronoun in each blank.

1. Would you please tell _____ Malia brings home that we will be home to greet Malia and her?

2. _____ told you that Jose was writing the report with me?

3. Just between you and me, _____ gets this job deserves it.

4. The briefcase _____ is sitting near the door belongs to Ms. Kwan.

5. Your family's kitchen table, _____ is much larger than ours, is beautiful.

Vocabulary Review

Directions: Match each vocabulary word with its definition.

1. _____ abstract

2. _____ antecedent

3. _____ gender

4. _____ noun

5. _____ possessive

6. _____ pronoun

7. _____ singular

A. classification by which pronouns are grouped according to sex

B. word that names a person, place, thing, or idea

C. expressing a quality apart from any material object

D. pronoun case expressing ownership

E. form of a word referring to one thing or person

F. word, phrase, or clause to which a pronoun refers

G. word that replaces or refers to a noun

Directions: Choose the <u>one best answer</u> to each question.

1. Which is the correct form of the underlined noun?

    Lupita says she will attend her <u>mothers</u> college and then pursue a career in politics.

    A. mothers
    B. mothers'
    C. mothers's
    D. mother's

2. Which noun in the following sentence is abstract?

    The audience showed its patriotism by pledging to the flag before the assembly began.

    A. audience
    B. patriotism
    C. flag
    D. assembly

3. What is the correct way to make the boldfaced noun plural in the following sentence?

    *The teacher introduced the **criterion** by which he would grade the students' essays.*

    A. criterions
    B. criteriones
    C. criteria
    D. criterion

4. Which is the correct form of the underlined noun?

    The <u>students</u> excuse for turning in their group project late was not believable.

    A. students'
    B. student's
    C. students's
    D. students

5. Choose the pronoun that **best** completes the following sentence.

    _____ *were the only guests that arrived on time.*

    A. Her
    B. Them
    C. Us
    D. They

6. Choose the pronoun that best completes the following sentence.

    Please send the tickets to Ms. Arocha or _____ .

    A. me
    B. he
    C. I
    D. theirs

Skill Review (continued)

7. Choose the pronoun that best completes the following sentence.

   Someone who forgets to pay _____ electric bill may end up without lights.

   A. their
   B. your
   C. his or her
   D. its

8. Choose the pronoun that best completes the following sentence.

   When Sergeant Lao tells you to do something, he expects _____ to do it.

   A. him
   B. them
   C. her
   D. you

9. Rewrite the following sentence to fix the unclear pronoun reference and make the language more precise.

   Remove the bike from the van and fix it.

   _____

   _____

10. Rewrite the following sentence to fix the unclear pronoun reference and make the language more precise.

    Although Professor Barnes was smart, she did not make use of it.

    _____

    _____

11. Choose the pronoun that best completes the following sentence.

    _____ told you that the meeting would begin at 8:00?

    A. Whom
    B. Who
    C. Whose
    D. Whomever

12. Choose the pronoun that best completes the following sentence.

    The lamp _____ sits on the table is dusty.

    A. who
    B. which
    C. whom
    D. that

Skill Practice

Directions: Edit each sentence to fix the underlined pronoun error.

1. My brother and I were bitten by mosquitoes, <u>that</u> appeared during the fireworks show.

_____

_____

_____

2. <u>Her</u> and Mary Beth reached their sales goals last month.

_____

_____

_____

3. No one is going to like what Ms. Chang has to tell <u>them</u> about the new production schedule.

_____

_____

_____

4. Gregory e-mailed Suzette's office yesterday, but <u>she</u> didn't respond.

_____

_____

_____

5. Sergio wants <u>me and you</u> to go to the training session with him.

_____

_____

_____

Writing Practice

Directions: Beginning with the sentence starter below or another one of your choice, write one or two paragraphs. Make sure to include at least two examples each of abstract, irregular plural, and possessive nouns. Underline these nouns. Use pronouns where appropriate. Underline pronoun examples twice.

They are going to have lots of questions when I tell them about . . .

_____

_____

_____

_____

_____

_____

_____

_____

_____

_____

_____

_____

_____

_____

_____

_____

_____

Writing Practice (continued)

Directions: When your writing is complete, use a colored pen to edit for the following conventions

_____ Are all abstract and plural nouns spelled correctly?

_____ Do all possessive nouns show the correct use of an apostrophe?

_____ Do all pronouns show the correct case?

_____ Do all pronouns agree with their antecedents in number, gender, and person?

_____ Do all pronouns have clearly stated antecedents?

_____ Do all relative pronouns show the correct case and usage?

Directions: Choose the <u>one best answer</u> to each question.

1. <u>While thousands of ducks</u> flew away from the lake.

   Which is the best way to write the underlined portion of the sentence? If the original is the best way, choose option (A).

   A. While thousands of ducks
   B. Because the ducks were nervous and
   C. Feeding on seeds
   D. Thousands of ducks

2. <u>Gave himself</u> a pepperoni pizza as a reward for his hard work.

   Which is the best way to write the underlined portion of the sentence? If the original is the best way, choose option (A).

   A. Gave himself
   B. Jevon gave hisself
   C. Jevon gave himself
   D. After finishing the job

3. <u>Because his cold</u> was so bad.

   Which is the best way to write the underlined portion of the sentence? If the original is the best way, choose option (A).

   A. Because his cold
   B. A cough that
   C. John stayed home from work because his cold
   D. Feverish and weak, which

4. During that cold <u>night around the fire.</u>

   Which is the best way to write the underlined portion of the sentence? If the original is the best way, choose option (A).

   A. night around the fire.
   B. night, the fire kept them warm.
   C. night as the snow fell.
   D. night without any food.

5. Eric and his brother both have their own businesses. Eric repairs old watches. His brother builds tables, chairs, and bookshelfs.

   Which correction should be made to these sentences?

   A. change <u>watches</u> to <u>watchs</u>
   B. change <u>tables</u> to <u>table's</u>
   C. change <u>chairs</u> to <u>chaires</u>
   D. change <u>bookshelfs</u> to <u>bookshelves</u>

6. The zookeeper told me to be careful when returning to my car. The ferocious lions had freed themselves. Had jumped over a wall.

   Which correction should be made to these sentences?

   A. replace <u>me</u> with <u>I</u>
   B. replace <u>my</u> with <u>mine</u>
   C. replace <u>themselves</u> with <u>theirselves</u>
   D. insert <u>They</u> before <u>had</u> in the last sentence

Review

7. As soon as Tony drove the car off their lot, it began backfiring. People pointed at him and his car. Smoke rose from under it's hood.

   Which correction should be made to these sentences?

   A. change their to their's
   B. replace it with his
   C. replace him with he
   D. replace it's with its

8. Will she go to their party with he?

   Which correction should be made to this sentence?

   A. replace she with her
   B. change their to theirs
   C. replace their with they
   D. replace he with him

9. Carla and three of her friends went bowling. When her friend dropped a bowling ball, she yelled, "Watch out!"

   Which is the best way to write the underlined portion of the sentence? If the original is the best way, choose option (A).

   A. she yelled, "Watch out!"
   B. Carla yelled, "Watch out!"
   C. she yelled, "Watch out."
   D. Carla yelled, "Watch out."

10. The car is on fire.

    Which correction should be made to this sentence?

    A. insert a subject in the sentence
    B. insert a verb in the sentence
    C. remove the period
    D. replace the period with an exclamation point

11. Mercedes and she were both hungry. They split a pizza between themselves. Whom do you think ate the most?

    Which correction should be made to these sentences?

    A. replace she with her
    B. replace themselves with theirselves
    C. replace Whom with Who
    D. replace the question mark with an exclamation point

12. Karen wants her son to be a basketball player. She teaches him herself. He already shoots better than her.

    Which correction should be made to these sentences?

    A. change the first her to hers
    B. replace She with Herself
    C. replace him with he
    D. replace the second her with she

13. Us Americans like our cars. We know public transportation is great, but whoever can afford a car has one, sometimes two.

    Which correction should be made to these sentences?

    A. replace Us with We
    B. change our to ours
    C. replace We with Us
    D. replace whoever with whomever

14. The artist's empty studio

    Which of these should be added to turn the fragment into a complete sentence?

    A. and the artist's home.
    B. which was old.
    C. was cold.
    D. on the third floor.

15. Write a paragraph comparing and contrasting an activity you enjoy with an activity your friends or family enjoy. Use appropriate nouns, pronouns, punctuation, and proper language conventions.

_____

_____

_____

_____

_____

_____

_____

_____

_____

_____

_____

_____

_____

_____

_____

_____

Review

Check Your Understanding

On the following chart, circle the number of any item you answered incorrectly in the Chapter 1 Review on pages 38–40. Next to each group of item numbers, you will see the pages you can review to learn how to answer the items correctly. Pay particular attention to reviewing skill areas in which you missed half or more of the questions.

Chapter 1 Review

Skill Area	Item Number	Review Pages
Sentences	1, 2, 3, 4, 10, 14, 15	16–23
Nouns and Pronouns	5, 6, 7,8, 9, 11, 12, 13, 15	24–37

Verbs

What is your favorite activity? Perhaps it's a baseball game, a soccer match, or just sitting back and observing others as they pass you by. Whatever activity you enjoy, you probably also enjoy talking to others about it. When you do, you are surely using verbs.

Read the following descriptions. Which sentence is more interesting? Why is it more interesting?

The batter hit the ball into left field.

The batter smashed the ball into left field.

Both sentences give the same information, but you probably said that the second sentence was more interesting. The word *smashed* helps readers picture the action more clearly than the word *hit*. Both words are verbs, but *smashed* makes the writing more exciting.

In this chapter you will learn about verbs and how choosing the right verb can bring your writing to life.

Lesson 2.1: Verbs and Verb Tenses
What did you do yesterday? Today? What will you do tomorrow? When writing or talking about what you did, are doing, or will do, you will need to use the proper verb tenses.

Lesson 2.2: Subject-Verb Agreement
What does it mean for subjects and verbs to agree? Learn about how choosing subjects and verbs that agree helps your writing.

Goal Setting

Becoming a better writer involves understanding the building blocks of language: the parts of speech. When you know what each part of speech is and how it works, you can make your writing more professional and more interesting.

Think about how certain words help you describe things you have seen or done. Many of these words are probably verbs. Verbs help bring your writing to life by vividly describing actions. Verbs also tell readers when an action takes place. In this chapter you will be learning about verbs. Check off each topic after you have read about it.

Types of Verbs

_____ Action Verbs

_____ Linking Verbs

_____ Regular Verbs

_____ Irregular Verbs

_____ Modal Verbs

Verb Tenses

_____ Simple Tenses

_____ Perfect Tenses

_____ Sequence of Verb Tenses

Subject-Verb Agreement

_____ Simple Subjects

_____ Compound Subjects

_____ Interrupters

_____ Inverted Sentences

_____ Clauses

What do you already know about verbs?

_____

_____

_____

Which of the above topics will help improve your writing?

_____

_____

_____

Verbs and Verb Tenses

KEY CONCEPT: Verbs tell what the subject of a sentence *is* or *does*, and the tense of a verb tells when the action occurs.

1. Select the correct pronoun in this sentence:

   Even though Victor and Dave are twin brothers, (*he, they*) have different interests.

2. Underline the subject once and the predicate twice:

   Rihanna and I bake something new every weekend.

Types of Verbs

Every sentence has a subject and a predicate. The key word in the predicate is the verb. A **verb** tells what the subject *is* or *does*. Verbs are divided into two types: action verbs and linking verbs.

Action Verbs

Action verbs are verbs that tell what the subject *does*.

   Paul <u>searches</u> for his car in the huge parking lot.

Searches is an action verb that tells what Paul, the subject, does. Here, the action is physical. Other action verbs tell what mental action the subject does. These can be more difficult to identify. *Know, wish, realize,* and *hope* are **common** [regularly used] verbs that tell about mental action.

   Helena <u>knows</u> where her car is parked.

Linking Verbs

Linking verbs tell what the subject *is*. They **link**, or connect, the subject with a word or words that describe it.

   Last night, Toshi <u>became</u> a father.

Note that some sentences contain more than one verb.

   When Toshi <u>became</u> a father, he <u>felt</u> proud.

Verbs also may be made up of more than one word. *Has been* and *did run* are examples of verb phrases.

Modal Auxiliary Verbs

Modal auxiliary verbs express several meanings. *Can* expresses ability or possibility.

Raj <u>can</u> dance very well.

May is used to ask for permission or to make a prediction.

<u>May</u> I sit with you at the meeting?

There <u>may</u> be some overtime work next week.

Must indicates the speaker's opinion.

You <u>must</u> balance your checkbook regularly!

Sometimes the words in a verb phrase may be separated by other words. These other words are not part of the verb. In the example below, the verb is *has watched*. *Always* is not part of the verb phrase.

Harrison <u>has</u> always <u>watched</u> boxing on television.

THINK ABOUT **WRITING**

Directions: On a separate sheet of paper, write a sentence that uses the type of verb in parentheses.

Example: (action) Julian <u>stayed</u> home from work.

1. (modal auxiliary)
2. (verb phrase)
3. (action)
4. (linking)
5. (action)

Verb Tenses

In addition to telling what something *is* or *does*, verbs also tell the time of the action. The time shown by a verb is called its **tense**.

Simple Tenses

There are three basic or simple tenses.

Present tense: Traci <u>plays</u> soccer on Wednesday.

Past tense: Traci <u>played</u> soccer on Wednesday.

Future tense: Traci <u>will play</u> soccer on Wednesday.

Infinitive and Base Form

Read the following sentence. Pay special attention to the underlined words.

Jim wants <u>to borrow</u> our barbecue grill.

The underlined words, *to borrow*, make up a verb form called an **infinitive**. The infinitive is the basic form of a verb and almost always begins with the word *to*. The verb form following *to* is the base form. The **base form** is what you begin with when you form all verb tenses.

Simple Present Tense

Verbs in the **simple present tense** are used in three situations. First, present-tense verbs tell what is happening or is true at the present time.

Andrea <u>pours</u> a second cup of coffee.

Second, present-tense verbs show actions that are performed regularly.

We <u>walk</u> for an hour every day.

Third, present-tense verbs tell about an action or state of being that is always true.

The Sonoran Desert <u>is</u> hot and dry.

The simple present tense is formed in three ways: base form (sometimes plus *s*), a form of the verb *to be* and the base form plus *ing*, and base form with *do* or *does*.

Base Form or Base Form plus *s*

Almost all verbs form their simple present tense from the base form of the verb or from the base form plus *s*. Study the following chart showing the simple present tense of the verb *walk*.

Simple Present Tense	
Singular	**Plural**
I walk you walk he, she, it walks	we walk you walk they walk

The only time a regular verb changes its form in the present tense is when the subject is *he, she, it,* or a singular noun. When the subject is one of these, an *s* is added (or *es* if the verb ends in *s, x, ch,* or *sh*).

Pedro <u>plays</u> basketball every evening.

Kathy <u>pushes</u> the pedal to the floor.

Base Form plus *ing*

Present Tense with *ing*		
I he, she, it we, you, they	am is are	walking

When the present tenses of verbs are formed in this way, they are used to tell about actions that are true now and are ongoing.

I am working too hard.

Evelyn and John are planning the company picnic.

Base Form with *do* or *does*

The present tense can also be formed by combining *do* or *does* with the base form of the verb. *Do* or *does* gives added emphasis to the verb.

My dog does eat at the table with everyone else.

Do you know what time it is?

Simple Past Tense

The **simple past tense** shows actions that occurred at a specific time in the past.

Ms. Chavez asked me for a ride home from work.

The simple past tense is formed by adding *ed* or *d* to the base form of the verb.

I hoped for a promotion.

Simple Past Tense	
Singular	**Plural**
I walked you walked he, she, it walked	we walked you walked they walked

Context clues are words that provide hints about a sentence's meaning.

Verbs can provide some information about whether an event is in the past, present, or future, but sometimes that is not enough. In those cases, other words, such as *before*, *yesterday*, and *next week*, can help make your writing clear and provide clues for readers.

In the following sentence, the word *tomorrow* and the verb *will* are clues that the party will take place in the future.

Tomorrow she will purchase the cake for the party.

Write three sentences to tell about something that happened in the past, is happening in the present, and will happen in the future. Include context clues, such as the words *yesterday*, *every morning*, and *next year*.

Simple Future Tense

The **simple future tense** shows an action that will occur in the future. The simple future tense is formed by combining *will* with the base form of the verb.

I will call you tomorrow.

Simple Future Tense	
Singular	**Plural**
I will walk	we will walk
you will walk	you will walk
he, she, it will walk	they will walk

THINK ABOUT **WRITING**

Directions: Write the correct tense of the base form of the verb in parentheses. Then underline any words that gave you a clue to the correct verb tense.

Example: (open) I __will open__ my birthday gifts <u>tomorrow</u>.

1. (call)   We _____ your daughter yesterday.

2. (wait)   Stan _____ for his children every afternoon after school.

3. (move)   The Rosellos _____ to Columbus two years ago.

4. (enjoy)   I always _____ a good mystery book.

5. (work)   Mrs. Haynes _____ on your furnace next week.

6. (happen)   What _____ to you last night?

7. (demand)   Today's consumers _____ higher-quality products than in the past.

8. (end)   You _____ your study of the Constitution next Tuesday.

9. (own)   Simon now _____ a car and a pickup truck.

10. (talk)   We _____ about you for hours yesterday.

Principal Parts of Verbs

As you have learned, there are three simple verb tenses: past, present, and future tenses. In addition to these simple tenses, there are perfect verb tenses. To understand the perfect tenses, you must understand the principal parts of verbs. These parts are used to form the perfect tenses.

The three principal parts of verbs are the base, past, and past participle. The past participle shows an action that was already complete before the sentence began.

The following chart shows the three principal parts, or forms, of the verb *help*.

Principal Parts of Verbs		
Base	**Past**	**Past Participle**
help	helped	helped

The base form is used to form the simple present and simple future tenses. The past form is used to form the simple past tense. The past participle form is used to form the perfect tenses, which you will learn about later in the lesson.

Regular Verbs

Regular verbs are verbs that form their past and past participle forms in a **regular**, or predictable, way. The **majority** [more than half] of verbs are regular verbs.

Most regular verbs form the past and past participle by adding *ed* to the base. If the verb ends with an *e*, only a *d* is added. In some cases, the final consonant is doubled. If the regular verb ends in a consonant plus *y*, the *y* is changed to *i* before *ed* is added. Here are examples:

Examples of Regular Verbs		
Base	**Past**	**Past Participle**
walk	walked	walked
praise	praised	praised
stop	stopped	stopped
reply	replied	replied

Irregular Verbs

Verbs that do not form their past and past participle forms by simply adding *ed* are called **irregular verbs**. There are no simple rules for forming the irregular forms of verbs. You will, however, notice patterns. You have to memorize the spellings of the principal parts of these verbs. Another tip is to look up the base form of the verb in a dictionary. You will find the past and past participle forms there.

Three irregular verbs are so common and so important they need special attention.

Have, Do, and *Be*			
Base	**Present**	**Past**	**Past Participle**
have	has, have	had	had
do	do, does	did	done
be	am, is, are	was, were	been

The following list gives the principal parts of common irregular verbs. Some verbs have more than one correct form for some parts.

Common Irregular Verbs		
Base	**Past**	**Past Participle**
awake	awoke, awaked	awaked, awoken
become	became	become
bend	bent	bent
bet	bet	bet
bid	bid	bid
bind	bound	bound
bite	bit	bitten
blow	blew	blown
build	built	built
burst	burst	burst
buy	bought	bought
cast	cast	cast
catch	caught	caught
cost	cost	cost
creep	crept	crept
cut	cut	cut
deal	dealt	dealt
dig	dug	dug

Common Irregular Verbs		
Base	**Past**	**Past Participle**
draw	drew	drawn
dream	dreamed, dreamt	dreamed, dreamt
drive	drove	driven
fall	fell	fallen
feed	fed	fed
feel	felt	felt
fight	fought	fought
find	found	found
fly	flew	flown
forget	forgot	forgotten
keep	kept	kept
lay	laid	laid
lead	led	led
leave	left	left
lend	lent	lent
lie	lay	lain
lose	lost	lost
make	made	made
mean	meant	meant
meet	met	met
pay	paid	paid
prove	proved	proved, proven
put	put	put
read	read	read
rid	rid	rid
ride	rode	ridden
rise	rose	risen
say	said	said
sell	sold	sold
send	sent	sent
set	set	set
shake	shook	shaken
shine	shone, shined	shone, shined
shoot	shot	shot
sit	sat	sat
sleep	slept	slept
spend	spent	spent
spin	spun	spun
stand	stood	stood
strike	struck	struck
swear	swore	sworn
teach	taught	taught
tell	told	told
think	thought	thought
throw	threw	thrown
understand	understood	understood

THINK ABOUT WRITING

Directions: Write the correct form of the missing verb. The base form is given in parentheses.

Example: (shake) Our house _____shook_____ violently during last week's earthquake.

1. (throw)   Brian _____ out the runner trying to steal second.

2. (freeze) The rain _____ as soon as it hits the pavement.

3. (give)   Please _____ this package to the delivery person.

4. (mean)   I didn't know what she _____ when she said she was skating home.

5. (cling)   Jill's children _____ tightly to her when she left home.

6. (deal)   Dilip is the most helpful real estate agent I have ever _____ with.

7. (swear)   Ms. Tso _____ to the judge that she was telling the truth.

Perfect Tenses

The simple tenses divide time into the three natural periods: the past, present, and future. Verbs also have three perfect tenses. **Perfect tenses** tell that an action has been completed before a certain time or will be continuing to a certain time. Two of the perfect tenses, the present perfect and the past perfect, are actually special forms of the past tense. The other perfect tense, the future perfect, is a special form of the future tense.

Although you may think of the past as one time, there are actually three levels of past tenses. You already know about the simple past tense. The other two types of past tense are the present perfect and the past perfect.

Present Perfect Tense

The **present perfect tense** tells that an action was started in the past and is continuing in the present or has just been completed.

Pat <u>has waited</u> for the bus since six o'clock.

I <u>have walked</u> the entire way home.

Form the present perfect tense of regular verbs by adding either *has* or *have* to the past participle of the main verb.

Present Perfect Tense	
he, she, it	has waited
I, you, we, they	have waited

Past Perfect Tense

The **past perfect tense** tells that an action was completed in the past before another event or before a certain time in the past. Form the past perfect tense of regular verbs by adding *had* to the past participle of the main verb.

Pat <u>had waited</u> for the bus for 10 minutes before we arrived.

Past Perfect Tense	
I, you, he, she, it, we, they	had waited

Future Perfect Tense

There are two types of verbs in the future tense. You already know about the simple future. It tells what will happen in the future. The other future tense is the future perfect tense.

The **future perfect tense** shows an action that will be completed by a specific time in the future.

Pat <u>will have waited</u> 10 minutes by the time we get there.

Form the future perfect tense of regular verbs by adding *will have* to the past participle of the main verb.

Future Perfect Tense	
I, you, he, she, it, we, they	will have waited

Using Verbs in a Cover Letter

When you write a cover letter to accompany a job application, you will include different types of verbs and you may use more than one tense.

Dear Mr. Smith:

    I <u>am interested</u> in the position of automotive service manager <u>advertised</u> on your website. My resume <u>is</u> attached. I <u>believe</u> I <u>have</u> the qualifications you <u>require</u>. In June I <u>graduated</u> from Silver Lake Community College with an associate degree in business. Prior to that, I <u>worked</u> for three years as an assistant service manager at Mega-Cars. I <u>will be</u> available for an interview any day next week. I <u>look</u> forward to hearing from you.

Best Regards,

Max Grafton

There are three perfect tenses: the present perfect, past perfect, and future perfect. Read the following sentence:

Max walks to work.

Now read the sentence rewritten in each of the three perfect tenses.

Max has walked to work every morning.

Max had walked to work before I even woke up.

Max will have walked to work by 8:00 a.m.

Rewrite the following sentence in a notebook using each of the three perfect tenses.

They watch the movie.

THINK ABOUT **WRITING**

Directions: Write the correct form of the verb in parentheses on the blank lines. These sentences review all six of the verb tenses: present, past, future, present perfect, past perfect, and future perfect.

Example: Ms. Luna ____will explain____ the new procedure next week. (explain)

1. (begin)   In two more weeks, I _____ my class.

2. (taste)   A cup of tea with lunch always _____ good to me.

3. (take)   Frank _____ a lot of pictures before he discovered that his lens cap was still on.

4. (swim)   Jose and Molly _____ more than 20 miles by the time they finish the race.

5. (say)   As I _____ before, I'm not going to be talked into taking the first offer I get.

Subjunctive Mood

The **subjunctive mood** is a verb form used in three situations: in commands, to express urgency, and to express wishes or a condition that is contrary to fact.

When used for commands or to express urgency, the subjunctive is formed in two ways.

1. Use the base form of the verb. Do not add an *s* to the end of the verb.

   <u>Be</u> careful. *(command)*

   It is important that Lee <u>complete</u> this questionnaire. *(urgency)*

2. Use the verb *be* plus the past participle of the main verb.

   Mr. Chino insists that this project <u>be finished</u> today. *(urgency)*

To express wishes or something that is contrary to fact, the subjunctive is formed using *were*. *Were* may be used by itself or with the infinitive, past participle, or the *ing* form of the main verb.

If I <u>were</u> taller, I could dunk the basketball.

If we <u>were to leave</u>, we would never know what happened.

If you <u>were elected</u> president, would you name me to the Supreme Court?

If he <u>were lying</u>, do you think it would show on his face?

THINK ABOUT **WRITING**

Directions: Choose the correct verb in the parentheses in each of the following sentences.

Example: If I (*was, were*) a fast runner, I would enter that 10K race.

1. It is necessary that the runner (*complete, completes*) the entire form.

2. If I (*was, were*) stronger, I would run a marathon.

3. It is important that lots of water (*is drunk, be drunk*).

4. If Naoshi (*was, were*) to see me in this race, he would be surprised.

5. The rules require that every runner (*pay, pays*) a small registration fee.

Active and Passive Voice

When a sentence is written in the **active voice**, the subject performs the action. When a sentence is written in the **passive voice**, the subject is acted upon.

Active: LeRoi poured the pancake batter onto the grill.

Passive: The pancake batter was poured onto the grill.

The first sentence is in the active voice. The subject, *LeRoi*, performs the action of pouring. The second sentence is in the passive voice. The subject, *pancake batter*, is acted upon by being poured.

Sentences in the passive voice can be written in any tense. To write regular verbs in the passive voice, use a form of the verb *be* and the past participle.

Passive Voice		
Present	I *am* he, she, it *is* we, you, they *are*	
Past	I, he, she, it *was* we, you, they *were*	shocked
Future	I, you, he, she, it, we, they *will be*	

THINK ABOUT **WRITING**

Directions: Rewrite each of the following passive voice sentences in the active voice.

Example: That wedding dress was worn by my grandmother 60 years ago.

My grandmother wore that wedding dress 60 years ago.

1. The old house was deserted by my grandparents.

    _____

2. The doorway is hidden by large shrubs.

    _____

3. The cellar door was jammed shut by that fallen tree.

    _____

4. The old house will be torn down by the wrecking crew.

    _____

Consistent Verb Tenses

Remember that verb tenses are used to show when an action takes place. As you write, use the correct tenses so your readers are not confused. Do not change tenses within a sentence or between sentences unless it is necessary to show a change in the time of the actions.

> **Incorrect:** Amy picked up the keys and walks to the door.
>
> **Correct:** Amy <u>picks</u> up the keys and <u>walks</u> to the door.
>
> **Correct:** Amy <u>picked</u> up the keys and <u>walked</u> to the door.

In the first sentence above, *picked* is in the past tense and *walks* is in the present tense. This change in verb tenses is confusing. Both verbs should be in the present tense, as shown in the second sentence, or in the past tense, as shown in the last sentence.

The following sentence contains two verbs in different tenses. How would you correct the sentence?

> Boris <u>stands</u> at the end of the diving board for five minutes before he <u>jumped</u>.

To correct the sentence, you could change both verbs to the present tense:

> Boris <u>stands</u> at the end of the diving board for five minutes before he <u>jumps</u>.

To correct the sentence, you could also change both verbs to the past tense:

> Boris <u>stood</u> at the end of the diving board for five minutes before he <u>jumped</u>.

Sometimes a change in tense is necessary to show that two actions occur at different times. In the following example, both events happened in the past. By using the past perfect and simple past tenses, the writer tells the reader that while both events took place in the past, one event (Abraham Lincoln had been a senator) preceded the other (he became president).

Abraham Lincoln <u>had been</u> (past perfect) a senator before he <u>became</u> (simple past) president.

When you write about two actions, you can give context clues to help your readers know if the actions occur at the same or different times. To do this use words such as *before, now, yesterday, after, while, next, then,* and *when.*

THINK ABOUT **WRITING**

Directions: Write the correct form of the verb in parentheses on the blank line.

Example: Before Yolanda (come) _____<u>came</u>_____ to see me, she (go) _____<u>had gone</u>_____ to the bakery.

1. Last year Lauren always (ride) _____ the bus to work, but now she always (ride) _____ her bike.

2. After we (buy) _____ a gas stove, we (discover) _____ we did not have a gas hookup.

3. Our company (begin) _____ a new hiring policy last month while I (be) _____ on vacation.

4. Jason (finish) _____ the book by the time class (begin) _____ next week.

5. Audrey (sweat) _____ when she (return) _____ from carrying the box of books up two flights of stairs.

6. I (hope) _____ that when you testified you (give) _____ the correct information.

7. Since last Tuesday, Sachi (memorize) _____ her lines for the play that (open) _____ next weekend.

8. Curtis didn't (reach) _____ his landlady until he (try) _____ six times.

9. Bill (run) _____ six miles by the time we (wake) _____ up in the morning.

10. The neighbor's dog (bite) _____ the mail carrier before it (run) _____ out of the yard.

Vocabulary Review

Directions: Complete each sentence with a vocabulary word. Then use the words to complete the puzzle.

common   link   majority   regular   verb

Across

2. There are only two girls in his class. The _____ of students are boys.

4. Serena used the chain to _____ her bike to the bike rack.

5. A word that tells what someone is or does is a _____.

Down

1. Tornadoes are a _____ occurrence in some parts of the country.

3. The seasons come and go in a _____ pattern.

Skill Review

Directions: Tell which words in the sentence are context clues that help you determine when the action happened. Then describe when it took place..

1. Before he left for work, Robert ate breakfast and walked his dog.

   _____

   _____

2. When Jordan finishes reading the book, he will read the next one in the series.

   _____

   _____

3. On her 80th birthday, my grandmother celebrated with all her children and grandchildren.

   _____

   _____

4. Yesterday, Sandy was feeling under the weather, so she did not have the energy to go for her usual run that day.

   _____

   _____

Skill Practice

Directions: Choose the <u>one best answer</u> to each question.

1. Javier crossed the finish line after John arrives at the track.

   Which correction should be made to the sentence?

   A. change <u>crossed</u> to <u>will have crossed</u>
   B. change <u>crossed</u> to <u>had crossed</u>
   C. change <u>arrives</u> to <u>had arrived</u>
   D. change <u>arrives</u> to <u>has arrived</u>

2. Scientists will study Jupiter when the satellite reachs the planet.

   Which correction should be made to the sentence?

   A. change <u>will study</u> to <u>study</u>
   B. change <u>will study</u> to <u>studied</u>
   C. change <u>reachs</u> to <u>reaches</u>
   D. change <u>reachs</u> to <u>will reach</u>

3. Before the lawyer asked any questions, the witness had swore she would tell the truth.

   Which correction should be made to the sentence?

   A. change <u>asked</u> to <u>asks</u>
   B. change <u>had swore</u> to <u>had sworn</u>
   C. change <u>had swore</u> to <u>swears</u>
   D. change <u>would tell</u> to <u>tells</u>

4. It is important that <u>Sid connects the wires properly</u> or the battery will go dead.

   Which is the best way to write the underlined portion of the sentence? If the original is the best way, choose option (A).

   A. Sid connects the wires properly
   B. Sid connect the wires properly
   C. Sid connected the wired properly
   D. Sid had connected the wired properly

5. <u>Marta exchange</u> the purple skirt for a white one so that she could wear more blouses with it.

   Which is the best way to write the underlined portion of the sentence? If the original is the best way, choose option (A).

   A. Marta exchange
   B. Marta will exchange
   C. Marta exchanged
   D. Marta had exchanged

6. After Ted gets his tax return, <u>he bought a computer</u>.

   Which is the best way to write the underlined portion of the sentence? If the original is the best way, choose option (A).

   A. he bought a computer
   B. he is buying a computer
   C. he will buy a computer
   D. he buy a computer

Writing Practice

Directions: On another piece of paper, write a paragraph about a place you like to go. Include examples of times that you have been there in the past. Use context clues to tell the reader more about when you went to this place. Use appropriate verb forms and tenses, punctuation, and proper language conventions.

Subject-Verb Agreement

Lesson Objectives

You will be able to

- Identify subject-verb agreement in sentences

- Identify clauses

- Identify collective nouns

Skills

- **Reading Skill:** Identify Sequence

- **Core Skill:** Understand Organization

Vocabulary

ascertain
confusion
distinguish
modify
sequence

KEY CONCEPT: A verb must agree with the subject of the sentence.

Choose the correct form of the verb in parentheses.

1. Koda (work; worked) nonstop since early this morning.

2. Minh (will have practiced; practice) for two months before opening night.

Simple Subjects

The key to making subjects and verbs agree is to look at the **simple subject**. The simple subject is the noun or pronoun that the sentence is about. Then look at the verb. If the simple subject is singular, the verb must also be singular. If the simple subject is plural, the verb must also be plural. How would you correct these sentences?

Juan leap up the stairs.   The birds flies to the feeder.

In the first sentence, the simple subject is *Juan*, a singular noun. *Leap* is the plural form of the verb, so use the singular verb *leaps*.

Juan <u>leaps</u> up the stairs.

In the second sentence, the simple subject is *birds*, a plural noun. To correct this sentence, you must **modify** [change] the singular verb *flies* to the plural verb *fly*. Another way to correct this sentence would be to change the plural noun *birds* to the singular noun *bird*.

The birds <u>fly</u> to the feeder.   The <u>bird</u> flies to the feeder.

To check whether you have correctly matched subjects and verbs in a sentence, replace the subject noun with a pronoun. The pronoun helps you see what is correct. Look at the pattern below.

Singular

I	
You	— **swim** in the pool.

He	
She	— **swims** in the pool.
It	

Plural

We	
You	— **swim** in the pool.

They —— **swim** in the pool.

Adding an *s* or an *es* to a present-tense verb makes it agree with the singular pronouns *he*, *she*, and *it*, as well as with all singular nouns that they replace.

IDENTIFY SEQUENCE

Sequence is the order in which events happen. Sometimes writers tell about events in the order they happen, and other times, they do not. Clue words such as *first, next, last, yesterday,* and *tomorrow* can help you figure out the order of events as you read. Another clue to the sequence of events is verb tense: past, present, future.

To order the events in a passage, ask yourself: *What happened first? Next? Last? What verb tense is used? Does the verb tense change anywhere in the passage?*

Read the following paragraph. Look for clue words and verb tense to help you figure out the order of events.

> (1) Yesterday, Luke completed his first marathon! (2) Today, he is thinking about all of his hard training. (3) First, he walked for an hour every other day for a week. (4) Next, he alternated between running and walking. (5) Finally, he ran 8 to 13 miles a day.

Sentence 1 tells about an event that has already happened. The word *yesterday* and the verb *completed* tells us that the event, a marathon, happened in the past. The word *today* and the present-tense verb phrase *is thinking* in sentence 2 are clues that the writer is talking about what is happening now. Sentences 3–5 tell about events in the past. We know this because the verbs *walked, alternated,* and *ran* are in the past tense. We also know the order in which each event happened in the past because of the clue words *first, next,* and *finally.*

Reading Skill
Identify Sequence

Remember that paying attention to verb tense is one way to make sense of what you are reading. Verb tense tells readers whether events happened in the past, are happening right now, or will happen in the future.

After you complete each sentence in the Think about Writing activity on this page, ask yourself: *Is this sentence telling about something that happened in the past, is happening now, or will happen in the future? Is it happening now and in the past? Is it happening now and in the future? How do I know?*

Subject-Verb Agreement with Linking Verbs

Linking verbs can cause **confusion**, or a mix-up, in subject-verb agreement. For example, which of the following is correct?

> Our best hope <u>is</u> our children.

> Our best hope <u>are</u> our children.

If you are not sure, find the simple subject of the sentence—*hope*. Since *hope* is singular, it should be used with the singular verb form *is*.

> Our best hope <u>is</u> our children.

THINK ABOUT **WRITING**

Directions: Find the simple subject in each sentence and underline it once. Then choose the correct verb form in parentheses and underline it twice.

Example: The <u>women</u> across the street (*is*, <u>*are*</u>) my aunts.

1. Those fish (*has*, *have*) been jumping since we got here.
2. Our problem (*is*, *are*) getting the tent set up.
3. We in the jury (*believe*, *believes*) he is innocent.
4. My muscles (*ache*, *aches*) from all the exercise.
5. The security guards at the store (*want*, *wants*) a raise.
6. I (*come*, *comes*) to all my son's baseball games.
7. The order (*include*, *includes*) paper clips, folders, and tape.

Compound Subjects

Sentences can have two or more nouns or pronouns as their subject. These are called **compound subjects**, and they can cause confusion in subject-verb agreement. Are the following sentences correct?

> Alicia and Patrick buy tickets to every concert.

> Alicia or Patrick buys tickets to every concert.

Both sentences are correct. To decide which verb form to use, look at how the parts of the compound subject are connected. In the sample sentences, they are connected by *and* and *or*.

When a compound subject is connected by *and*, the subject is plural. Use the present-tense verb that does not end in *s*.

Incorrect: Juanita <u>and</u> George <u>plays</u> tennis every week.

Correct: Juanita <u>and</u> George <u>play</u> tennis every week.

Words such as *or* and *neither...nor* split the parts of a compound subject. Each noun or pronoun in the compound subject is considered separately. The verb agrees with the part closer to it.

Neither Helen nor Maria <u>wants</u> to go to the game.

Either David or the twins <u>take</u> the dog for a walk.

THINK ABOUT **WRITING**

Directions: Underline the correct verb in each sentence.

Example: Either Sarah or her two children (*does*, <u>*do*</u>) the dishes.

1. Mr. Fletcher and Ms. Ortega (*were*, *was*) a good sales team.

2. Three books and a new DVD (*appear*, *appears*) on my son's Christmas list.

3. My favorite lunch (*are*, *is*) fruit and cheese.

4. Neither the twins nor Jeffrey (*plan*, *plans*) to go to the reunion.

5. Either Veronica or they (*has*, *have*) the keys to my apartment.

6. My roommate and best friend, Mitch, often (*give*, *gives*) parties.

7. My car and Stan's pickup (*is*, *are*) in the repair shop.

8. Zelda, Pearl, and Tonya (*complain*, *complains*) constantly.

Interrupters

Many sentences look more complicated than they really are because they have interrupting phrases. An **interrupting phrase** is a group of words that comes between the simple subject and the verb. Because of these interrupters, it's easy to make an error in subject-verb agreement.

Many interrupters are prepositional phrases. A **prepositional phrase** is a word group that starts with a preposition and ends with a noun or pronoun. A **preposition** is a word that connects a noun with another part of the sentence. A prepositional phrase can be removed, and the sentence will still be complete.

The building <u>with the white shutters</u> needs painting.

There are many prepositions in the English language. Here are a few.

Some Common Prepositions			
above	by	into	through
at	for	near	to
before	from	of	under
between	in	on	with

When you write a sentence with a prepositional phrase, use these three steps to **ascertain** [make sure] that the subject and verb agree.

1. Draw a line through any prepositional phrases.

   My mother's biscuits and barbecued chicken ~~off my father's grill~~ (is, are) my favorite foods.

2. Find the simple subject.

   My mother's <u>biscuits and</u> barbecued <u>chicken</u> ~~off my father's grill~~ (is, are) my favorite foods.

3. Choose the verb that agrees with the subject.

   My mother's <u>biscuits and</u> barbecued <u>chicken</u> ~~off my father's grill~~ (are) my favorite foods.

A special group of words can make interrupting prepositional phrases especially troublesome. These are words that seem to make the subject plural. Actually, they introduce an interrupting phrase.

as well as   besides   including   together with

along with   in addition to   like

These words usually introduce phrases that are set off by commas. Treat the phrase as an interrupter, not as part of the subject.

My <u>sister</u>, along with my brother, <u>likes</u> horror movies.

Inverted Sentences

In most sentences, the subject comes first and is followed by the verb. Sometimes, however, the subject and verb are **inverted** [reversed]. Inverted sentences can cause confusion in subject-verb agreement. Which of the following is correct?

In her hand <u>is</u> two red roses.

In her hand <u>are</u> two red roses.

Notice that this sentence begins with a prepositional phrase, *in her hand*. The phrase is followed by the verb and the subject comes last. Often, it is easier to **distinguish** [recognize the difference] between correct and incorrect subject-verb agreement in an inverted sentence by rephrasing it in normal order.

Two red roses <u>is</u> in her hand.

Two red roses <u>are</u> in her hand.

Now it is easy to see that the subject is *roses*, and the correct verb is *are*.

Sentences Beginning with *Here* and *There*

Sentences beginning with *here* and *there* can also be confusing. Which of the following sentences is correct?

Here <u>is</u> my new car.   Here <u>are</u> my new car.

Neither *here* nor *there* is a noun or pronoun, so they cannot be the subject of a sentence. You know, then, that this is an inverted sentence. Rearrange the sentence in normal subject-verb order. Then choose the verb.

My car <u>is</u> here.   My car <u>are</u> here.

Car is a singular subject, so it takes the singular verb *is*.

THINK ABOUT WRITING

Directions: Choose the correct verb in parentheses.

Example: On top of the suitcase (*is*, <u>*are*</u>) my tennis shoes.

1. At the end of the dusty road (*stand*, *stands*) two old water pumps.

2. There (*is*, *are*) no clues to tell who the robber is.

3. Antonio, along with his two sons, (*waits*, *wait*) beneath the tree.

4. Across the front windows (*stretch*, *stretches*) a yellow ribbon.

5. Three lost dogs, including my collie, (*walk*, *walks*) into the yard.

6. Here (*is*, *are*) my old hiking boots.

7. Later in the day, the clouds in the west (*grow*, *grows*) thick and dark.

8. Why (*do*, *does*) those two dead plants still sit on your desk?

Clauses

Another group of words that often causes problems in subject-verb agreement is a clause. A **clause** is a group of words that contains a subject and a verb. Sentences often contain more than one clause.

An article <u>that explains the scandals</u> appears in today's newspaper.

When a sentence has more than one clause, you must be careful to identify which verb goes with which subject. When you are not sure, draw a line under the interrupting clause. Then check the subject-verb agreement in the main sentence and also in the clause.

In the sample sentence, *article* is the main subject of the sentence and should agree with the verb *appears*. *That explains the scandals* is a clause. *That* is a pronoun and goes with the verb *explains*.

Errors in subject-verb agreement are often caused by the pronouns that introduce interrupting clauses. Many pronouns can be either singular or plural, depending on the nouns they replace. *That*, *who*, and *which* are examples. To be sure subject-verb agreement is correct, you need to know if the pronoun refers to a plural or a singular noun.

Kioko is one of those people <u>who love to read mystery novels</u>.

In the sample sentence, the clause is *who love to read mystery novels*. The verb of the main sentence is *is*, which agrees with the simple subject, *Kioko*. The verb in the clause is *love* and its subject is *who*. In this sentence, *who* replaces *people*, a plural noun. *Love* is a plural verb, so the subject and verb do agree.

THINK ABOUT WRITING

Directions: In each of the sentences below, underline the correct verb form in parentheses.

Example: Do you know the woman who (<u>is</u>, *are*) selling those plants?

1. Molly is one of those people who (*argue*, *argues*) about everything.

2. Pang is taking all the orders that (*is*, *are*) placed this morning.

3. He has two lamps that (*need*, *needs*) new shades.

4. The solution, which (*seems*, *seem*) quite simple, is to hire more help.

5. Larry reads books that (*require*, *requires*) a lot of concentration.

6. The speakers have suggested a plan that (*appear*, *appears*) to be logical.

7. My niece is one of those children who (*love*, *loves*) being outdoors.

8. June's office has several computers that (*are*, *is*) no longer needed.

9. This childproof cap is one of many useful inventions that (*make*, *makes*) life more difficult.

10. The two brothers, who (*like*, *likes*) to go fishing, usually go to Beck Lake.

11. The answer, which (*appear*, *appears*) to be correct, is, in fact, incorrect.

12. Mr. Lee, who has several tables and chairs to refinish for his customers, (*plan*, *plans*) to finish them by Tuesday.

13. His nephews, who (*arrive*, *arrives*) next week, plan to meet Don at Metro Airport at noon.

Singular Subjects That Seem Plural

One of the most common mistakes in subject-verb agreement is caused by a certain group of pronouns. They look plural but are really singular. Which sentence is correct?

Everybody on the team win.

Everybody on the team wins.

Everybody seems to refer to all people. So it is plural, right? No. What it really says is *every body*, and *body* is singular. The second sentence, which has the singular verb *wins*, is correct. All of the following pronouns are singular.

Singular Pronouns		
another	either	no one
anybody	everybody	nothing
anyone	everyone	one
anything	everything	somebody
each	neither	someone
each one	nobody	

Neither of the whales is happy living in the tank.

Each of those sharks weighs more than 500 pounds.

Here is a way you can easily remember most of these words. Look at the second part of the words. The words *one*, *thing*, and *body* are all singular. The words they are part of are also singular.

Vocabulary Review

Directions: Complete each sentence below using one of the following vocabulary words:

ascertain   confusion   distinguish   modify   sequence

1. When you _____ something, you find out something for certain.

2. When you make a change to something, you _____ it.

3. The _____ is the order in which events happened.

4. A person might feel _____ about something that is unclear or misunderstood.

5. Looking carefully, you can _____ the different types of pronouns.

Skill Review

Directions: Read the sentences. Use the verb tenses to help you answer the questions about the sequence of events.

> Graciela is always busy. On Monday, she had a doctor's appointment. On Wednesday, she had a piano lesson. Tomorrow, she will have soccer practice.

1. Which two events happened in the past? _____

_____

2. Which event happened first—the doctor's appointment or piano lesson? How do you know?

_____

_____

3. What event will happen in the future? When will it happen? _____

Directions: The order of the subject and verb are reversed in the following inverted sentences. Which sentence is correct?

4. _____ In the tree is two tiny kittens.
   _____ In the tree are two tiny kittens.

5. _____ Around her neck were a strand of pearls.
   _____ Around her neck was a strand of pearls.

Skill Practice

Directions: Choose the one best answer to each question.

1. Shen and Mike plan to visit the National Air and Space Museum, which is part of the Smithsonian Institution. Neither of them want to miss the historic airplanes. The collection includes many famous planes.

   Which correction should be made to these sentences?

   A. change plan to plans
   B. change is to are
   C. change want to wants
   D. change includes to include

2. Rosa, along with her sister, jump out of the stalled car and walks the rest of the way home. The sisters, who get there at the same time, rush through the front door.

   Which correction should be made to these sentences?

   A. change jump to jumps
   B. change walks to walk
   C. change get to gets
   D. change rush to rushes

3. Here is your tickets. When the band plays tonight, it will be before a full house. Jose and Kathy, as well as the Tucker family, seem eager to hear it. Everyone wants to hear this hot band.

   Which is the best way to write the underlined portion of the sentence? If the original is the best way, choose option (A).

   A. Here is your tickets.
   B. Here are your tickets.
   C. Here is yours tickets.
   D. Heres is your ticket.

4. Jan, along with her sister Cindy, run 10 miles a day. They plan to compete in the marathon and win.

   Which is the best way to write the underlined portion of the sentence? If the original is the best way, choose option (A).

   A. run 10 miles a day
   B. running 10 miles a day
   C. runs 10 miles a day
   D. are running 10 miles a day

Writing Practice

Directions: On a piece of paper, describe a trip you have taken or a trip you would like to take. Make sure to describe the events of the trip in the correct sequence. Remember to keep your verb tenses accurate and to make sure your subjects and verbs agree.

Directions: Choose the one best answer to each question.

1. The security guard who walk the long halls is exhausted at the end of his shift.

   Which correction should be made to this sentence?

   A. change walk to walks
   B. change walk to had walked
   C. change is exhausted to are exhausted
   D. change is exhausted to had been exhausted

2. The computer class will start next week. Everyone who is interested in computers are welcome. A fee of $25.00 has been set.

   Which correction should be made to these sentences?

   A. change will start to will have started
   B. change who is to who are
   C. change are welcome to is welcome
   D. change has been to was

3. Lucinda arrived at the store after the sale has ended.

   Which correction should be made to this sentence?

   A. change arrived to has arrived
   B. change arrived to arrive
   C. change has ended to had ended
   D. change has ended to ends

4. Somebody whom I do not know send me a birthday card every year.

   Which correction should be made to this sentence?

   A. change do not know to does not know
   B. change do not know to do not knows
   C. change send to will send
   D. change send to sends

5. Ana had given the package to Curtis while they stood at the door talking.

   Which correction should be made to this sentence?

   A. change had given to had give
   B. change had given to gave
   C. change stood to have stood
   D. change stood to stand

6. It is necessary that the club manager signs this contract or the band will quit.

   Which is the best way to write the underlined portion of the sentence? If the original is the best way, choose option (A).

   A. It is necessary that the club manager signs
   B. It is necessary that the club manager sign
   C. It was necessary that the club manager signs
   D. It is necessary that the club manager signed

7. Sonia, along with her two little brothers, were given tickets to the game.

Which is the best way to write the underlined portion of the sentence? If the original is the best way, choose option (A).

A. Sonia, along with her two little brothers, were given
B. Sonia, along with her two little brothers, was given
C. Sonia, along with her two little brothers, are given
D. Sonia, along with her two little brothers, were gave

8. Before the amusement park had opened, neither Martha nor Kim had ever seen such a large roller coaster.

Which is the best way to write the underlined portion of the sentence? If the original is the best way, choose option (A).

A. Before the amusement park had opened,
B. Before the amusement park opened,
C. Before the amusement park is opened,
D. Before the amusement park has opened,

9. Shawna has overslept. She hurries to leave so she will not be late. Her daughter has hid her car keys.

Which is the best way to write the underlined portion of the sentence? If the original is the best way, choose option (A).

A. Her daughter has hid her car keys.
B. Her daughter is hiding her car keys.
C. Her daughter have hide her car keys.
D. Her daughter has hidden her car keys.

10. Simon stoops to pick up the broken plate, and his eyeglasses slips down his nose.

Which is the best way to write the underlined portion of the sentence? If the original is the best way, choose option (A).

A. and his eyeglasses slips down his nose
B. and his eyeglasses slipping down his nose
C. and his eyeglasses slip down his nose
D. and his eyeglasses had slipped down his nose

11. Beside the new garage rests three tired carpenters. They will be going home when the work is done.

Which is the best way to write the underlined portion of the sentence? If the original is the best way, choose option (A).

A. rests three tired carpenters
B. rest three tired carpenters
C. is resting three tired carpenters
D. had rested three tired carpenters

12. <u>He opens his birthday gifts</u> after he had eaten some cake.

Which is the best way to write the underlined portion of the sentence? If the original is the best way, choose option (A).

A. He opens his birthday gifts
B. He will open his birthday gifts
C. He is opening his birthday gifts
D. He opened his birthday gifts

13. Her daughter's clothes is always dirty after playing at the park.

Which correction should be made to this sentence?

A. change <u>is</u> to <u>are</u>
B. change <u>is always</u> to <u>had been</u>
C. change <u>playing</u> to <u>played</u>
D. change <u>playing</u> to <u>had played</u>

14. My brothers, along with my youngest sister, likes to put ketchup on everything they eat.

Which correction should be made to this sentence?

A. change <u>likes</u> to <u>like</u>
B. change <u>likes</u> to <u>have liked</u>
C. change <u>eat</u> to <u>ate</u>
D. change <u>eat</u> to <u>have eaten</u>

15. The size of those berries seem larger than usual.

Which correction should be made to this sentence?

A. change <u>those berries</u> to <u>that berry</u>
B. change <u>seem</u> to <u>is seeming</u>
C. change <u>seem</u> to <u>are seeming</u>
D. change <u>seem</u> to <u>seems</u>

16. Write a paragraph or two about a skill or talent that you have. Describe how you first recognized that you had this skill or talent. Explain the steps you have taken to develop it and how you plan to continue to use it in the future. Remember to keep your verb tenses consistent and to make sure your subjects and verbs agree.

_____

_____

_____

_____

_____

_____

_____

_____

Review

Check Your Understanding

On the following chart, circle the number of any item you answered incorrectly in the Chapter 2 Review on pages 70–72. Next to each group of item numbers, you will see the pages you can review to learn how to answer the items correctly. Pay particular attention to reviewing skill areas in which you missed half or more of the questions.

Chapter 2 Review

Skill Area	Item Number	Review Pages
Verb and Verb Tenses	3, 5, 8, 9, 12, 16	44-59
Subject-Verb Agreement	1, 2, 4, 6, 7, 10, 11, 13, 14, 15, 16	60-69

Modifiers

Read the following description of a cat:

> The cat is fat.

What does this sentence tell you about the cat? All you know is that the cat is fat.

Now read this description of the same cat:

> The playful, black-and-white cat has a fat belly.

This sentence gives us so much more information about the cat. It tells us that the cat is playful, that its fur is black and white, and that the cat has a fat belly. The second sentence shows how modifiers can bring a sentence to life.

Modifiers are words that describe other words. In this chapter you will learn about how modifiers can transform dull writing into something colorful and interesting. Modifiers help readers imagine what they are reading about.

Here is what you will learn about in this chapter:

Lesson 3.1: Adjectives and Adverbs
Adjectives and adverbs are words that describe other words. They add interest to your writing. Writing without adjectives and adverbs is like cooking without spices—it's uninteresting.

Lesson 3.2: Modifying Phrases
Want to add detail and precision to your writing? Learn about the different kinds of modifying phrases that can make your writing interesting and precise.

Goal Setting

Using modifiers builds on what you have already learned about the parts of speech and sentence basics. Think about how modifying your sentences can make your writing more personal and more interesting.

What would you like to learn about modifiers? How do you think they will help change/improve your writing?

_____

_____

_____

In the chart below, write down new ways to modify, or describe, the objects around you and the actions you perform in your daily life. Add to the chart as you complete each lesson in the chapter.

Objects and Actions	Modifiers

Adjectives and Adverbs

Lesson Objectives

You will be able to

- Recognize the functions of adjectives and adverbs in sentences
- Use adjectives and adverbs to write sentences

Skills

- **Core Skill:** Use Details
- **Reading Skill:** Visualize

Vocabulary

adjective
adverb
exception
modify
negative
visualize

KEY CONCEPT: Adjectives and adverbs are modifiers, words that describe [tell about] other words in a sentence.

1. Underline the correct verb form in this sentence:
   Don's nephews, who (*arrive*, *arrives*) today, plan to meet him at the airport at noon.

2. Underline the correct pronoun choice in this sentence:
   Anyone can learn to play piano as long as it is something that (*he or she*, *they*) wants to do.

Adjectives

Adjectives are words that **modify**, or describe, a noun or pronoun.

An adjective can modify a noun in several ways. It can tell *what kind, which one, or how many.*

what kind	⟶	**worst** storms	**mountainous** waves
which one	⟶	**this** hurricane	**that** shore
how many	⟶	**one** town	**countless** choices

Often a noun is modified by more than one adjective.

safer, **higher** land

Adverbs

Adverbs are words that modify, or describe, a verb, an adjective, or another adverb.

modifying a verb	⟶	moved **slowly**
modifying an adjective	⟶	**already** gigantic
modifying an adverb	⟶	**far** away

Adverbs can modify words in several ways. They can tell *how, when, how often, where,* and *to what extent.*

how	⟶	moved **slowly**
when	⟶	**already** gigantic
where	⟶	land **far** away
how often	⟶	calls **daily**
to what extent	⟶	**nearly** empty

VISUALIZE

When you form a mental picture in your mind from a written or spoken description, it is call visualizing. To **visualize** is one of the best ways to understand and to remember something. To help you visualize what you are reading, writers provide colorful and interesting details. One way they do this is by adding adjectives and adverbs to sentences. Adjectives and adverbs help readers "see" what they are reading. They provide a visual picture for the reader.

Read these two sentences:

> (1) Miguel has a new motorcycle.
>
> (2) Miguel has a shiny, black, powerful new motorcycle.

Sentence 1 provides a detail about Miguel's motorcycle, but Sentence 2 helps readers to visualize, or picture in their minds, what Miguel's motorcycle is like.

THINK ABOUT WRITING

Directions: Look at the underlined modifier in each sentence. Circle the word that is modified, or described. State whether the modifier is an adjective or an adverb.

Example: _adjective_ The snow fell on the red (flower)

1. _____ The mail arrived <u>late</u> today.

2. _____ A <u>late</u> dinner was served at the restaurant.

3. _____ <u>Four</u> children came to my door this afternoon.

4. _____ Andrew moved too <u>quickly</u> in the darkness and fell.

The more specific an adjective is, the better it describes what you are talking about. For example, *small* is an adjective that describes size. *Tiny* is an adjective that also describes size but is more precise and helps readers to better visualize what you are writing about.

In a notebook, write these three adjectives: *good, nice, loud*. Next to each one, write as many adjectives as you can that provide more specific details.

small ⟶ tiny

Adjectives and Adverbs Forms

Adjectives do not have a special form. Many adverbs, however, are formed by adding *ly* to an adjective.

Adverbs Formed with *ly*	
Adjectives	**Adverbs**
loud screaming	scream **loudly**
warm clothes	**warmly** dressed
beautiful painting	paints **beautifully**

Some adverbs are formed from adjectives in other ways.

If the adjective ends in

ll, add only a *y*	full ⟶	fully
y, change the *y* to *i* and add *ly*	happy ⟶	happily
le, change the *e* to *ly*	horrible ⟶	horribly
ic, add *al* before adding *ly*	frantic ⟶	frantically

Some adjectives and adverbs have the same form. The chart below shows some of these. Note that words ending in *ly* are not always adverbs.

Adjectives and Adverbs with the Same Form			
daily	fast	ill	right
early	hard	low	straight
far	high	near	weekly

THINK ABOUT **WRITING**

Directions: Identify the adjective or adverb in each sentence. Write the correct form.

Example: <u>slowly</u> The parks committee worked slow.

1. _____ The runners moved rapid toward the finish line.

2. _____ This new calculator is supposed to work easy.

3. _____ The extremely heat and lack of rain is hard on the crops.

4. _____ I read the contract careful before signing it.

5. _____ Molly hurt her foot bad.

Problems with Adjectives and Adverbs

Adverbs can often be moved around in a sentence without changing the meaning or making the sentence unclear. Sometimes, however, putting an adverb in the wrong position can change the meaning of a sentence. Compare the meanings of the following two sentences.

Mia **actually** told me that they eat worms.

Mia told me that they **actually** eat worms.

When an adverb is placed too far from the word it modifies, it can make the meaning of the sentence unclear. A reader might wonder exactly what is meant in the first sentence. Moving the adverb will make it clear.

I'll **just** give you two hours to finish that project.

I'll give you **just** two hours to finish that project.

Modifiers Used with Linking Verbs

Linking verbs, such as *is*, *are*, *seems*, *appears*, and *looks*, connect a noun with another word that describes it or renames it. The following verbs can be used as either linking verbs or action verbs:

Both Linking and Action Verbs			
appear	feel	look	smell
become	grow	seem	taste

A modifier that follows these words can be an adjective or an adverb.

Incorrect: That box looks **heavily**.

Correct: That box looks **heavy**. *(a heavy box)*

THINK ABOUT **WRITING**

Directions: Read each sentence below. If an underlined modifier is incorrect, write the correct form.

Example: *delighted* Laura seemed delightedly to see us.

1. _____ The early morning sky became darkly with thunderclouds.

2. _____ Will you be sadly if you don't see him again?

3. _____ When the two dogs looked fiercely at Gopal, he crossed quick to the other side of the street.

4. _____ The doctor felt Ann's swollen arm careful.

Adjectives and Adverbs in Comparisons

Adjectives are used to compare people, places, things, and ideas. Adverbs are used to compare actions. There are three degrees or levels of comparison. The first level uses the basic form of the adjective or adverb.

Adjective	Adverb
Claudia is **tall**.	Phuong walks **quickly**.

Compare Two Things or Actions

When two things or actions are compared, the correct adjective or adverb is usually formed in one of two ways. If the modifier is short—one or two syllables—add *er*. If the modifier is longer—three or more syllables—use the word *more* or *less* plus the adjective or adverb. Always use *more* or *less* with adverbs ending in *ly*. If an adjective ends in a consonant plus *y*, change the *y* to *i* before adding *er*.

Adjectives

Kathy's job is **harder** than his.

That house is **more expensive** than ours.

Adverbs

Steve's band played **louder** than Ken's band.

Of those two stars, that one sparkles **less brightly**.

Compare Three or More Things or Actions

There are two ways to form modifiers that compare three or more things or actions. For short adjectives and adverbs, add *est* to the end. For longer modifiers—and all adverbs ending in *ly*—use *most* or *least* plus the regular form of the adjective or adverb. For adjectives ending in a consonant plus *y*, change the *y* to *i* before adding *est*.

Adjectives

Of the three children, John is **sleepiest**.

The book is the **least interesting** one I've read all year.

Adverbs

Our team plays the **hardest** of all.

Elvira works the **most carefully** of the four employees.

Irregular Forms of Comparisons

Adjectives and adverbs that are used to make comparisons have both regular and irregular forms.

Irregular Comparisons		
Describing One Thing or Action	**Comparing Two Things or Actions**	**Comparing Three or More Things or Actions**
bad	worse	worst
far	farther	farthest
good	better	best
little	less	least
many	more	most
much	more	most
well	better	best

WRITE TO LEARN

A goal of good writing is to create visual images for readers. This helps them connect to your writing. In a notebook, write a paragraph about a movie or TV show you recently watched. As you write, choose words that describe people, places, and events. In addition, use words that appeal to the reader's senses to create vivid, interesting images.

Comparison Problems with Modifiers

When making comparisons, check how many things or actions are being compared. If two items are being compared, use the *er*, *more*, or *less* forms. If more than two items are being compared, use the *est*, *most*, or *least* forms. Errors often result from not using these forms correctly.

Incorrect: Of the **two** sisters, she is the **shortest**.

Correct: Of the **two** sisters, she is the **shorter**.

Be alert to comparisons between one thing and a group of things. It may seem as though you are comparing many things. In fact, it is two things—one thing and one group.

Incorrect: He speaks **most slowly** than the **other men**.

Correct: He speaks **more slowly** than the **other men**.

THINK ABOUT WRITING

Directions: Write the correct form of each modifier in parentheses.

Example: *hungrier* Elena is (*hungry*) than Margo.

1. _____ Rice, beans, and macaroni are the (*cheap*) items I buy at the store.

2. _____ Mark always dresses (*neat*) than Tamiko.

3. _____ Susan has never been (*happy*) than she is now.

4. _____ Helena is (*serious*) about starting a business than I am.

More Problems with Adjectives and Adverbs

There are four common mistakes in the use of modifiers.

Well or Good; Badly or Bad

Well and *badly* are adverbs. *Good* and *bad* are adjectives.

Adjectives	**Adverbs**
Take a **good** look at this example.	She plays **well**.
Do you think this is a **bad** idea?	The toast is **badly** burnt.

Be especially careful when using linking verbs. They connect a subject to its modifier, which is always an adjective.

The book is **good**. Those rotten apples smell **bad**.

There is an important **exception** [case when the rule does not apply] to this rule. When the modifier after a linking verb refers to health, use *well* instead of *good*.

Are you feeling **well**?

Double Negatives

A **negative** is a word that means *no* or *not*.

Negatives		
hardly	nobody	nothing
neither	none	nowhere
never	no one	*n't* in contractions
no	not	scarcely

Never use more than one **negative** in a clause.

Incorrect: I do **not** want **nothing**.

Correct: I do **not** want **anything**.

Look for contractions that end with *n't*. The *n't* stands for "not," so these words are negatives. Do not use them with another negative.

Incorrect: She **can't** go **nowhere**.

Correct: She **can't** go **anywhere**.

Correct: She can go **nowhere**.

A common mistake is to forget that *hardly* and *scarcely* are negatives.

Incorrect: Teresa **can't hardly** see well enough to drive.

Correct: Teresa can **hardly** see well enough to drive.

Correct: Teresa **can't** see well enough to drive.

This, That, These, Those, and Them

This and *that* are adjectives used to point out singular nouns. *This* refers to something that is close by. *That* refers to something that is not close.

This book goes in **that** bookcase.

These and *those* are adjectives used to point out plural nouns. *These* refers to things that are nearby. *Those* refers to things that are not nearby.

These books go in **those** bookcases.

Because *this* and *these* mean "here," do not use *this here* or *these here*. For the same reason, do not use *that there* or *those there*.

Incorrect: These pencils **here** are mine.

Correct: **These** pencils are mine.

Them cannot be used in place of *those* to point out a noun. *Them* is always an object pronoun.

Incorrect: Did you see **them** cars?

Correct: Did you see **those** cars?

A and An

The words *a* and *an* are articles, or special adjectives and are always used with a noun. They modify nouns to show they are singular. *An* is used before all words that begin with a vowel sound. (The vowels are *a, e, i, o, u*.) Use *a* before all other words.

an ape	**an** opinion	**an** unusual day
a boring speech	**a** lazy dog	**a** flower

Use *an* before a word that begins with an *h* if the *h* is not pronounced.

an hour	**an** honor	but: **a** hospital

There is one vowel to watch out for. Use *a* before words beginning with a *u* that is pronounced like *you*.

a unicorn	**a** usual day	**a** union

THINK ABOUT **WRITING**

Directions: In each sentence below, underline the correct answer in the parentheses.

Example: Hilda visited (<u>a</u>, an) university last week.

1. I have already read (*those, them*) books.

2. Sarah (*hadn't scarcely, had scarcely*) begun to clean her house.

3. That coffee tastes (*bitter, bitterly*).

4. Jill is (*a, an*) ideal candidate for mayor.

5. We don't have time to sponsor (*no, any*) special events.

6. We couldn't find the little girl (*anywhere, nowhere*).

Vocabulary Review

Directions: Complete the sentences below using one of the following words:

adjective   **adverb**   **exception**   **modify**   **negative**   **visualize**

1. When you _____ a word or a phrase, you describe it.

2. If you want to tell how often something happened, you should use a(n) _____.

3. You make a(n) _____ when you make something different from other things.

4. You use a(n) _____ to modify a noun.

5. Using more than one _____ in a clause is always incorrect.

6. When you create mental pictures in your mind, you _____ what is being said or written.

Skill Review

Directions: Underline the words or phrases in this paragraph that help you picture or visualize the scene.

1. (1) One of nature's worst storms moved slowly toward the unprotected land. (2) Worried people were preparing for this hurricane. (3) It would hurl powerful winds and mountainous waves at them. (4) Already, gigantic waves were beating savagely against that shore. (5) One town was nearly empty. (6) Wisely, its people had run toward higher land far away from the dangerous sea.

Directions: Use the word web to write modifiers—adjectives and adverbs—that you think of when you hear the word *hero*.

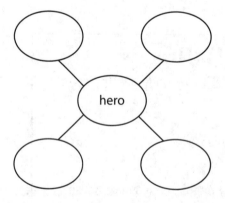

2. Write two sentences about someone you would consider a hero using the modifiers you included in your word web.

_____

_____

Skill Practice

Directions: Choose the <u>one best answer</u> to each question.

1. <u>The nervous man drove careful down the busy street.</u> He seemed glad when he turned onto the side road.

   Which is the best way to write the underlined sentence? If the original is the best way, choose option (A).

   A. The nervous man drove careful down the busy street.
   B. The nervous man drove carefully down the busy street.
   C. The nervously man drove careful down the busy street.
   D. The nervous man drove careful down the busily street.

2. The oak tree is highest than the maple tree in our yard. We get more shade early in the morning from the oak tree.

   Which correction should be made to these sentences?

   A. change <u>highest</u> to <u>high</u>
   B. change <u>highest</u> to <u>higher</u>
   C. replace <u>more</u> with <u>most</u>
   D. change <u>early</u> to <u>earliest</u>

3. <u>I didn't hardly ever do anything fun</u> while I lived in that city. After a few months, I moved back to this city, where I know more people.

   Which is the best way to write the underlined portion of the sentence? If the original is the best way, choose option (A).

   A. I didn't hardly ever do anything fun
   B. I did hardly never do anything fun
   C. I didn't hardly ever do nothing fun
   D. I hardly ever did anything fun

4. My manager wants our small department to be the most successful in the company. She tries to hire the better people she can find.

   Which correction should be made to these sentences?

   A. change <u>small</u> to <u>smaller</u>
   B. change <u>most successful</u> to <u>successfullest</u>
   C. change <u>most successful</u> to <u>more successful</u>
   D. replace <u>better</u> with <u>best</u>

Writing Practice

Directions: On a piece of paper, describe a type of weather you have experienced, such as a snow storm, thunder storm, hurricane, or tornado. Use adjectives and adverbs to create an accurate and compelling description. Use appropriate verb forms and tenses, punctuation, and proper language conventions.

Modifying Phrases

Lesson Objectives

You will be able to

- Understand the use of modifying phrases

- Identify prepositional phrases as modifiers

- Identify verb phrases as modifiers

- Identify renaming phrases as modifiers

Skills

- **Core Skill:** Clarify and Explain

- **Reading Skill:** Recognize Supporting Details

Vocabulary

adjacent
ambiguous
phrase

KEY CONCEPT: A group of words called a *phrase* can modify another word in a sentence.

Underline the adjectives in each sentence. Tell what each modifies.
1. The spotted dog wagged its tail.

2. Enormous raindrops fell from the dark clouds.

Underline the adverb in each sentence. Tell what it modifies.
3. The kids giggled loudly while playing with their puppets.

4. We watched as the kite dipped and turned wildly.

Modifying Phrases

Sometimes a whole group of words acts to modify, or describe, another word in a sentence. A **phrase** is a group of words that contains either a noun (or pronoun) or a verb, but not both. A phrase also includes other words that describe the noun or verb or that tie the group of words to the rest of the sentence.

Prepositional Phrases

As you learned in Chapter 2, a **prepositional phrase** is a group of words that begins with a preposition and ends with a noun or pronoun. In a sentence, a prepositional phrase works as an adjective or an adverb. When it serves as an adjective, it modifies a noun or a pronoun.

> The water **in the pool** is clear.

When a prepositional phrase is used as an adverb, it modifies a verb, an adjective, or an adverb.

> Cindy jumped **off the high board**.
> She is skillful **at diving**.
> Cindy began diving soon **after her older sister**.

A prepositional phrase can be placed either before or after the word it modifies. However, the sentence will be clearer if the phrase is **adjacent**, or next to, the word it modifies.

> **Confusing:** Cindy teaches children to jump off the low board from the grade school.

> **Better:** Cindy teaches children from the grade school to jump off the low board.

RECOGNIZE SUPPORTING DETAILS

Details are words and phrases that give information. Supporting details describe or tell more about the subject or verb of a sentence or about the main idea of a passage. They can be factual details, commonly in a nonfiction piece, or descriptive details, commonly in fiction.

In this lesson, you will learn about how modifiers add details that describe another word in a sentence.

Read the following sentences and find the supporting details. Think about whether they support the subject or the verb.

> (1) The smell of freshly baked cookies made her mouth water.
>
> (2) The tiny white-and-black speckled kitten napped in the sun.

In sentence 1, the supporting detail *freshly baked cookies* tells more about the subject, *smell*. In sentence 2, the words *tiny white-and-black speckled* give details about the kitten. These words help us picture what the kitten looks like.

21st Century Skill
Communication and Collaboration

Work with a partner. Make a list of several modifying prepositional phrases. Give your list to your partner. Each partner should then write a paragraph that uses the phrases. Exchange paragraphs and check to see that the phrases have been used correctly.

THINK ABOUT WRITING

Directions: Read each sentence and underline the prepositional phrase. Then write whether the phrase is an adjective or adverb, what the phrase modifies, and what information it gives you.

1. The sign at the end of the road had been blown down during the storm.

    _____

    _____

2. During the storm, the dog hid under the bed.

    _____

    _____

3. Kyle had to clear all the branches that blew off the trees.

    _____

    _____

When writing is **ambiguous**, or unclear, it makes it difficult for readers to understand what they are reading.

In this lesson, you are learning about using modifiers in your writing. Modifiers help explain or clarify what you are trying to tell your readers. They can help "paint" a clear image in the readers' minds.

Read the following sentences:

The baby stopped crying.

The tired baby stopped crying as he finally fell asleep.

Although the first sentence is a complete sentence, it gives little information and leaves you wondering: *Why was the baby crying? When did he stop crying?* The second sentence uses modifiers, which help clarify and explain what is happening.

Read the sentences below. In a notebook, revise each sentence. Add more detail to clarify and explain.

The cake was ruined.

Luis missed the performance.

The bird chirped.

Verb Phrases

Another group of words that acts as a modifier is a **verb phrase**. A verb phrase begins with a verb form.

Tired after a long day, José took his dog for a walk.

José used a leash **to walk his dog**.

Breaking the leash, the dog was free.

THINK ABOUT **WRITING**

Directions: Underline the modifying phrase in each sentence below. Then write the word it modifies.

Example: ___Jan___ <u>Walking home</u>, Jan watched dark clouds gather.

1. _____ Louis saw the bus at the corner.

2. _____ Opening the door, Shen looked outside.

3. _____ The smell of barbecued chicken made Shawna hungry.

4. _____ The exhausted runner, seeing the finish line, speeded up.

5. _____ Julie was sorry to lose the watch.

6. _____ Jacob left his books at the library.

7. _____ Already soaked from the rain, Ms. Cardenas opened her umbrella.

8. _____ The basketball game ended soon after sunset.

9. _____ The police car arrived at the accident scene in a hurry.

10. _____ Hoping to get more customers, the store manager lowered prices.

11. _____ Mrs. Cosmos crossed over the Canadian border.

12. _____ Sitting between her parents, Lenore felt quite happy.

Renaming Phrases as Modifiers

A **renaming phrase**, also called an **appositive**, is a group of words that gives more information about a noun in a sentence. It is made up of a noun and other words that modify it.

John Santos, **a truck driver**, left the warehouse at noon.

As with other phrases, a renaming phrase must be placed carefully in the sentence. Otherwise, it can be confusing or misleading. A renaming phrase usually comes directly after the noun it modifies. Occasionally, it may come before the noun.

A retired state senator, Margaret Fisher stayed active in politics.

Usually, renaming phrases are separated from the rest of the sentence by commas. If the renaming phrase occurs in the middle of a sentence, a comma comes before and after it.

THINK ABOUT WRITING

Directions: Find the renaming phrase in each sentence below and punctuate it correctly.

Example: Neil Armstrong, the astronaut, was the first person on the moon.

1. Yuri Gagarin the first human in space was from the Soviet Union.

2. Ham a chimpanzee tested the US spacecraft.

3. Alan Shepard the first American in space wrote a book about the early space program.

4. Shepard went into space in Redstone 3 a tiny spacecraft.

5. Shepard an astronaut and test pilot went to the moon years later.

Reading Skill
Recognize Supporting Details

Remember that adjectives, adverbs, and modifying phrases are supporting details that help paint a clear picture in readers' minds.

As you complete the Think about Writing exercise on this page, ask yourself: *What is this sentence about? What details support, or tell more about, the main idea of the sentence?*

WRITE TO LEARN

A modifying phrase is often used to begin a sentence. When you do this in your writing, use a comma to separate it from the rest of the sentence. A comma is not always needed if the phrase occurs somewhere else in the sentence.

Stumbling over the curb, Mindy almost fell.

In a notebook, write five sentences that include modifying phrases. At least three of the sentences should begin with a modifying phrase.

Vocabulary Review

Directions: Complete the sentences below using the following words:

adjacent   **ambiguous**   **phrase**

1. The group of words *hoping to win*, is an example of a _____.

2. The dog owner is happy to live _____ to a beautiful park.

3. His answer was _____, so I am not sure if he is coming to the party.

Skill Review

Directions: Read the sentences. Underline the supporting details.

1. Pang loves to play baseball. He practices every chance he gets. On Saturday mornings, he's the first one up and ready to go hit some balls.

2. Zihna just completed her third marathon. She has always been an active person. She ran, and won, her first race when she was only eight years old!

3. Lian cried and cried. When Dad tried to give her a bottle, she just turned her head away and rubbed her eyes. She didn't even want to play with her favorite toy. Dad knew it was time to put the baby to bed.

4. Walter likes to plan ahead. Every Sunday, he picks out the clothes he will wear during the week. He also plans what he will eat for breakfast, lunch, and dinner each day.

Directions: Read each sentence. Then rewrite it, inserting a modifier to clarify and explain what is happening.

5. The dog sits.

_____

_____

6. His shoes were wet.

_____

_____

7. They walked home together.

_____

_____

8. Liz cooked for hours.

_____

Skill Practice

Directions: Choose the <u>one best answer</u> to each question.

1. Jumping up Isabel, my mother's friend, ran after the children.

   Which correction should be made to the sentence?

   A. move <u>jumping up</u> to the end of the sentence
   B. insert a comma after <u>up</u>
   C. remove the commas after <u>Isabel</u> and after <u>friend</u>
   D. insert a comma before <u>after the children</u>

2. <u>After we left the movie we stopped for some coffee.</u> My friend Albert, an avid film buff, discussed the movie with me.

   Which is the best way to write the underlined portion of the sentence? If the original is the best way, choose option (A).

   A. After we left the movie we stopped for some coffee.
   B. After we left, the movie, we stopped for some coffee.
   C. After we left the movie, we stopped, for some coffee.
   D. After we left the movie, we stopped for some coffee.

3. Losing his wallet, Jerome called the security office to report his loss. <u>Leonard Chino, chief of security,</u> told him the wallet had been found.

   Which is the best way to write the underlined portion of the sentence? If the original is the best way, choose option (A).

   A. Leonard Chino, chief of security,
   B. Leonard Chino, chief of security
   C. Leonard Chino chief of security,
   D. Leonard Chino chief of security

4. <u>To rescue her cat Ann called the fire chief, an old friend.</u> He sent a young firefighter up a long ladder to save the cat.

   Which is the best way to write the underlined portion of the sentence? If the original is the best way, choose option (A).

   A. To rescue her cat Ann called the fire chief, an old friend.
   B. To rescue her cat, Ann called the fire chief, an old friend.
   C. To rescue her, cat Ann called the fire chief, an old friend.
   D. To rescue her cat Ann called the fire chief an old friend.

Writing Practice

Directions: Think about the many workplace skills that you have. Write a letter to a prospective employer. Describe your workplace skills in detail. Use prepositional phrases, verb phrases, and appositives to enhance and clarify your descriptions.

Directions: Choose the <u>one best answer</u> to each question.

1. Ann Watson, manager of the grocery store, hired two new employees. The younger one will help Sid the produce manager.

   Which correction should be made to these sentences?

   A. change <u>new</u> to <u>newer</u>
   B. change <u>younger</u> to <u>youngest</u>
   C. change <u>younger</u> to <u>more young</u>
   D. insert a comma after <u>Sid</u>

2. Noriko can't hardly go to work today. Her car, a beat-up old jalopy, won't start. It has seen better days.

   Which correction should be made to these sentences?

   A. change <u>can't</u> to <u>can</u>
   B. replace <u>hardly</u> with <u>scarcely</u>
   C. remove the commas before and after <u>a beat-up old jalopy</u>
   D. replace <u>better</u> with <u>best</u>

3. After I put them cans in this cooler, I added a big bag of ice. In yesterday's hot weather, the ice melted fast.

   Which correction should be made to these sentences?

   A. replace <u>them</u> with <u>those</u>
   B. remove the comma after <u>cooler</u>
   C. remove the comma after <u>weather</u>
   D. change <u>fast</u> to <u>fastest</u>

4. To buy that new car, Sheri signed a application for a loan.

   Which correction should be made to this sentence?

   A. replace <u>that</u> with <u>these</u>
   B. remove the comma after <u>car</u>
   C. change <u>a application</u> to <u>an application</u>
   D. change <u>a loan</u> to <u>an loan</u>

5. Taro's car looks much shinier than it did. That there wax really makes it look good.

   Which correction should be made to these sentences?

   A. replace <u>much</u> with <u>more</u>
   B. change <u>shinier</u> to <u>shiniest</u>
   C. remove <u>there</u>
   D. replace <u>good</u> with <u>well</u>

6. The letter carrier looks nervous at the dog. It is the most ferocious of all the dogs on that street.

   Which correction should be made to these sentences?

   A. change <u>nervous</u> to <u>nervously</u>
   B. change <u>most ferocious</u> to <u>more ferocious</u>
   C. change <u>most ferocious</u> to <u>ferocious</u>
   D. replace <u>most</u> with <u>much</u>

7. <u>Those steaks smell bad.</u> They looked fresh when I picked them out.

   Which is the best way to write the underlined portion of the sentence? If the original is the best way, choose option (A).

   A. Those steaks smell bad.
   B. Them steaks smell bad.
   C. Those steaks smell badly.
   D. Those steaks smell more bad.

Review

8. The funnier book I have ever read is *Roughing It*. Mark Twain, a nineteenth-century writer, is the author.

Which is the best way to write the underlined portion of the sentence? If the original is the best way, choose option (A).

A. The funnier book I have ever read
B. The most funny book I have ever read
C. The funniest book I have ever read
D. The more funny book I have ever read

9. Lee Chung did not feel very good yesterday. He feels even worse today.

Which is the best way to write the underlined portion of the sentence? If the original is the best way, choose option (A).

A. did not feel very good yesterday
B. did not feel very well yesterday
C. did not feel good yesterday
D. did not feel weller yesterday

10. If I were more smarter, I would have bought this television last week. That sale was better than the sale this week.

Which is the best way to write the underlined portion of the sentence? If the original is the best way, choose option (A).

A. If I were more smarter
B. If I were most smarter
C. If I were smarter
D. If I were more smartest

11. That basketball player has scarcely any competition. Watch how he sets up the play so easy.

Which is the best way to write the underlined portion of the sentence? If the original is the best way, choose option (A).

A. Watch how he sets up the play so easy.
B. Watch how he sets up the play more easy.
C. Watch how he sets up the play easy.
D. Watch how he sets up the play so easily.

12. That computer is less expensive than this one. However, it isn't hardly the best one that I have ever seen.

Which is the best way to write the underlined portion of the sentence? If the original is the best way, choose option (A).

A. it isn't hardly the best one
B. it isn't hardly the bestest one
C. it is hardly the best one
D. it isn't hardly the better one

13. Waving frantically, the hungry, shipwrecked sailor screamed loud at the passing ship.

Which is the best way to write the underlined portion of the sentence? If the original is the best way, choose option (A).

A. the hungry, shipwrecked sailor screamed loud
B. the hungry shipwrecked sailor screamed loud
C. the hungrily, shipwrecked sailor screamed loud
D. the hungry, shipwrecked sailor screamed loudly

14. Patty seemed extremely happy when <u>she was given those tickets there</u>.

Which is the best way to write the underlined portion of the sentence? If the original is the best way, choose option (A).

A. she was given those tickets there
B. she was given them tickets
C. she was given them tickets there
D. she was given those tickets

15. Sarin and Ann like to walk together, but <u>Sarin prefers to walk more faster than Ann</u>.

Which is the best way to write the underlined portion of the sentence? If the original is the best way, choose option (A).

A. Sarin prefers to walk more faster than Ann
B. Sarin prefers to walk faster than Ann
C. Sarin prefers to walk fastest than Ann
D. Sarin prefers to walk fast than Ann

16. Mrs. Vega my teacher can hardly believe that she has taught children for thirty years.

What correction should be made to this sentence?

A. insert commas before and after <u>my teacher</u>
B. change <u>can hardly</u> to <u>can't hardly</u>
C. change <u>believe</u> to <u>not believe</u>
D. insert a comma after <u>children</u>

17. All the athletes trained hard, but Lisa trained the most hardest.

What correction should be made to this sentence?

A. change <u>trained hard</u> to <u>trained hardest</u>
B. change <u>most hardest</u> to <u>hardest</u>
C. change <u>the most hardest</u> to <u>more harder</u>
D. insert a comma after <u>Lisa</u>

18. Write a brief paragraph about a hobby that you enjoy. Use several prepositional phrases, verb phrases, and appositives in your paragraph. Make sure to include clear descriptions to help readers visualize and to punctuate your sentences correctly.

_____

_____

_____

_____

_____

_____

_____

Review

Check Your Understanding

On the following chart, circle the number of any item you answered incorrectly in the Chapter 3 Review on pages 92–94. Next to each group of item numbers, you will see the pages you can review to learn how to answer the items correctly. Pay particular attention to reviewing skill areas in which you missed half or more of the questions.

Chapter 3 Review

Skill Area	Item Number	Review Pages
Adjective and Adverbs	2, 3, 4, 5, 6, 7, 8, 9, 10, 11, 12, 13, 14, 15, 17, 18	76–85
Modifying Phrases	1, 16, 18	86–91

Mechanics

We live in a fast-paced, high-tech world. It seems as though no one worries about capitalization and punctuation when texting or e-mailing, so why does it matter when writing? The real reason is that these skills, along with proper spelling, represent standard usages in written English. Employers, for example, expect potential employees to demonstrate an understanding of these skills when filling out job applications, writing cover letters, or corresponding in the business world in general.

In this chapter you will learn about what words should be capitalized, when to use commas and other types of punctuation, and the importance of accurate spelling.

Lesson 4.1: Capitalization
Learn about basic capitalization, including how to handle names and titles in written materials and capitalized words you may encounter in the workplace.

Lesson 4.2: Punctuation
Learn about basic punctuation rules, including how to use commas, end marks, and other common punctuation and how the wrong punctuation can change the meaning of text.

Lesson 4.3: Spelling
Spelling homophones, contractions, possessives, and affixes can pose a challenge to any writer. This lesson will teach you the rules you need to follow to spell these kinds of words and parts of words correctly so that your writing is clear and understandable to others. You will also learn some helpful spelling patterns and generalizations.

Goal Setting

Writing correctly and precisely shows readers that you are a careful and thoughtful writer. Think about what you already know concerning capitalization, punctuation, and spelling. Then answer these questions to clarify your goals for this chapter.

What would you like to learn in this chapter about the mechanics of writing?

_____

_____

_____

_____

How will you use what you learn? In what ways will this information help you with your writing?

_____

_____

_____

_____

Capitalization

Lesson Objectives

You will be able to

- Edit to ensure correct use of capitalization, including titles and the beginnings of sentences

- Edit to ensure correct use of capitalization in proper nouns

Skills

- **Core Skill:** Demonstrate Command of Standard English Conventions

- **Core Skill:** Use Precise Language

Vocabulary

capitalization
narrator
occupation
quotation
standard

KEY CONCEPT: Correct capitalization—beginning certain words with capital letters—helps make your writing clear and effective.

You may remember learning to write capital and lowercase letters in primary school. You probably wrote line after line of capital As. However, capital letters are not simply a handwriting exercise. Look around and you will notice that you use capital letters every day.

For example, proper nouns, names, book and movie titles, and each complete sentences begin with capital letters.

When to Capitalize

Capital letters are used in three basic situations to make your writing easy for readers to understand: 1) to start the first word in a sentence, including quotations; 2) to start the first word, last word, and important words in titles; and 3) to start proper nouns.

Beginnings of Sentences

Use a capital letter, or **capitalization**, to begin the first word in every sentence.

> *My friend lives in a large city.*

When you write a sentence that is a **quotation**, or a person's exact words, follow the same rule. If the quotation is not a complete sentence, do not use capitalization.

> *Dionne asked, "Should we order toner now or wait until next month?"*

> *Rhashan described the color of his new car as "seasick green."*

If the quotation is divided by the words of the **narrator**—the person telling the story—use capitalization at the beginning of the complete sentence.

> *"A fire broke out at Martinez Manufacturing," the newscaster reported, "and three people were injured."*

Titles

When you include the title of a book, movie, piece of artwork, poem, song, or television show in a sentence, capitalize the first, last, and main words of the title.

Use lowercase letters with articles (*a, an, the*), coordinating conjunctions (*and, but, or*), and **prepositions** (*at, in, of*) unless they appear as the first or last words in titles.

Book	*Of Mice and Men*
Movie	*Gone with the Wind*
Song	*"Can't Help Falling in Love"*
Television Show	*Once Upon a Time*

A different kind of title is used to refer people who have specific jobs—*Doctor Singh, Judge Gomez, Captain Smith*. Capitalize words used as titles that refer to specific people.

> *When Senator Jones spoke, her audience listened carefully.*

Sometimes, titles are used by themselves as though they are names. This occurs when the speaker directly addresses someone. Use a capital letter in this case as well. If a title refers only to an **occupation**, or job, do not capitalize it.

> *Tell me how you will reduce crime, Mayor.*
> *The judge gave her decision.*

PROPER NOUNS

Remember that there are two types of nouns: common and proper. Common nouns refer to whole groups or general types of people, places, things, or ideas. Proper nouns name specific people, places, things, or ideas. While proper nouns are more precise than common nouns, they also require special capitalization.

	Common Noun > Proper Noun
Calendar References	• day > Monday • month > April • holiday > Labor Day Seasons are not capitalized: *spring*.
Geographic Locations	• city > San Francisco • building > Capitol • street > Maple Street Directions are not capitalized unless they refer to a specific region: *the South*.
Historical References	• government document > Declaration of Independence • economic depression > Black Monday • civil rights > Civil Rights Movement
Names	• president > Barack Obama • country > Japan • organization > American Heart Association Abbreviations and initials are also capitalized: *Ph.D., Jr., NFL, Susan R. Snow*.

Proper nouns may take adjective, or describing, forms. These are also capitalized: Shakespearean drama, Chinese tea, or African American president.

Standard English is spoken and written English that is widely recognized as correct and acceptable. In standard English, capital letters have three specific purposes:

- To start a new sentence
- To start a name
- To signal important words in titles

If a word does not fall into one of these categories, use a lowercase letter. Additionally, in formal writing, do not use capital letters to create emphasis.

In a notebook, draw charts like the ones shown below, and use them to categorize the words in the passage as you edit for capital letters.

For example, *regularly, geraldo stops for coffee and a Community Paper at a café he passes each day.*

Sentence Start
Regularly

Name
Geraldo

Title

Lowercase
community paper

Directions: As you read the passage below, use a sheet of paper to make notes about capitalization. In one column, list words that should have been capitalized. In a second column, list words that are incorrectly capitalized and should begin with a lowercase letter. Review the guidelines for use of capital letters as necessary.

geraldo takes the Train to work every morning. He is lucky because he lives on east street, which is a short walk to the Station. Geraldo walks every day, regardless of the weather. If it is raining, he brings an umbrella. If it is snowing, he wears boots. He enjoys the brisk walk to the train station. Regularly, Geraldo stops for coffee and a community paper at a café he passes each day. This physical activity gives Geraldo time to prepare mentally for his day.

Taking the train gives Geraldo many opportunities he might not otherwise have. Frequently, he uses the time to read. He may read the community paper he picked up at the café or he may read a book. Currently, he is reading a biography about president john adams called *john adams speaks for freedom*. Geraldo may also use the time to respond to E-mails or Text Messages on his SmartPhone. Sometimes the day ahead is so busy that Geraldo may NOT get to these tasks at mcClain and dunn, where he works. Sometimes Geraldo allows himself the pleasure of people-watching. He likes feeling as if he is part of a community of workers who travel to the city each day to make their individual contributions to the world.

No matter how Geraldo spends his daily train rides, he wouldn't give them up for a car. The time that his morning train trip allows Geraldo to prepare for the day is something he values above speed or privacy.

THINK ABOUT **WRITING**

Directions: Edit each sentence below for correct capitalization.

1. geraldo takes the Train to work every morning.

   _____

2. He is lucky because he lives on east street, which is a short walk to the Station.

   _____

3. Currently, he is reading a biography about president john adams called *john adams speaks for freedom*.

   _____

4. Geraldo may also use the time to respond to E-mails or Text Messages on his SmartPhone.

   _____

THINK ABOUT WRITING

Directions: Read the passage below. Then rewrite the passage, replacing or revising the underlined common nouns and phrases with proper nouns and phrases to make the writing more precise. Use correct capitalization with proper nouns.

My vacation begins <u>next week</u>. I plan to travel to <u>another state</u>, where I will visit <u>family</u>. I am looking forward to the visit because I haven't seen my <u>sister</u> or my <u>nephews</u> in several years.

My sister lives near <u>a big city</u>. We plan to take the boys to <u>a fun family location</u>. The boys are in good enough shape to walk around all day because they play baseball. However, I'm worried about whether I will be able to keep up! Hopefully, <u>my favorite restaurant</u> will be open for some air conditioning and refreshments.

<u>The school I attended</u> is nearby, too. I hope to have time to stop and visit with <u>my instructor</u>, who taught <u>my favorite classes</u>. I can show the boys <u>the library</u>, where I spent many hours studying.

_____

_____

_____

_____

_____

_____

_____

_____

_____

_____

_____

_____

_____

_____

_____

_____

_____

_____

Core Skill
Use Precise Language

Using proper nouns and the adjective form of proper nouns can make your writing clearer, more interesting, and more precise.

In a notebook, list proper nouns to replace the common nouns shown below.

For the word *date*, ask yourself: *What are some more specific ways to refer to the calendar?* Use this same questioning method as you think about the remaining words.

Common Nouns

date
state capital
employer
physician
computer
cell phone
political party
address
search engine
car

Write directions for getting from your home to a nearby market, shop, park, or school. Make sure to include street names, landmarks, and **cardinal directions**: *north, south, east,* and *west.* You may write the directions in list or paragraph form, but make sure to use capital letters correctly to begin sentences and in proper nouns. When your directions are complete, have a partner read them for clarity. Revise by responding to any questions your partner may have.

THINK ABOUT **WRITING**

Directions: Read each sentence below. Underline the word that has incorrect capitalization. Then write the word with the correct capitalization.

1. _____ To get to the employment office, turn East on Riverdale Road.

2. _____ A famous monument to president Lincoln is in Springfield, Illinois.

3. _____ "Don't drink water from the stream," my sister warned, "Unless you want to get sick."

4. _____ A production of the play *My Fair Lady* will be presented by southeast High School.

5. _____ Susan Cordova, Ph.D., teaches biology 340 on Wednesday evenings.

Vocabulary Review

Directions: Match each vocabulary word with its definition.

1. _____ capitalization

2. _____ narrator

3. _____ occupation

4. _____ quotation

A. trade, profession, or business

B. words spoken or written by one person that are repeated or used by someone else

C. person who relates a story or an account

D. act of converting a lowercase letter to a capital letter

Directions: Choose the <u>one best answer</u> to each question.

1. Which word in the following sentence should be capitalized?

   in the spring, I will visit my friend Omarr, who lives in a large city.

   A. In
   B. Spring
   C. Large
   D. City

2. Which word in the following sentence should be capitalized?

   at the restaurant, the family ordered garlic bread and spaghetti.

   A. At
   B. Restaurant
   C. Family
   D. Garlic

3. Which word in the following sentence should be capitalized?

   we drove south to the coast and then northeast to the foothills.

   A. We
   B. South
   C. Coast
   D. Northeast

4. Which words in the following sentence should be capitalized?

   He memorized the poem jazz fantasia for the music festival.

   A. He Memorized
   B. The Poem
   C. *Jazz Fantasia*
   D. Music Festival

5. How should the title in the following sentence be capitalized?

   I read the book harry potter and the sorcerer's stone before I saw the movie.

   A. Harry Potter and the Sorcerer's stone
   B. Harry Potter and the sorcerer's stone
   C. Harry Potter And The Sorcerer's Stone
   D. Harry Potter and the Sorcerer's Stone

6. Which answer choice correctly completes the sentence that follows?

   I asked _____ to look at my arm.

   A. doctor Garcia
   B. Doctor Garcia
   C. doctor garcia
   D. Doctor garcia

Skill Review (continued)

7. Which word in the following sentence should be capitalized?

Tanaka's Dry cleaning is her favorite place to clean her clothes.

A. Place
B. Clean
C. Clothes
D. Cleaning

8. Which word in the following sentence should be capitalized?

Let's visit the Empire state Building, which is the tallest building in the city.

A. State
B. Tallest
C. Building
D. City

9. Which word in the following sentence should be capitalized?

Madison street is a grand avenue lined with stately oak trees.

A. Street
B. Grand
C. Avenue
D. Oak

10. Rewrite the following sentence to replace the underlined common noun phrase with a proper noun.

We visited a city, which is located in the Southwest.

_____

_____

11. Rewrite the following sentence to fill in the blank with a proper adjective.

Because we were having spaghetti, I bought some _____ bread to eat with dinner.

_____

_____

12. Rewrite the following sentence to replace the underlined common noun phrase with a proper noun.

While visiting Washington, DC, the Kowalski family toured the historical site.

_____

_____

Skill Practice

Directions: Edit each sentence to fix errors in capitalization. Then, explain your edits.

1. Winton's Father works for the department of justice.

   _____

   _____

   _____

2. I am taking a Biology Class and History 101.

   _____

   _____

   _____

3. Did you see the movie *The Return Of The King*?

   _____

   _____

   _____

4. Kathy Chung, ph.D. is a spokesperson for the American diabetes association.

   _____

   _____

   _____

Directions: Beginning with the sentence starter below, write one to two paragraphs. Make sure to include at least three examples each of titles and proper nouns or adjectives. Underline each example.

I visited _____, *which is located* _____

_____

_____

_____

_____

_____

_____

_____

_____

_____

_____

_____

_____

_____

_____

_____

_____

_____

_____

Writing Practice (continued)

Directions: When your writing is complete, use a colored pen to edit for the following conventions.

_____ Have you used a capital letter at the beginning of each sentence, including quotations?

_____ Have you used a capital letter to begin each proper noun or adjective?

_____ Have you used a capital letter at the beginning of each personal title and for the first word, last word, and important words in each title of a work?

_____ Have you avoided using capital letters elsewhere, with the exception of abbreviations or initials?

Punctuation

Lesson Objectives

You will be able to

- Use punctuation marks correctly, including end marks, commas, colons, semicolons, apostrophes, and quotation marks

- Write clearly and demonstrate command of standard English conventions

Skills

- **Core Skill:** Demonstrate Command of Standard English Punctuation

- **Core Skill:** Edit to Ensure Correct Use of Punctuation

Vocabulary

abbreviations
appositive
clauses
compound sentence
conjunction
phrase
punctuation

KEY CONCEPT: Along with correct capitalization, correct punctuation will make your writing clear and effective.

You have learned that writing in complete sentences helps to make your ideas clear. Using punctuation marks helps to further clarify the meaning of the sentences you write. Read the following sentences, paying close attention to punctuation. After each sentence, write a "C" if the meaning is clear and write a "U" if the meaning is unclear.

Anna I said I don't want to go to the game with you.
The menu had a salad with olives, tomatoes, lettuce, and cheese.
Slow animals crossing.
Do you want to eat Patrick.

Punctuation

There are many types of **punctuation** marks that separate and clarify parts of a sentence, such as periods, commas, question marks, apostrophes, and quotation marks. There are also rules for each type. Using punctuation correctly will help you clarify your meaning to readers.

End Marks

End marks are the types of punctuation used to end sentences. You may end a sentence with a period, a question mark, or an exclamation point.

When stating information, feelings, or wishes, use a period. When asking for a response, use a question mark. When showing strong excitement or emotion, use an exclamation point.

- The Riveras will arrive tomorrow.

- Why does Jonathan always work late?

- Help! Please hurry, Doctor!

Comma

The comma has several uses. One is to separate parts of a sentence, such as items in a series, **appositives**, and other nonessential elements. Appositives are phrases that rename or further identify nouns. A **phrase** is a group of words that has a subject or verb, but not both.

Commas in a Series

When you use more than two nouns, verbs, adjectives, or adverbs in a series, separate them with commas. The final item in the series of nouns or verbs is usually introduced by a **conjunction** such as *and* or *or*. A conjunction is a word that connects other words or phrases. Use a comma before the conjunction. Do not use the comma and conjunction to write a series of adjectives.

- We had hamburgers, baked beans, and salad.
- That big, smelly, ill-tempered dog is a nuisance.

Use commas to set off phrases or **clauses** that are written as a series. Clauses are groups of words that contain subjects and verbs.

- Thomas grabs the ball, dribbles to his left, pulls up, and shoots.

With Appositives and Other Non-Essential Elements

Appositives and other nonessential elements are not necessary parts of sentences. They interrupt sentences to add information. If you remove the phrase or word, the sentence retains its meaning. Three types of interrupting phrases are set off from the rest of a sentence by commas.

Type of Phrase	Examples
Appositive, or a phrase that renames or further identifies a noun	Manuel Suarez, the man behind the desk, is an accountant.
Direct Address, or a sentence directed to a named specific person	If you will go with me, Latona, we can carpool to the conference.
Extra or Contrasting Information	Mary Ellen, in fact, refused to leave. Pavel will work today, not on Friday.

Before setting off a phrase with commas, make sure the phrase is not essential to the meaning of the sentence. In the example below, if the underlined phrase is removed, the sentence loses its meaning, so do not use commas to set it off.

- Anyone who submits the assignment early will be rewarded.
- Anyone will be rewarded.

Periods are used with
abbreviations that
end in a lower case
letter and with initials.
They are not used in
abbreviations with full
capitals, including the
abbreviation for United
States. For example:

Dec. 3 (December 3)
*John F. Kennedy (John
Fitzgerald Kennedy)*
*Chicago, IL (Chicago,
Illinois)*
*the US Fish and Wildlife
Service*

Use commas to separate
parts of an address or
date. Commas are used
in dates that include
the day of the month,
but are not used if only
the month and year are
given. For example:

*20 Any Street, Akron, OH
44303*
May 7, 2013
June 2013

Commas are used after
both greetings and
closings in letters. For
example:

*Dear friends, (informal
usage only)*
*Sincerely, (informal and
formal usage)*

In a notebook, correctly
punctuate these
abbreviations and parts
of letters.

John Q Adams
Boston, M.A.
August, 2013
Dear Mr. Grant

THINK ABOUT **WRITING**

Directions: Read the following sentences, noticing the
end marks used. Then rewrite any that require commas or
need a different end mark. If a sentence is correct as it
is, write "Correct."

1. Caitlin look out for that bus.

   _____

2. Did Deisha finish her résumé yet?

   _____

3. It was in fact the best cheesecake Ms. Littleshield ever had.

   _____

4. Why don't you ever wear your yellow sweater Malik?

   _____

5. Yolanda the woman who got me this job has now quit.

   _____

DEMONSTRATE COMMAND OF STANDARD ENGLISH PUNCTUATION

Some end marks and commas are found frequently in workplace
documents.

Abbreviations and Initials

Use periods with **abbreviations** and initials, which are shortened
forms of words or names. However, periods are not used in
abbreviations that appear in full capitals, including US postal
abbreviations of state names.

Addresses, Dates, Greetings, and Closings

Use commas to separate parts of an address or date. Commas are
used in dates that include the day of the month, but commas are not
used if only the month and year are given. Commas are also used
after greetings or closings in a letter.

Directions: Do an online search to find and print out a sample
letter of recommendation. Label the special usages of end marks or
commas for abbreviations, initials, addresses, dates, greetings, or
closings. With a partner, discuss why print or online publishers may
prefer to use abbreviations.

Edit to Ensure Correct Use of Punctuation

You can edit errors in the use of end marks and commas by thinking of the meaning of your sentences.

Editing for End Marks

To edit for end marks, consider the message that your sentence conveys.

You can recognize a statement or command because it supplies a fact or gives an order. Use a period at the end of the sentence.

- The paper is due on Friday.

You can recognize a question because it asks for a response.

- When is the paper due?

Context can help you to recognize an expression of strong feelings.

- I made a mistake. The paper is due on Friday, not Monday!

Editing Commas in a Series

To edit commas in a series of words, consider their part of speech. Nouns, verbs, and adverbs in a series use commas, a conjunction such as *or* or *and* before the last word in the series, and a comma before the conjunction.

- The clerk answered my questions cheerfully, quickly, and helpfully.

Adjectives in a series use commas but do not include a conjunction.

- Look at that big, funny, colorful hat!

Editing Commas with Appositives and Nonessential Elements

To edit using commas with appositives and other nonessential elements, reread your sentence without the phrase within the commas. If the sentence has lost its original meaning, delete the commas.

- I'm giving you this gift, <u>Kyoko</u>, to say thank you.

Colon

A **colon** introduces something, or several things, that tell more about a complete thought. Use a colon after a complete thought that introduces a list. Do not use a colon if the introduction to the list is not a complete thought.

- We packed the following items: apples, cheese, and bread. (correct)

- We packed: apples, cheese, and bread. (incorrect)

Use a colon after the greeting in a very formal or business letter, rather than the more informal comma.

- Dear Sir or Madam:

Use a colon to separate the hour from minutes in written time.

- It is now 6:45.

Advertisers are sometimes so focused on selling their ideas or products to the public that they neglect the rules of punctuation. For example, while stopped at a red light, you may find yourself reading a cardboard sign that reads as follows: *Neighborhood Yard Sale "Today."* Why has the writer used quotation marks in this way? Is he or she capturing someone's direct words?

Find a print or digital advertisement that makes use of quotation marks, ellipses, or exclamation points within the copy or text. In a notebook, evaluate whether the writer has used the punctuation correctly.

Respond to these questions:

How does the writer's intended meaning compare or contrast with the actual meaning conveyed by the punctuation?

How should the ad copy or text be rewritten to show correct punctuation?

How do errors in punctuation in advertising affect your impression of the advertiser and/or his or her ideas or product?

Semicolon

A semicolon is used in two ways to form **compound sentences**. A compound sentence is made up of two simple sentences, or **independent clauses**, that are joined together. When the clauses in a compound sentence are linked using a conjunctive adverb, place a semicolon before the adverb.

- Emily sets two alarm clocks before going to bed; otherwise, she is likely to oversleep.

You can also link closely related clauses in a compound sentence without using either a conjunction or a conjunctive adverb. Use the semicolon by itself to show that the two clauses are independent.

- It is a beautiful day; I should be spending it outdoors.

A semicolon can also be used to separate items in a series when there are already commas within the items.

- The contestants in the dog show were Fido, a brown and white mutt; Fifi, a French poodle; and Farley, a golden retriever.

THINK ABOUT WRITING

Directions: In a notebook, edit the following informal letter for correct punctuation.

Dear Great-uncle Quincy:

I am excited about seeing you when you come for a visit next week we will pick you up at Kennedy Airport on Saturday March 15 at 7 pm Please be sure to bring a bathing suit towel and sunscreen could you also please bring the latest family photos I cannot wait to see you

Love
Cantrice

Quotation Marks

Use quotation marks to show the exact words of a speaker. Do not use quotation marks in a statement about what someone says or for an indirect quotation.

- "Stop yelling," Ernesto said, "or we will go home."

- Ernesto said that we should stop yelling or we will go home.

When using other punctuation with quotation marks, follow these rules.

Periods and commas are always placed inside the quotation marks. Use commas to separate quotations from the rest of the sentence.

- "Elephants," Tyrell said, "can be dangerous."

Colons and semicolons are always placed outside quotation marks.

- The zookeeper said, "Have your tickets ready"; they ignored her directions.

Question marks and exclamation points are placed inside the quotation marks if they are part of the quotation. Use a comma to introduce a quotation. If question marks or exclamation points are not part of the quotation, they are placed outside the quotation marks.

- Did Keith say, "That elephant is loose"?

- "Is that elephant loose?" Marisol asked.

Apostrophe

The apostrophe has two main uses. The first is to show **possession**. When used for possession, an apostrophe shows that one thing belongs to another.

- Piri's laptop helps her take notes in meetings.

The second use for apostrophes is to form **contractions**. A contraction is one word that is made up of two words with one or more letters left out. The apostrophe is used in place of the missing letters.

- "There's a fire!" Akira yelled into the phone. "Please send help quickly!"

Ellipsis

An ellipsis, three periods with spaces between each, is used to leave out part of a quotation.

- "We the people of the United States, in order to form a more perfect Union, establish Justice . . . and secure the Blessings of Liberty to ourselves and our Posterity, do ordain and establish this Constitution for the United States of America."

An ellipsis can also be used to show a pause in dialogue or speech.

- As Maxine looked all over her house, she moaned, "Where . . . are . . . my . . . keys?"

Parentheses

Use parentheses to highlight interruptions in a sentence that provide useful, but nonessential, information such as dates, definitions, or explanations.

- The Bombers will play (Jan. 3) at Johnson Field in Omaha, Nebraska.

- The ant used its mandibles (jaws) to collect its food.

- I can't wait to show you our new dog (a beagle).

Dash

Use a dash, a horizontal line, to separate parts of a sentence. It can be used in place of a comma, semicolon, or colon to show sudden breaks, expressions, or emphasis. However, the dash should not be overused, or it loses its impact.

- Mr. Chung—after getting the mysterious call—raced from his house!

- She received top honors in her class—how impressive!

- The doctor explained the test—the one for bone density.

WRITE TO LEARN

Choose a family member or a friend and write an informal letter or e-mail message to this person. Make sure the letter includes a minimum of three paragraphs, along with a date, greeting, and closing. You may either write about a topic of your choosing or use this sentence starter: *I am excited to . . . .* Make sure to use correct punctuation, including end marks and commas. Use colons, semicolons, quotation marks, apostrophes, ellipses, parentheses, or dashes, as needed. Include at least one example of a series and an appositive or other non-essential element. Underline each example. When you are finished, you can send your letter or e-mail to the person you chose.

Vocabulary Review

Directions: Match each vocabulary word with its definition.

1. _____ abbreviations
2. _____ appositive
3. _____ clauses
4. _____ compound sentence
5. _____ conjunction
6. _____ phrase

A. made up of two simple sentences, or independent clauses

B. word that connects other words, phrases, or clauses

C. groups of words that have a subject and a verb

D. shortened forms of words or names

E. renaming word, phrase, or clause

F. group of words that does not have both a subject and a verb

Skill Review

Directions: Which is the best way to write the underlined portion of the sentence?
Choose the one best answer to each question. If the original is the best way, choose
the first option (A).

1. "Is Mark's new company located in Philadelphia," Julie asked.

   A. located in Philadelphia," Julie asked.
   B. located in Philadelphia," Julie asked?
   C. located in Philadelphia?" Julie asked.
   D. located in Philadelphia?" Julie asked?

2. Teresa really wanted to go to Mexico; nevertheless, she agreed to spend her vacation at the lake.

   A. Mexico; nevertheless,
   B. Mexico, nevertheless;
   C. Mexico, nevertheless,
   D. Mexico; nevertheless;

3. He gave these reasons for moving a bigger yard, more bedrooms, lower taxes, and a better school district.

   A. moving a bigger yard,
   B. moving: a bigger yard,
   C. moving, a bigger yard,
   D. moving; a bigger yard

4. It is now 7:00, Stan just got here.

   A. 7:00, Stan
   B. 7:00: Stan
   C. (7:00), but Stan
   D. 7:00, and Stan

5. Kalindi yelled to her brother, Who's going to feed the dog?

   A. brother, Who's going to feed the dog?
   B. brother, "Who's going to feed the dog?"
   C. brother, Whos going to feed the dog?
   D. brother "Who's going to feed the dog?"

6. Theyre looking for a new car; the one they have is worn out.

   A. Theyre looking for a new car;
   B. They're looking for a new car,
   C. Theyre looking for a new car because
   D. They're looking for a new car;

7. Paulo wished he could remember <u>everything; he was always forgetting the details.</u>

    A. everything; he was always forgetting the details.
    B. everything, he was always forgetting the details.
    C. everything: he was always forgetting the details.
    D. everything, and he was always forgetting the details.

8. When the engine caught on fire <u>Sachi yelled "Get out of the car!"</u>

    A. Sachi yelled "Get out of the car!"
    B. Sachi yelled, "Get out of the car!"
    C. Sachi yelled "Get out of the car."
    D. Sachi yelled "Get out of the car?"

9. Ricardo and Felicia went to a <u>basketball game their school won 88–72.</u>

    A. basketball game their school won 88–72.
    B. basketball game, their school won 88–72.
    C. basketball (game their school won 88–72).
    D. basketball game (their school won 88–72).

10. "I pledge allegiance to the flag of the United States of <u>America one nation under God</u>, indivisible, with liberty and justice for all."

    A. America one nation under God,
    B. America (one nation under God)
    C. America . . . one nation under God
    D. America—one nation under God—

11. Lucita's <u>favorite play which she has read ten times is</u> *Death of a Salesman.*

    A. favorite play which she has read ten times is
    B. favorite play which she has read ten times is:
    C. favorite play—which she has read ten times—is
    D. favorite play which she has read (ten times) is

12. When Trivets, Inc., didn't hire her, Gina wanted to know <u>what she had to do to get a job</u>

    A. what she had to do to get a job
    B. what she had to do to get a job?
    C. what she had to do to get a job.
    D. what she had to do to get a job;

Skill Practice

Directions: Rewrite the passage below, correcting any errors in punctuation.

Marcela checked the schedule one last time! The train was due to arrive at 6 45: she had fifteen minutes more to wait in the bitter cold. It would be worth it in spite of the fact that she forgot her gloves at home she could still hear her mothers voice urgently calling down the hall Don't forget your gloves. Marcela refused to dwell on her forgetfulness instead she imagined the look she would see on her friends faces when she stepped off the train. ten years was a long time Would they recognize each other. Marcela was certain, that memories of their years together at Middletown High School would make it feel as if they were together just yesterday.

_____

_____

_____

_____

_____

_____

_____

_____

_____

_____

_____

_____

_____

_____

_____

Directions: Find a print or online employment source, such as a job listing or a job search site. Locate an advertisement for a job for which you are qualified. In response to this listing, write a formal cover letter that might accompany your résumé. Remember to include the date, a greeting, and a closing. Make sure to describe your qualifications for the job.

_____

_____

_____

_____

_____

_____

_____

_____

_____

_____

Directions: When your writing is complete, use a colored pen to edit for the following conventions.

_____ Do all possessive nouns and contractions show the correct use of an apostrophe?

_____ Do all sentences end with the appropriate end mark?

_____ Have you used commas correctly in a series?

_____ Have you edited to ensure the correct use of punctuation, including colons, semicolons, quotation marks, ellipses, dashes, and parentheses?

_____ Have you used commas correctly with appositives and other non-essential elements?

Spelling

Lesson Objectives

You will be able to
- Spell possessives, contractions, and homophones correctly
- Spell words with affixes correctly
- Use spelling patterns and generalizations
- Use resources and strategies to ensure correct spelling

Skills

- **Core Skill:** Use a Dictionary
- **Reading Skill:** Understand Compound Words

Vocabulary

affixes
contraction
generalization
homophones
interpret
possessives

KEY CONCEPT: Accurate spelling is an important skill in effective writing.

Rewrite the following sentences with the correct capitalization and punctuation.

1. The nice woman said, Take a left on main street. village restaurant is on the left.

2. The alarm went off at 6 00 but sebastian was still tired?

3. Would you like toast fruit or eggs.

Possessives, Contractions, and Homophones

Homophones are words that sound the same but are different in meaning and sometimes in spelling. A **contraction** is a shortened way to write two words. A **possessive** is a form of a word that shows ownership. Several possessives and contractions are homophones. Here are some examples:

> All of the forklift operators are good at their jobs.

> They're good drivers on the open road, too.

> Are there any questions?

The words *their*, *they're*, and *there* are homophones. *Their* is a possessive pronoun meaning "belonging to them." *They're* is a contraction meaning "they are." *There* is an adverb that specifies where something is. All three words have different meanings and different spellings, but they all sound alike. A common writing error is to use the wrong homophone in a sentence. What is the spelling error in the sentence below?

> There should be a bonus for they're hard work.

The spelling error in the sentence is the contraction *they're*. *They are* makes no sense in this sentence, but *their*, the possessive pronoun that shows who did the hard work, does.

> There should be a bonus for their hard work.

Here is a review of some confusing contractions and possessive pronouns that are homophones. Notice how they follow a simple rule: Contractions need apostrophes; possessive pronouns do not have apostrophes.

Possessive Pronoun	Contractions
its (the cat's)	it's (it is, it has)
theirs (the workers')	there's (there is)
your (belonging to you)	you're (you are)
whose (Maggie's)	who's (who is)

Incorrect: That cat must be controlled by **it's** owner.

Correct: **It's** a cat without fear.

Correct: It knows **its** claws are sharp.

Incorrect: **Who's** dog wandered onto Ahmik's street?

Correct: **Who's** looking for a pet?

Correct: I know **whose** dog it is.

Another common homophone error is using an apostrophe to form a plural noun. This error is often made because a plural noun sounds just like a possessive noun—but it's spelled differently.

Incorrect: The **computer's** have stopped working.

Correct: The **computers** have stopped working.

Correct: Jane's **computer's** keyboard is broken.

Correct: All three **computers'** keyboards are broken.

The first sentence is incorrect because it uses an apostrophe in a plural noun that does not show possession. The next three sentences are correct. The first correct sentence shows a simple plural, the next shows a singular possessive, and the last shows a plural possessive.

In the English language, there are many homophones that are not contractions, possessives, or plurals. The chart on page 122 provides you with just a few examples of the many homophones that exist.

WRITE TO LEARN

After reviewing the example sentences on this page, write your own sentence for each of the possessives and contractions listed at the top of the page.

If you use a contraction, try replacing it with the two words it stands for to see if the sentence still makes sense. If it does not, you probably need to replace it with a possessive. For example:

If you write: It's handle broke off.

Try substituting It is: It is handle broke off.

You can see this does not make sense. **Replace it's with a possessive:** Its handle broke off.

UNDERSTAND COMPOUND WORDS

When you read, you might see a long word made up of two smaller words. Words like this are called **compound words**. The English language is full of compound words. For example, *laptop, daytime,* and *seacoast* are all compound words.

In order to understand compound words, use the two smaller words to **interpret**, or explain, how the parts combine to form a new word. Ask yourself: *Can I break this long word down into two smaller words? What do the smaller words mean? What does the context of the sentence tell me?*

Read the following passage. Identify the compound words and explain what they mean.

Ade loves to work in his garden. He plants flowers that attract butterflies, so he can study them. Yesterday, Ade spotted a butterfly he had never seen before. He wanted to get a closer look, so he put on his eyeglasses. Ade grabbed a notebook and sketched the butterfly before it fluttered off.

The words *butterflies, eyeglasses,* and *notebook* are compound words. The definition of some compound words, like *butterflies,* cannot be determined by looking at the meanings of the smaller words. But, the context around the word helps us understand the word's meaning. *Eyeglasses* is made up of the words *eye* and *glasses* and literally means "glasses for one's eyes." *Notebook,* made up of the words *note* and *book* means "a book for writing notes."

You can also use the two smaller words to figure out how to spell a compound word. Think about how each of the smaller words is spelled. When you combine the two smaller words, you have the correct spelling of the compound word. For example, *snow* and *flake* together spell *snowflake*. *Basket* and *ball* together spell *basketball*.

THINK ABOUT WRITING

<u>Part A</u> **Directions:** Underline the word in parentheses that will correctly complete each sentence below.

Example: What is the (*affect*, <u>*effect*</u>) of the new rules?

1. I (*brake*, *break*) for unicorns.

2. I (*know*, *no*) that you think I'm crazy, but I did see it.

3. The start of the concert season is finally (*hear*, *here*).

4. Does it matter (*whether*, *weather*) or not it rains if we're going to be indoors?

5. Marta (*passed*, *past*) the history book to Alex.

6. The directions say to turn (*right*, *write*) at the next corner.

7. His family is going on vacation next (*weak*, *week*).

8. It was fun to drive (*threw*, *through*) the long tunnel.

9. The dog's fur felt very (*coarse*, *course*).

10. Think carefully before you (*choose*, *chews*) your answer.

<u>Part B</u> **Directions:** Find and correct the spelling errors in the passage below.

The founders of the United States didn't no whether they wood succeed in winning independence from Great Britain, but they new they had to try. They're goal was freedom. This country was founded on the principal of equality for all. The founders past on to us there belief in democracy. The Constitution guarantees our write to free speech. That means everyone is allowed to say whatever he or she thinks, weather anyone else wants to here it or not.

Core Skill
Use a Dictionary

When you come across an unfamiliar word, the context, or words around it, can often help you figure out the word's meaning. Sometimes, however, this does not work. When that happens, use a dictionary.

A dictionary is a book that lists words in alphabetical order. It explains what each word means. Guide words, which appear at the top of each page, are the first and last words on the page. Use the guide words to find your word more easily.

Use a dictionary to look up the meaning of each homophone pairs below. Then write a sentence for each word to show its meaning.

sea/see   pleas/please
gait/gate   pause/paws

When you read, it is not unusual to come across unfamiliar words. Sometimes you can **interpret** the meaning of the word by looking at its parts. In compound words, often, but not always, the meanings of the smaller words can help you understand the compound word. Here are some examples:

seashell—a shell found near the sea

bedroom—a room with a bed

headache—an ache or a pain in one's head

Some compound words are also homophones. When you write, you must choose the homophone whose spelling shows the meaning you want. Use the meanings of the smaller homophones in the compound word to help you.

Read the pairs of compound homophones below. Write two sets of sentences. Each sentence should use one homophone.

- overseas/oversees
- overdo/overdue

Homonym	Meaning	Example Sentence
affect effect	act upon result	The change will **affect** marketing. The **effect** of the change was minor.
all ready already	completely ready previously	Delores is **all ready** for the meeting. She **already** discussed that issue.
brake break	stop; stopping device fall to pieces; take a rest	Victor repaired the **brake** line. After four hours of work, we get a short **break**.
hear here	listen; use one's ears in this place	I couldn't **hear** the speaker It's noisy in **here**.
knew new	was aware of not old	Betty **knew** how to use a computer. She didn't know the **new** program.
know no	be aware of opposite of yes	Do you **know** what time it is? **No**, I don't. I forgot my watch.
passed past	went by; succeeded before the present; gone by	The deadline **passed** with no answer. In the **past**, we wouldn't have let that happen.
principal principle	main; most important theory; belief	John's **principal** aim is to do a good job. In **principle**, he believes in honesty.
right write	opposite of left; correct put words on paper or screen	The **right** answer was "none of the above." I'm going to **write** a memo.
through threw	finished; into and out of did throw	They drove **through** the business district. Jan **threw** a stick for the dog to catch.
to two too	word before a verb; in a direction number after one also; more than enough	Steve is going **to** Pittsburgh. He's spending **two** days there. He's going to Cleveland **too**.
weather whether	atmospheric conditions if	The **weather** is warm. We're going **whether** he likes it or not.
week weak	seven days not strong	I learned a lot in just one **week**. Leo's performance was **weak**.
whole hole	entire empty place	The **whole** conference was canceled. That left a **hole** in my schedule.
wood would	product of trees helping verb	The floorboards are old **wood**. Marie **would** help if you asked.

Affixes

Affixes are word parts that are added to the beginning or the end of a base word. A **prefix** is added to the beginning, while a **suffix** is added to the end. Some spelling rules apply when adding prefixes and suffixes. Read the spelling rules and the examples on the two charts.

PREFIXES

Rule	Examples
Do not change the spelling of a prefix when you add it to the base word.	**mis**spell **re**charge **un**do **bi**cycle

SUFFIXES

Rule	Examples
Do not change the spelling if the base word ends with a consonant.	child**hood** smooth**ness** repent**ance**
Drop the final e of the base word if the suffix starts with a vowel.	bak**ing** (bake) activ**ate** (active) fam**ous** (fame)
Keep the final e of the base word if the suffix starts with a consonant.	state**hood** care**less** strange**ly**
Double the final consonant if the base word has one syllable, or if the final syllable is stressed.	begg**ar** (beg) referr**al** (refer) admitt**ing** (admit)
When a base word ends with a vowel followed by y, keep the y.	annoy**ance** joy**ous**
When a base word ends with a consonant and y, change the y to i before adding the suffix.	beauti**ful** (beauty) librari**an** (library) histori**an** (history)

Spelling Patterns

The English language has some tricky or confusing spelling patterns. When you learn the patterns, it will be easier to remember how to spell many words.

Silent Letters

The letter *b* is silent in these words.

debt	climb	numb
doubt	comb	limb

The letter *g* is silent in words with a *gn* combination.

gnat	gnaw	gnarled
sign	campaign	design

The letter *h* is silent in these words.

exhaust	rhyme	khaki
vehicle	heir	honest
herb	hour	graham

Commonly Misspelled Words

These words are often difficult to spell. Memorize as many of them as you can.

all right	another	arctic
bargain	because	believe
chief	desert	dessert
February	friend	grammar
interesting	interrupt	license
many	opinion	people
thought	together	tried
very	wanted	when

Spelling Generalizations

Spelling **generalizations**, or rules, apply to most words in English. When you learn the generalizations, spelling correctly will be much easier.

1. Add *s* to form the plural of most nouns.

   computer–computer**s**   automobile–automobile**s**

2. Add *es* to form the plural of nouns ending in s, ss, sh, ch, or x.

   gas–gas**es**   glass–glass**es**

   dish–dish**es**   watch–watch**es**   fax–fax**es**

3. Add *s* when a vowel comes before the final *y*.

   day–day**s**   turkey–turkey**s**

4. Change the *y* to *i* and add *es* when a consonant comes before the final *y*.

   daisy–dais**ies**   county–count**ies**

5. Change the *f* to *v* and add *es* when a word ends in *f* or *fe*.

   leaf–lea**ves**   wife–wi**ves**

6. Add *s* when a vowel comes before the final *o*.

   radio–radio**s**   studio–studio**s**

7. Add *es* when a consonant comes before the final *o*.

   tomato–tomato**es**   potato–potato**es**

Irregular Plurals

You need to memorize these irregular plurals to spell them correctly.

   tooth–**teeth**   man–**men**

   mouse–**mice**   foot–**feet**

   ox–**oxen**   goose–**geese**

   child–**children**   woman–**women**

Spell Correctly in the Workplace

When you are at work, spelling correctly is extremely important. If you work in the medical profession, exact spelling is crucial. You don't want to misspell a diagnosis, or the name of a drug on a prescription. One or two incorrect letters, or letters in incorrect placement, might cause serious complications for someone taking a medication.

Sloppy spelling in a memo to your boss or coworkers makes you look unprofessional and unprepared. It might cost you a promotion, too. Before you send any memo, double check your spelling.

In a notebook, rewrite the memo below from James to his boss, Karen. Fix any spelling errors. Then write a sentence or two explaining why it is important to avoid errors in business communication.

Too: Karen

From: James

Re: Recycling

Strating next Monday, March 5, recycling pickup will occur precisely at noon. The recycleing company will invoice accounting directly four this servise.

Ensuring Correct Spelling

No matter what you write, strive to make your spelling correct. Use these tips to help you achieve that goal.

- Pay attention when you read. You'll begin to recognize common spelling patterns.

- Consult a print or online dictionary when you are not sure of a spelling. You may need to consult a specialized dictionary for highly technical terms.

- Use the spell check feature on your computer composing software program. But beware—the feature on some programs is sometimes inaccurate, so double check with a dictionary.

- Ask a friend or a colleague who has good spelling skills to check your work.

- Write a list of words you frequently misspell. Check the list as you write until you can spell the words on your own.

- Create mnemonic (memory assistance) devices for words that are difficult to spell.

- Playing spelling-related board or computer games is a fun way to enhance your skills.

THINK ABOUT **WRITING**

Directions: You may need to check the spelling of a word in more places than just a dictionary. Read each situation below. Write how you could find or check the correct spelling.

1. You are writing a paper about a rare insect, and you are not sure how to spell the plural form of the insect name.

_____

2. You are typing a paper, and you want to make sure you have not made any spelling errors.

_____

3. You are hand writing a note to a colleague, and you are nervous that you've spelled something wrong.

_____

4. You are updating the company directory, and you need to spell workers' names correctly.

_____

Vocabulary Review

Directions: Match each word in column 1 with its definition in column 2.

Column 1

1. _____ affixes

2. _____ contractions

3. _____ generalizations

4. _____ homophones

3. _____ interpret

4. _____ possessive

Column 2

A. to explain the meaning of something

B. word that shows ownership

C. words that sound the same but have different meanings

D. shortened form of words

E. word parts that are added to the beginning or the end of a base word

F. rules that apply in most situations

Skill Review

Directions: Underline the compound word in each sentence. Then write the word's definition.

1. I play basketball every Saturday morning.

   _____

2. She served a homemade apple pie for dessert.

   _____

3. The kids played with their new dollhouse for hours.

   _____

Directions: Read each pair of guide words in column 1. Find the word in column 2 that would be found on the same page in the dictionary. Draw a line to connect them.

4. holly/home   cousin

5. thud/tick   blueberry

6. cry/cup   homage

7. blow/board   culture

8. cotton/cover   thunder

Skill Practice

Directions: Choose the one best answer to each question.

1. Jean's younger sister accidentally hit the baseball threw the window.

   Which correction should be made to the sentence?

   A. replace Jean's with Jeans
   B. replace threw with through
   C. replace Jean's with Jeans'
   D. insert a comma after sister

2. It's safe to return to you're homes now.

   Which correction should be made to the sentence?

   A. replace it's with its
   B. insert a comma after homes
   C. replace it's with they're
   D. replace you're with your

3. Who's coffee grounds have clogged the sink's drain?

   Which correction should be made to the sentence?

   A. replace grounds to grounds'
   B. replace sink's with sinks
   C. replace Who's with Whose
   D. replace sink's with sinks'

4. The Martin familys' house has been affected by all three storms.

   Which correction should be made to the sentence?

   A. replace Martin with Martin's
   B. replace familys' with family's
   C. replace affected with effected
   D. replace storms with storms'

5. I wood think twice before turning in their report with your name on it.

   Which is the best way to write the underlined portion of the sentence? If the original is the best way, choose option (A).

   A. I wood think twice before
   B. I woodn't think twice before
   C. I wood think twice, before
   D. I would think twice before

6. It's not easy to ride a bike in rainy whether.

   Which is the best way to write the underlined sentence? If the original is the best way, choose option (A).

   A. It's not easy to ride a bike in rainy whether.
   B. Its not easy to ride a bike in rainy whether.
   C. Its' not easy to ride a bike in rainy whether.
   D. It's not easy to ride a bike in rainy weather.

7. "Their's a reason your mother said no," Dad explained.

   Which is the best way to write the underlined portion of the sentence? If the original is the best way, choose option (A).

   A. Their's a reason your mother
   B. Their's a reason you're mother
   C. There's a reason your mother
   D. They'res a reason your mother

Directions: What would happen if spelling rules went away? How would communication change if all writers spelled words however they wanted? In the space below, write how you think people's lives would change without spelling rules. Be sure to include how people would respond to confusion among homonyms and possible confusion in the workplace. In your writing, be sure to follow correct spelling rules.

_____

_____

_____

_____

_____

_____

_____

_____

_____

_____

_____

_____

_____

_____

_____

_____

_____

_____

_____

_____

Directions: Choose the <u>one best answer</u> to each question.

1. When Dr. Mendez announced her <u>retirement, the Doctors at the hospital organized a party</u>.

   Which is the best way to write the underlined portion of the sentence? If the original is the best way, choose option (A).

   A. retirement, the Doctors at the hospital organized a party
   B. retirement, the Doctors at the Hospital organized a party
   C. retirement, and the Doctors at the hospital organized a party
   D. retirement, the doctors at the hospital organized a party

2. When Annie reached home, she found the door wide open. It's lock was broken. She ran to the neighbor's house and telephoned the police.

   Which correction should be made to these sentences?

   A. replace the comma after <u>home</u> with a semicolon
   B. remove the comma after <u>home</u>
   C. replace <u>It's</u> with <u>Its</u>
   D. insert a comma after <u>house</u>

3. "Are you going to the concert, two?"

   Which correction should be made to this sentence?

   A. insert a comma after <u>going</u>
   B. replace <u>to</u> with <u>too</u>
   C. remove the comma after <u>concert</u>
   D. replace <u>two</u> with <u>too</u>

4. <u>Lupita plays three sports, tennis, basketball, and softball.</u> She won't say which she likes best, but she's a great softball player.

   Which is the best way to write the underlined sentence? If the original is the best way, choose option (A).

   A. Lupita plays three sports, tennis, basketball, and softball.
   B. Lupita plays three sports: tennis, basketball, and softball.
   C. Lupita plays three sports; tennis, basketball, and softball.
   D. Lupita plays three sports, tennis, and basketball, and softball.

5. That movie <u>was great, I'd love to see it again</u>. I can't remember the star's name; nevertheless, I think she's great.

   Which is the best way to write the underlined portion of the sentence? If the original is the best way, choose option (A).

   A. was great, I'd love to see it again
   B. was great, Id love to see it again
   C. was great: I'd love to see it again
   D. was great; I'd love to see it again

6. The people of the state of Colorado are in fact satisfied with who's running their government.

   Which correction should be made to this sentence?

   A. change <u>state</u> to <u>State</u>
   B. change <u>Colorado</u> to <u>colorado</u>
   C. insert commas before and after <u>in fact</u>
   D. replace <u>who's</u> with <u>whose</u>

Review

7. "The person who's lucky enough to pick the winning number," shouted the host, "Will be the proud owner of this new car!"

Which correction should be made to this sentence?

A. replace who's with whose
B. change "Will to "will
C. change number," to number",
D. change car!" to car"!

8. The schedule couldn't be changed, because many of the club members are from out of town.

Which correction should be made to this sentence?

A. change couldn't to could'nt
B. remove the comma after changed
C. replace the comma with a semicolon
D. insert a comma after because

9. "Dad, will you tell me a story about your Uncle, the one who went gold prospecting in Alaska?"

Which is the best way to write the underlined portion of the sentence? If the original is the best way, choose option (A).

A. Dad, will you tell me a story about your Uncle
B. Dad, will you tell me a story about your uncle
C. Dad, will you tell me a story about you're Uncle
D. Dad will you tell me a story about your Uncle

10. The old saying that money does'nt grow on trees is a good one to remember.

Which correction should be made to this sentence?

A. insert quotation marks before money and after remember
B. change money to Money
C. change does'nt to doesn't
D. replace the period with an exclamation point

11. Is your date of birth June, 12, 1961, or am I confusing you with Phil?

Which correction should be made to this sentence?

A. remove the comma after June
B. remove the comma after 1961
C. replace the comma after 1961 with a semicolon
D. insert a comma after birth

12. Write a letter to a friend telling about a party you attended. Include the names of the people who attended, where and when it occurred, and quotations of conversations you heard or were a part of during the party. Be sure to use correct capitalization, punctuation, and spelling.

Check Your Understanding

On the following chart, circle the number of any item you answered incorrectly in the Chapter 4 Review on pages 130–131. Next to each group of item numbers, you will see the pages you can review to learn how to answer the items correctly. Pay particular attention to reviewing skill areas in which you missed half or more of the questions.

Chapter 4 Review

Skill Area	Item Number	Review Pages
Capitalization	1, 7, 9, 12	98–107
Punctuation	4, 5, 6, 8, 11, 12	108–117
Spelling (Possessives, Contractions, Homophones, Patterns, Generalizations, and Affixes)	2, 3, 10, 12	118–129

UNIT 2

Writing

Sentence Structure

Have you ever heard the phrase "Less is more"? When it comes to writing, this is often true. Read the following sentences:

Earlier this week, it was three days ago, I went for a long walk with my dog by putting on my sneakers and going for an hour-long stroll.

Earlier this week, I walked my dog for an hour.

Which sentence is longer? Which is easier to understand? The second sentence has fewer words but is clearer and more effective.

In this chapter you will learn how to write effective sentences. You will also learn how to avoid some common mistakes that many writers make. These skills will help you to improve your writing and make it more interesting and enjoyable to read.

Here is what you will learn about in this chapter:

Lesson 5.1: Combine Ideas in Sentences
If you would like your writing to be easily read and understood, then you will want to learn about how to add variety and interest to your sentences.

Lesson 5.2: Write Effective Sentences
This lesson will help you avoid making common mistakes in your sentences by understanding modifiers, parallel structure, verb sequence, and pronoun references.

Lesson 5.3: Style and Diction
The difference between good and great writing can be your word choices and how you use them to express your meaning.

Goal Setting

This chapter is about adding your own personal style to your writing and recognizing other writers' styles. Think about how your style of writing can represent who you are. Ask yourself these questions:

Why is it important to write clear, effective sentences?

_____

_____

_____

What might happen if your writing isn't clear?

_____

_____

_____

How do you want to improve your writing?

_____

_____

_____

Combine Ideas in Sentences

Lesson Objectives

You will be able to
- Form compound and complex sentences
- Use conjunctions correctly
- Use commas and semicolons correctly

Skills

- **Core Skill:** Use Commas
- **Core Skill:** Sequence Events

Vocabulary

altered
combined
implement
logical
precedes

KEY CONCEPT: By combining simple sentences in your writing, you create more variety in sentence length and structure.

Write the correct form of each modifier in parentheses.

1. The cat napped *(happy)* in the afternoon sun.

2. Zach studied *(hard)* than Amy for the test.

Choose the correct words in the parentheses.

3. We *(hadn't scarcely, had scarcely)* begun watching the movie when the power went out.

4. There isn't *(anything, nothing)* I like better than the beach.

Combine Sentences

Read the following two paragraphs. Which do you like better?

> The US Army is dumping tanks into the Gulf of Mexico. They are trying to improve fishing. Old tanks are cleaned up. The army no longer wants them. All poisonous chemicals are removed. Then the tanks are taken out to sea on ships. The tanks are dumped overboard. This part of the gulf is flat. It has few natural hiding places for fish. Dumping the tanks creates artificial places. Fish can hide and reproduce.

> The US Army is dumping tanks into the Gulf of Mexico in order to improve fishing. Old tanks that the army no longer wants are cleaned up, and all poisonous chemicals are removed. Then the tanks are taken out to sea on ships and dumped overboard. This part of the gulf is flat; it has few natural hiding places for fish. Dumping the tanks creates artificial places where fish can hide and reproduce.

Both paragraphs are correct and give the same information. The first one, however, is made up entirely of simple sentences and sounds choppy. In the second paragraph, the sentences have been joined, or **combined,** to create variety in sentence length and structure. Ideas are more closely linked so you know how they are related.

Forming Compound Sentences

The most basic form of a sentence is the **simple sentence**. It contains one subject and one predicate and expresses a complete thought.

Yolanda wanted a radio for her birthday. She got two.

Simple sentences can often be combined to make a more interesting sentence.

Yolanda wanted a radio for her birthday, and she got two.

This new sentence has two subject-predicate sets. The two original simple sentences were linked by the word *and*. The result is a compound sentence. A **compound sentence** contains two or more connected simple sentences.

Conjunctions

Compound sentences are most often linked by a **conjunction**. Conjunctions link sentences by showing how ideas are related. Each conjunction shows a certain kind of connection between ideas.

Conjunctions and Their Uses	
Conjunction	**Use**
and	adds extra information
but, yet	shows how ideas are different
or	shows a choice between ideas
nor	shows a rejection of both ideas
for	connects an effect to a cause
so	connects a cause to its effect

In most compound sentences, a comma **precedes**, or comes before, the conjunction. Here are some examples of compound sentences.

Laura bought a coat, *and* Sara bought a pair of gloves.

Pan hated painting, *yet* he finished the whole room.

The Tuckers had a long trip before them, *so* they left early.

Jim's baby wouldn't be quiet, *nor* would she keep still.

Notice that when two simple sentences are combined using a conjunction, the original sentences are not **altered**, or changed. The only exception is when you use *nor*. Then the subject and verb in the second sentence are reversed.

Other Conjunctions

Some conjunctions are made up of two parts and used in pairs.

both...and	either...or
not only...but also	neither...nor

Place the second part next to the words that are being connected.

Not only do I take sugar in my coffee, **but** I **also** take milk.

Either it rains when I go fishing, **or** it's sunny when I work.

Join Ideas with a Semicolon

Semicolons with Conjunctive Adverbs

Simple sentences can also be joined using a semicolon and a conjunctive adverb. A conjunctive adverb is a word or phrase that works like a conjunction. As with conjunctions, it is important to choose the right conjunctive adverb to say what you mean.

Conjunctive Adverbs		
To show contrast	however otherwise	nevertheless on the other hand
To explain	for example furthermore besides	in other words in fact moreover
To show a result	consequently as a result	then therefore

These words are used like conjunctions to join sentences. Place a semicolon before the conjunctive adverb. Put a comma after all conjunctive adverbs except *then*.

Food prices keep rising; in fact, our weekly grocery bill is 10 dollars higher than last year.

Noriko took tennis lessons; then she beat me all the time.

Semicolons without Conjunctions

You can also join two simple sentences without using a conjunction or a conjunctive adverb. A semicolon shows the ideas are linked.

Benito likes to barbecue; ribs are his specialty.

One common error in forming compound sentences is caused by forgetting to **implement**, or put into use, one of these methods. The result is a **run-on sentence**.

Incorrect: Hieu needed new shoes he bought some at the sale.

Run-ons can be corrected with one of the methods you've learned for forming compound sentences—joining ideas with a comma or a semicolon with a conjunction, or joining ideas with a semicolon without a conjunction.

Correct: Hieu needed new shoes, so he bought some at the sale.

A second common error in forming compound sentences is caused by stringing several sentences together with the word *and*.

Incorrect: He went on vacation to New Mexico and visited Pueblo villages and saw hot-air balloons and rode on a tram up the mountain.

Correct: He went on vacation to New Mexico and visited Pueblo villages; he also saw hot-air balloons and rode on a tram up the mountain.

A third common error in forming compound sentences is caused by a **comma splice**. This occurs when a writer separates two sentences with a comma instead of the correct punctuation (period, question mark, etc.).

Incorrect: I keep sneezing, I think I'm catching a cold.

Correct: I keep sneezing, so I think I'm catching a cold.

Correct: I keep sneezing; I think I'm catching a cold.

THINK ABOUT WRITING

Directions: Rewrite the following pairs of simple sentences as compound sentences. Use a conjunction, conjunctive adverb, or semicolon shown in parentheses to connect the sentences. Add correct punctuation.

Example: Bill likes sports. He especially enjoys touch football. (and)
Bill likes sports, and he especially enjoys touch football.

1. Ann starts a new job soon. She hasn't told her present boss. (but)

   _____

2. There are no good movies in town. A great rock band is playing. (however)

   _____

3. My house is a mess. I never seem to have time to clean it. (semicolon)

   _____

4. The plane's wings were covered with ice. The departure was delayed. (as a result)

   _____

Prashant sat at his desk, then opened his laptop. Before he came to work, he had finally remembered to grab his extra keyboard. After he plugged it into his laptop, he felt like his whole work style would change.

Notice that the events are not presented in the order they happened, but the reader can still understand them. The words *before* and *after* are clues to tell the reader when the actions in the rest of the sentence took place.

Read the following list of events. In a notebook, write two short paragraphs. The first paragraph should present the events in the exact order they happened. The second paragraph should present the events in a different order but use sequence words to tell the reader what happened when.

Alice walked to the movie theater.
She bought a ticket.
She bought popcorn
She watched the movie and ate popcorn.

Form Complex Sentences

Another kind of sentence is the **complex sentence**. It is made up of two or more clauses. You have learned that a clause is a group of words that contains a subject and a predicate. A clause may express a complete thought, or it may not. In a complex sentence, only one of the clauses expresses a complete thought and can stand alone as a sentence. Look at the clauses in the following sentence:

While Rosa loaded the car, Michael got the kids ready to go.

The first clause in this sentence, *While Rosa loaded the car*, is not a complete thought. When you read it, you want to know what happened while Rosa loaded the car. This clause is called a **dependent clause** because it depends on the second clause to make it a complete thought. The second clause, *Michael got the kids ready to go*, is an independent, or main, clause. An **independent clause** expresses a complete thought and can stand alone.

A complex sentence is made up of one or more dependent clauses linked to one independent clause.

Simple sentences can be combined to form complex sentences. One simple sentence will be the independent clause. A second sentence will be linked to it by a type of conjunction that makes it dependent. The dependent clause can come before or after the independent clause. If it comes after the independent clause, no comma is needed.

You are such a good friend. I'll help you out.

becomes

Because you are such a good friend, I'll help you out.

or

I'll help you out because you are such a good friend.

Marty grilled some hamburgers. Denise fixed a salad.

becomes

While Marty grilled some hamburgers, Denise fixed a salad.

or

Denise fixed a salad while Marty grilled some hamburgers.

Here is a list of conjunctions that can make dependent clauses.

Conjunctions	
To show time before after while when whenever until as soon as as long as	**Before** I got out my camera, the bear had Manuel up a tree. Sylvia hurried home **while** it was still light.
To show reason because in order that since so that	Alicia went home early **because** she was sick.
To show conditions if unless whether	**Unless** you want trouble, don't pester that bee.
To show contrast though although even though in spite of the fact that despite the fact that whereas	**Even though** Pak Ku was tired, he helped fix dinner. Jennifer went to the meeting **despite the fact that** she had lost the election.
To show similarity as though as if	The day looked **as if** it would be clear and warm.
To show place where wherever	Jan went **wherever** her sister went.

When forming complex sentences, the dependent clause can come before or after the independent clause. When it comes before, use a comma to separate it from the independent clause; for example:

Because Jerry arrived late, he was criticized.

Jerry was criticized because he arrived late.

In a notebook, write a complex sentence in two ways: once with the dependent clause first, and once with the dependent clause after the independent clause.

When combining sentences, be careful to choose the conjunction that says what you mean. Think about which conjunction you would use to combine these two clauses:

Phillip forgot to open the door _____ he saw the ghost following him.

Combining the clauses with *when* or *because* is **logical** here. It makes sense. Try some other conjunctions, like *unless* or *as though*. They do not make sense at all. Make sure your sentence makes sense when you use a conjunction. Here is another example. Think of what relationship there is between the clauses.

Lana went to the show _____ she hated gangster movies.

Several conjunctions would work here—*although, even though, in spite of the fact that, despite the fact that*. All of them show contrast between the ideas. Try other conjunctions from the chart on page 141. You will see that most of them do not make sense here.

THINK ABOUT WRITING

Directions: Complete each complex sentence below. Link the clauses together by choosing the conjunction in the parentheses that makes sense. Write it on the line.

Example: ___When___ the hurricane approached, people left the island. *(When, As though)*

1. _____ backing into the garage, Sarah loaded the truck. *(Because, After)*

2. Melissa wants to go to the zoo _____ the weather turns cold. *(unless, so)*

3. _____ I tell Santwana I saw a spider, she will want to leave. *(As soon as, Where)*

4. _____ that dog has a loud bark, it's really very friendly. *(Before, Even though)*

5. The doctor says the wound will heal _____ I keep it bandaged. *(if, wherever)*

6. I have to finish this project _____ I like it or not. *(in order that, whether)*

Vocabulary Review

Directions: Match each word in column 1 with its definition in column 2.

Column 1

1. _____ altered
2. _____ combined
3. _____ logical
4. _____ precedes

Column 2

A. comes before something else

B. reasonable; sensible

C. changed or adjusted in some way

D. joined together

Skill Review

Directions: Read each sentence and determine if it is missing a comma. If it is, rewrite the sentence correctly.

1. Because the sky darkened I knew it was about to rain.

_____

2. Oscar helped me wash the car even though he was tired.

_____

3. I do not like coffee but I enjoy drinking tea.

_____

4. My brother does not like the cold yet he helped me build a snow fort.

_____

5. Ms. Ruiz does not have a lawn mower and she doesn't want one.

_____

6. Mom filled the cooler with water while Dad packed the bags.

_____

Skill Practice

Directions: Choose the <u>one best answer</u> to each question.

1. <u>I feel tired I think I need a nap.</u>

   Which is the best way to write the sentence? If the original is the best way, choose option (A).

   A. I feel tired I think I need a nap.
   B. I feel tired; I think I need a nap.
   C. I feel tired, then I think I need a nap.
   D. I feel tired as if I think I need a nap.

2. I usually read a magazine. I eat lunch.

   Which is the most effective combination of these sentences?

   A. I usually read a magazine while I eat lunch.
   B. Since I usually read a magazine, I eat lunch.
   C. I usually read a magazine until I eat lunch.
   D. So that I eat lunch, I usually read a magazine.

3. Michiko bought healthy plants, all of them are wilted now.

   Which correction should be made to the sentence?

   A. Insert <u>but</u> after the comma.
   B. Insert <u>so</u> after the comma.
   C. Insert <u>or</u> after the comma.
   D. Remove the comma.

4. You will receive only one more issue. Renew your subscription.

   Which is the most effective combination of these sentences?

   A. Because you renew your subscription, you will receive only one more issue.
   B. Renew your subscription, but you will receive only one more issue.
   C. You will receive only one more issue as if you renew your subscription.
   D. Unless you renew your subscription, you will receive only one more issue.

5. Will you please answer the phone despite the fact that I am in the shower?

   Which correction should be made to the sentence?

   A. replace <u>despite the fact that</u> with <u>in order that</u>
   B. replace <u>despite the fact that</u> with <u>while</u>
   C. insert a comma after <u>phone</u>
   D. move <u>despite the fact that I am in the shower</u> to the beginning of the sentence

6. He won't pay his bills on time whether he didn't get his paycheck.

   Which correction should be made to the sentence?

   A. Replace <u>whether</u> with <u>while</u>.
   B. Insert a comma after <u>time</u>.
   C. Replace <u>whether</u> with <u>because</u>.
   D. Remove <u>on time</u>.

Skill Practice (continued)

7. <u>Serena was late for work however she stayed late</u> to make up the time.

   Which is the best way to write the underlined portion of the sentence? If the original is the best way, choose option (A).

   A. Serena was late for work however she stayed late
   B. Serena was late for work; however she stayed late
   C. Serena was late for work; however, she stayed late
   D. Serena was late for work however, she stayed late

8. <u>In the morning edition of the newspaper Mayor Gonzalez</u> is quoted as saying that she will run for re-election.

   Which is the best way to write the underlined portion of the sentence? If the original is the best way, choose option (A).

   A. In the morning edition of the newspaper Mayor Gonzalez
   B. In the morning edition, of the newspaper, Mayor Gonzalez
   C. In the morning, edition of the newspaper Mayor Gonzalez
   D. In the morning edition of the newspaper, Mayor Gonzalez

9. We are out of milk. I will go to the store to buy some.

   Which is the most effective combination of these sentences?

   A. We are out of milk, so I will go to the store to buy some.
   B. Unless we are out of milk, I will go to the store to buy some.
   C. We are out of milk I will go to the store to buy some.
   D. We are out of milk, I will go to the store to buy some.

10. It is supposed to rain today. We should postpone the picnic.

    Which is the most effective combination of these sentences?

    A. It is supposed to rain today, because we should postpone the picnic.
    B. It is supposed to rain today, however, we should postpone the picnic.
    C. It is supposed to rain today, we should postpone the picnic.
    D. It is supposed to rain today; therefore, we should postpone the picnic.

Writing Practice

Directions: In a notebook, write two paragraphs about an event you organized and hosted or about an event you would like to organize. Include details about the steps you took to make sure that the event was successful. Make sure to clearly show what sequence the events occurred in. Include at least one dependent clause that uses a conjunction to show time. Include several compound and complex sentences. Use conjunctions, commas, and semicolons correctly.

Lesson Objectives

You will be able to

- Avoid misplaced and dangling modifiers in writing

- Identify parallel structure

- Use correct verb sequence in writing

- Keep pronoun references clear

Skills

- **Core Skill:** Avoid Excess Commas

- **Core Skill:** Use Precise Language

Vocabulary

conditional
excess
intended
precise
recognize
reposition

KEY CONCEPT: To write effective sentences, place modifiers close to the words they are modifying. Also, use parallel sentence structure, correct verb sequence, and clear pronoun references.

Combine each of the following into one sentence.
1. Luisa wants to go on vacation. She is afraid to fly.

2. I went grocery shopping. I put the food away.

Reposition Misplaced Modifiers

Modifiers—whether they are words, phrases, or clauses—should be placed as close as possible to the words they modify. When they are not, confusing ideas sometimes result. In the following sentence, who or what is wearing the yellow sneakers?

> Julian is following a stray cat wearing yellow sneakers.

The writer probably meant that Julian, not the cat, was wearing yellow sneakers. However, that is not what the sentence says. This is an example of a misplaced modifier. A **misplaced modifier** is a word or phrase whose meaning is unclear because it is in the wrong place.

To correct a misplaced modifier, **reposition**, or move, the modifier closer to the word it modifies.

> Wearing yellow sneakers, Julian is following a stray cat.

Here are some examples of how to correctly reposition misplaced modifiers:

> **Incorrect:** Sameer is talking about eating ice cream on the telephone.

In this example, it seems like Sameer wants to eat ice cream that has been placed on a telephone.

> **Correct:** Sameer is talking on the telephone about eating ice cream.

> **Incorrect:** The mayor is travelling to the rally in a car.

This example makes it seem like there is a political rally being held in a car, and the mayor is on his or her way there.

> **Correct:** The mayor is travelling in a car to the rally.

> **Incorrect:** Vanessa loves reading about astronauts in the library.

Sometimes, you may have to rearrange the sentence a little more to make the meaning clear.

> **Correct:** Vanessa loves reading in the library, and she loves to read about astronauts.

Simple sentences can often be combined to make a more interesting sentence, but make sure the modifiers are in the correct place.

Here are some examples of how to correctly combine two simple sentences:

> Carmen bought milk from the grocery store. The milk was spoiled.

Incorrect: Carmen bought milk from the grocery store that was spoiled.

Correct: Carmen bought milk that was spoiled from the grocery store.

> Sharon read a story about a woman who won the lottery. Sharon was in the elevator.

Incorrect: Sharon read a story about a woman who won the lottery in the elevator.

Correct: In the elevator, Sharon read a story about a woman who won the lottery.

Fix Dangling Modifiers

Another common mistake writers make when forming sentences is called a **dangling modifier**. A dangling modifier is a phrase or clause that does not modify any word in the sentence. This error is sometimes more difficult to identify than the misplaced modifier.

> While entering the cave, bats flew out of the darkness.

Who entered the cave? The bats? You probably know what the writer **intended**, or meant, to say, but the message isn't quite clear. *While entering the cave* does not modify a word in the sentence.

There are two ways to correct a dangling modifier. One way is to change the dangling modifier into a dependent clause by adding a subject.

> While I was entering the cave, bats flew out of the darkness.

A second way to correct a dangling modifier is to add a word for the phrase to modify. When rewriting the sentence, place the modifier as close as possible to the word it modifies.

> While entering the cave, I heard bats fly out of the darkness.

Here is another example:

Incorrect: To get home quickly, a creepy path by the river was taken. (*Who* wants to get home quickly?)

Correct: To get home quickly, they took a creepy path by the river.

Correct: Because they wanted to get home quickly, a creepy path by the river was taken.

THINK ABOUT WRITING

Directions: Underline the misplaced or dangling modifier in each sentence. Then rewrite the sentence to correct it.

Example: <u>While reading an exciting book</u>, Gretchen's telephone rang.
While Gretchen was reading an exciting book, her telephone rang.

1. Your bill should be paid before going on vacation.

   _____

   _____

2. Hanging on the wall, Javier stared at the beautiful painting.

   _____

   _____

3. The parade included clowns, elephants, and bands beginning on Main Street.

   _____

   _____

Parallel Structure

Many sentences have compound parts connected by a conjunction, such as *and* or *or*. These parts may include adjectives, verbs, adverbs, phrases, or other sentence parts. Compound parts should always have the same form.

> Combining ingredients, stirring the mixture, and kneading the dough are steps in making bread.

The words *combining, stirring,* and *kneading* have the same form; they all end in *-ing*. The sentence has **parallel structure**. Using parallel structure makes a sentence easier to read. Now look at the following sentence:

> Naoko's goals are to build a boat, to quit his job, and sailing around the world.

This sentence does not have parallel structure. The words *build, quit,* and *sailing* do not have the same form. Here are two ways to correct this:

> Naoko's goals are <u>to build</u> a boat, <u>to quit</u> his job, and <u>to sail</u> around the world.

> Naoko's goals include <u>building</u> a boat, <u>quitting</u> his job, and <u>sailing</u> around the world.

In the first correction, each verb uses the infinitive verb form including the word *to: to build, to quit, to sail*. In the second correction, each verb ends in *-ing: building, quitting, sailing*.

Nonparallel structure can occur with compound verbs, nouns, adjectives, and adverbs.

Incorrect: This morning I <u>did</u> the grocery shopping, <u>bought</u> a bus pass, and <u>had looked</u> for a job.

Correct: This morning I <u>did</u> the grocery shopping, <u>bought</u> a bus pass, and <u>looked</u> for a job.

In the incorrect sentence above, *did* and *bought* are in the simple past tense. The other verb, *had looked*, is in the past perfect tense. The corrected sentence changes them all to the simple past.

Incorrect: The clothes were <u>wrinkled</u>, <u>smelly</u>, and <u>needed washing</u>.

Correct: The clothes were <u>wrinkled</u>, <u>smelly</u>, and <u>dirty</u>.

The incorrect sentence includes two adjectives and a verb phrase. The corrected sentence changes them all to adjectives.

THINK ABOUT **WRITING**

Directions: Rewrite each sentence below to create parallel structure.

Example: Carlota told me to sit back, relax, and enjoying the afternoon.

Carlota told me to sit back, relax, and enjoy the afternoon.

1. I spent the weekend working in the yard, painting a door, and to fix a cracked window.

   _____

2. Regina said she would fix supper, set the table, and that she would clean up afterward.

   _____

3. That candidate has energy, concern, and she is honest.

   _____

4. When Taro got home, he found mud on the carpet, scratch marks on the furniture, and having broken glass on the floor.

   _____

5. The workshop leader explained how to speak clearly, appearing skilled, and how to ask for a raise.

   _____

Commas are used in writing to make the meaning of your writing clear. Commas tell readers when to pause and help them know which words go together.

Sometimes, however, commas are used in **excess**, or too frequently. When that happens, it can be difficult to understand what you're reading.

Read the following sentences:

I placed my clothes, and shoes, on the bed, and I began to pack.

I placed my clothes and shoes on the bed, and I began to pack.

In the first sentence, too many commas make the writing choppy and confusing. The second sentence is clear and easy to read.

In a notebook, rewrite the following sentences without excess commas:

- He missed the train because, his alarm did not go off, and he overslept.
- We walked down the beach, and wondered, if it would rain, soon.

Correct Verb Sequence

Sequence of Verbs

Verbs have tenses to show when actions occur. When a sentence has more than one verb, the verbs must work together to tell when the different actions happened. This is called the **verb sequence**. Notice the verb sequence in the following sentence:

It rained for five days before the sun had come out.

Rained is the simple past tense. *Had come* is the past perfect tense. The past perfect tells that an event occurred in the past before another event in the past. Here, the verb tenses say that the sun came out before it rained for five days. That doesn't make sense. Here is the correct verb sequence:

It had rained for five days before the sun came out.

To check verb sequence, first determine if the action of each verb occurs in the past, present, or future. If both actions are in the past, decide if they happened at the same time or if one happened before another. Here are some examples of correct verb sequence:

I eat too much when I worry.

(Both verbs are in the present tense.)

I ate too much yesterday because I worried about work.

(Both verbs are in the past because both actions were completed in the past and happened at the same time in the past.)

I had eaten three sandwiches before I realized it.

(Both actions happened in the past. One action—eating the sandwiches—took place before the other action—realizing it. The earlier action is correctly shown by the past perfect tense.)

Conditionals

A **conditional** [subject to requirements being met] clause is one that begins with the word *if*.

If Marie Valdez is elected, taxes will increase.

Sentences with conditional clauses must have certain verb sequences. In the example above, the conditional clause uses the present tense verb *is*. The main clause uses the future tense verb *will increase*. Here are some examples using the past, subjunctive, and past perfect tenses in the conditional clause.

If you had a million dollars, you could buy any car.

If Estevan were rich, he would give his money to charity.

If Minh had been more careful, this accident would have been avoided.

The following chart summarizes the correct verb sequences to use in sentences containing conditional clauses.

Conditional Verb Tenses	
Form of verb in *if* clause	Form of verb in main clause
present (*is elected*)	future (*will increase*)
past (*had*) subjunctive (*were*)	*would, could*, or *should* plus the base form of the verb (*could buy, would give*)
past perfect (*had been*)	*would have, could have*, or *should have* plus the past participle (*would have been*)

Helping Verbs

A **helping verb** is a verb such as *is, was, have, has*, or *had*. A helping verb is used to form different tenses of a verb. These helping verbs must be used in the correct combination with verbs in the rest of the sentence. Some cannot be used when another verb in the sentence is in the past tense.

Helping Verbs	
Not used in past tense	**Can be used in past tense**
can may must will shall	could might had to would should

Incorrect: When I <u>looked</u> at my study habits, I <u>decided</u> that I really <u>can work</u> harder.

Correct: When I <u>looked</u> at my study habits, I <u>decided</u> that I really <u>could work</u> harder.

In the example, *looked* and *decided* are both in the past tense. *Can*, therefore, is an incorrect choice as a helping verb with *work*. The helping verb *could* is correct. Try some other verbs from the chart that can be used in the past tense. All of them could be used correctly in this sentence.

21st Century Skill
Collaborative Learning

Work with a partner. In a notebook, write several conditional clauses while your partner writes several main clauses. Trade notebooks and add conditional clauses to your partner's main clauses. Your partner should add main clauses to your conditional clauses. Trade back and discuss your sentences.

Then write several main clauses while your partner writes conditional clauses. Trade notebooks and complete each other's sentences. Discuss these sentences together.

Find a valid informational blog on the Internet. As you read the blog, evaluate the effectiveness of the sentences. In a notebook, make a three-column chart. In the first column, list the skills you learned in this chapter about writing effective sentences. In the second column, write an example from the blog in which the skill is used correctly and effectively. In the third column, write an example of ineffective or incorrect use. Then show how you would revise the sentence.

THINK ABOUT WRITING

Directions: If the underlined verb shows correct verb sequence, write C. If the verb shows incorrect verb sequence, write the correct form of the verb.

Example: I am sure that I <u>would be</u> a better soccer player if I go to the training camp. **will be**

1. Toni was convinced that she <u>will get</u> lost. _____

2. We were so hungry at noon that we ate the meal we <u>had prepared</u> for supper. _____

3. Leroy finally realized that he <u>locked</u> himself out of his apartment. _____

4. Maria's neighbor asked her whether he <u>can</u> borrow a hammer. _____

5. We would buy a new refrigerator if we <u>are</u> able to afford one. _____

Pronoun References

Pronouns are words that take the place of nouns or refer to nouns. Errors in using pronouns occur when it is not clear what noun the pronoun refers to. This happens in two situations: when more than one noun comes before the pronoun and when there is no noun before the pronoun.

Pronouns with More Than One Preceding Noun

Read the following example of an unclear pronoun reference.

> Amy glanced at Sara as she entered the room.

To which noun does the pronoun *she* refer? You cannot tell whether it is to *Amy* or *Sara*.

There are different ways to correct sentences with unclear pronoun references. Here are two ways to correct the example:

> Amy glanced at Sara as <u>Amy</u> entered the room.

> As Amy entered the room, she glanced at Sara.

Here is another example of a sentence with an unclear pronoun reference:

Confusing: I'm reading a story in this book, <u>which</u> is very good.

Clear: I'm reading a very good story in this book.

Pronouns Without a Preceding Noun

Sometimes pronouns are used without any noun preceding them.

> After we put seeds in the birdfeeder, <u>they</u> never came around.

What is probably meant is that the birds never came around. However, it is better to be specific.

> After we put seeds in the birdfeeder, the <u>birds</u> never came around.

Another common mistake is to use a pronoun to refer to a general idea.

> The Changs give a lot of money to charity, <u>which</u> is admirable.

Here, *which* refers generally to giving money to charity. However, pronouns should refer to specific nouns. Then the sentence's meaning cannot be misunderstood.

> The Changs give a lot of money to charity; <u>their generosity</u> is admirable.

One other common problem occurs with the use of pronouns like *they*, *you*, and *it*.

> <u>They</u> say that too much salt is not good for <u>you</u>.

Who are *they*? Who is *you*? Notice how the following sentence makes the meaning more **precise**, or exact.

> <u>Health experts</u> say that too much salt is bad for <u>people</u>.

THINK ABOUT **WRITING**

Directions: Decide if each of the following sentences has a clear pronoun reference. If it does, write C on the line. If the reference is not clear, rewrite the sentence correctly.

Example: Mr. Berg and his son David took his car to the mechanic.
Mr. Berg and his son David took David's car to the mechanic.

1. Cathy told her son to clean his closet and his room since it was a mess.

   _____

2. The walls were bright green and the carpeting pale gray, which we thought was really ugly.

   _____

3. People are actually living without heat and hot water, and this must be changed.

   _____

4. They say that crime is increasing in our city.

   _____

It is often difficult to **recognize**, or become aware of incorrect language use, As the writer, it is easy to assume that everyone knows what you intended to write. However, it is easy to make mistakes or mislead your readers. Vague words or phrases contribute to this problem. Read the following example invitation:

> Please come to my party. It will be next week. Games will be after dinner. See you then!

The reader doesn't have enough information to know what's going to happen. Next week is not a useful time in this situation. The invitation mentions that games will be after dinner, but it doesn't state if dinner will be served, or if guests should eat dinner and then come to the party. Because there is no time listed, the reader cannot make inferences.

In a notebook, revise the invitation so that precise, necessary information is included. Reread your work when you are finished to make sure you have eliminated vague details and removed any misplaced modifiers.

Vocabulary Review

Directions: Complete each sentence with a vocabulary word. Then complete the puzzle.

conditional   excess   intended   precise   recognize   repositioned

Across

2. I _____ to wake up early, but I overslept.

4. After we _____ the furniture, there was room to dance.

5. It is important to be _____ when giving someone directions.

6. The agreement was _____ upon all requirements being met.

Down

1. I did not _____ anyone at the party.

3. Nam bought dog food in _____. Unfortunately, there is no place to store it all.

Skill Review

Directions: Read each sentence below. If it is written correctly, write C. If there are excess commas, rewrite the sentence correctly.

1. Acacia always dreamed, of riding a horse across a large field.

_____

2. Vanessa, who loves to cook, returned from the store with fresh fruits and vegetables.

_____

3. Yesterday's news, surprised and saddened us, all.

_____

Skill Practice

Directions: Choose the one best answer to each question.

1. It had snowed overnight, but the sun had come out by 7:00 a.m. Looking outside, Juan told his son that it would be great skiing.

   Which correction should be made to the sentence?

   A. change had snowed to snowed
   B. change had come to came
   C. replace his son with Juan's son
   D. change would be to can be

2. If Marsha had gone to the movie, she will take her little sister with her.

   Which correction should be made to the sentence?

   A. change had gone to has gone
   B. replace she with Marsha
   C. change will take to would have taken
   D. replace with her to with Marsha

3. Isabel told her daughter that she would go on vacation after all.

   Which correction should be made to the sentence?

   A. change told to tells
   B. replace her daughter with Isabel's daughter
   C. replace she with Isabel
   D. change would go to goes

4. Mr. Ho rides the train to work because it gives him time to read. He read a short story about a haunted house on the train.

   The most effective revision of the second sentence would begin with which group of words?

   A. A haunted house,
   B. A short story,
   C. About a haunted house,
   D. On the train,

5. If you will go to the store, pick up some milk, and rent a movie, I will cook dinner.

   Which is the best way to write the underlined portion of the sentence? If the original is the best way, choose option (A).

   A. I will cook dinner
   B. I would cook dinner
   C. I will have cooked dinner
   D. I had cooked dinner

6. Barry told Boris that he is a better athlete because he can run faster.

   Which is the best way to write the underlined portion of the sentence? If the original is the best way, choose option (A).

   A. he is a better athlete
   B. him is a better athlete
   C. Boris is a better athlete
   D. it is a better athlete

Writing Practice

Directions: In a notebook, write a story about an experience you have had. As you write, be sure to avoid confusion by making sure your ideas are clearly stated.

Style and Diction

KEY CONCEPT: Make the meaning of your writing clear by choosing and using words carefully.

Rewrite each sentence to make it clear.

1. I left several messages, but he never called back.

2. If I had more time, I will learn a new language.

3. Tomorrow I will do the laundry, bake a cake, and I washed the car.

Formal and Informal English

There are two types of standard English—formal and informal. You use formal English for serious writing, such as official documents or speeches, books, business communication, and job applications. Formal English is also used in academic writing, including textbooks and class presentations. It uses longer, more complicated sentences without slang or too many contractions.

You use informal English in your daily speech. You would also use informal English to write friendly letters, texts, blogs, or journal entries. Sometimes your teacher may allow you to use informal English to write a story. The sentences in informal English are shorter and simpler, and may contain slang, contractions, or popular expressions.

Read the following examples.

Formal English: The tenant was shocked at the large amount of the rent increase.

Informal English: The tenant was blown away at the humongous jump in the rent.

Formal English: Your presence is requested at the wedding of Ms. Amy Papas and Mr. Matthew Ling.

Informal English: Hey, we're having a party! Wanna come?

Style and Diction

Sometimes unclear writing is not caused by errors in grammar or sentence structure. In fact, writing can be grammatically and mechanically correct, and yet the meaning may still be unclear. This lack of clarity can result from problems with style or mistakes in diction.

Style is how you use words and sentences to express your meaning. **Diction** refers to your choice and use of words.

Economy and Precision in Writing

When you write, your most important goal should be to make your meaning clear. To write clearly, do not confuse your reader by adding more words than are necessary. Choose words that are as exact as possible. Here is an example of a sentence in which too many words make the meaning unclear:

> An article in a book that Sue was reading states that walking in which the walker moves briskly is exercise that is excellent.

Grammatically, there is nothing wrong with this sentence. However, to know what is said, you must read carefully. The problem is too many words. To make this kind of writing easier to understand, simplify it.

> An article in a book Sue was reading states that brisk walking is excellent exercise.

Even more simplification makes the meaning clearer.

> An article states that walking is excellent exercise.

When the sentence was made so **concise**, or brief, some ideas were lost. However, that information may not be important to the reader. The message in the final revision is what the writer really wants readers to understand.

When writing, the words you choose can make a big difference in how the reader responds.

Read the following sentences:

When the little girl smiled, I could see a space between her teeth.

When the little girl smiled, I could see a gaping hole where her front teeth used to be.

Both sentences say the same thing; however, it is easier to form a mental picture of what the girl looks like after reading the second sentence.

Read the following sentences. Then rewrite them in a notebook, choosing precise words that help readers visualize what they are reading.

- A lot of smoke was coming out of the building's windows.

- The lunch was prepared by Vicki.

- The dog made a noise to be let outside.

Here are some suggestions for making writing more **economical**, or getting the most meaning with the fewest words, and more precise, meaning each word states the exactly what you intended.

Avoid Repeating Ideas

Writers often unnecessarily repeat ideas. For example:

Lemonade is <u>equally as refreshing as</u> orange juice.

Equally refreshing and *as refreshing as* mean the same thing.

Better:　Lemonade is as refreshing as orange juice.

<u>or</u>

Lemonade and orange juice are equally refreshing.

A common example of repetition occurs when writers want to avoid sounding too sure of themselves. Then phrases such as *I think* creep into the writing.

In my opinion, I think you should use a hammer.

In my opinion and *I think* repeat the same idea. Sometimes this is important information. Often it is not, because it is already understood that the writer is expressing a personal opinion.

Better:	I think you should use a hammer.
Best:	You should use a hammer.
Repetitious:	In my opinion, it seems to me that nowadays there's too much violence on TV.
Better:	In my opinion, nowadays there's too much violence on TV.
Best:	There's too much violence on TV.

Use the Active Voice

Most verbs have both an active and a passive form. Remember that the subject of an **active verb** is the performer of the action. The subject of a **passive verb** has the action done to it. Sentences using passive forms usually need more words to say the same thing. To identify a verb in the passive voice, look for a phrase beginning with *by*. It tells who performs the action.

Passive:	The bread was baked by Maya.
Active:	Maya baked the bread.

Besides needing fewer words, active verbs make sentences more direct.

Passive: The lamp was broken by me.

Active: I broke the lamp.

Passive: The movie was enjoyed by the whole audience.

Active: The whole audience enjoyed the movie.

Passive: Carrie's column is read by many people each day.

Active: Many people read Carrie's column each day.

THINK ABOUT **WRITING**

Directions: Rewrite each sentence to state the idea more economically and precisely.

Example: My neighborhood has several new buildings that were recently built near my house last year.

In my neighborhood, several buildings were built last year.

1.   Heatwise, the temperature should get to eighty degrees warm.

   _____

   _____

2.   People's names are often forgotten by me all the time.

   _____

   _____

3.   The first step is to make a detailed list of each of the necessary ingredients right away.

   _____

   _____

4.   The reason I don't write letters is because I never have enough time to write them.

   _____

   _____

On this page, you
learned about idioms.
The example passage
showed you how details
in the text can often
help readers understand
an idiom's meaning.

The following passage
includes an idiom. Read
the passage and look
for details that help you
figure out the meaning
of the underlined idiom.
Then write the meaning
in your notebook.

When Serena
accidentally learned
about the party for
Marco, she was asked
to keep it under
her hat. Everyone
wanted Marco to be
completely surprised.

Common Errors with Diction

Idioms

Idioms are groups of words that have developed a special meaning.
The phrase *break the ice* is an example of an idiom. It means to help others
feel relaxed and more comfortable at a social gathering. When
you look at the meaning of each word, it does not help you understand the
meaning of the idiom.

Here are some other common idioms and their meanings:

Idiom: raining cats and dogs

Meaning: raining very heavily

Idiom: draw a blank

Meaning: to fail to recall a memory

Idiom: hit the ground running

Meaning: get off to a quick, successful start

When you **encounter**, or come across, an unfamiliar idiom in your
reading, look for clues to its meaning in the surrounding text. Sometimes
the author will include details that help readers figure out the meaning of
the idiom.

Read the following passage. **Examine**, or look carefully at, the underlined
idiom. What do you think it means? Use details in the text to support
your understanding.

It seemed as though everyone was having a good time at the party.
Everyone, that is, except Adela. Adela sat off to the side, away from
the crowd of happy people. She didn't feel like smiling or talking to
anyone. Adela was down in the dumps.

If you determined that *down in the dumps* means "unhappy," you are
correct. Details in the passage, such as *Everyone...except Adela; sat off to
the side;* and *didn't feel like smiling or talking*, support your conclusion.

Before you use idioms in your writing, make sure you understand their
meaning. Otherwise, your writing will not be clear—and it may also be
incorrect.

Prepositions

Prepositions tell how things relate. In spoken, informal English, people often use prepositions incorrectly. When you write, be sure to use the correct preposition for your sentence.

1. Use *different from*, not *different than*.

   Incorrect: Pecans are different than walnuts.

   Correct: Pecans are different from walnuts.

2. Use the preposition *at* or *in* with the verb *to be*, not the preposition *to*.

   Incorrect: Juan was to the game yesterday.

   Correct: Juan was at the game yesterday.

3. Use the preposition *as* when a subject-verb combination follows, even if the verb is implied. Use the preposition *like* in all other cases.

   Incorrect: My daughter looks as me.

   Correct: My daughter looks like me.

   Incorrect: Like you know, she is already as tall as I am.

   Correct: As you know, she is already as tall as I am.

4. Use *between* when referring to only two things. Use *among* when referring to more than two things.

   Incorrect: The argument was among the two brothers.

   Correct: The argument was between the two brothers.

   Incorrect: The four couples divided the cost between themselves.

   Correct: The four couples divided the cost among themselves.

5. Use the preposition *from* after the word *borrow*, not *off* or *off of*.

   Incorrect: I will borrow the bicycle off Melissa.

   Incorrect: I will borrow the bicycle off of Melissa.

   Correct: I will borrow the bicycle from Melissa.

6. Use the preposition *off*, not *off of*.

   Incorrect: Warner got off of the train from Kansas City.

   Correct: Warner got off the train from Kansas City.

7. After the verbs *could*, *should*, and *would*, do not use the preposition *of*. The correct phrase is *could have, would have,* or *should have*. A contraction is also acceptable.

   Incorrect: I should of known the answer.

   Correct: I should have known the answer.

   Correct: I should've known the answer.

Verbs

Do not use incorrect verbs. The following are a few common errors.

1. Do not use the phrase *try and*. Use *try to* instead.

    Incorrect: Ms. Clemente says she will <u>try and</u> be here by three.

    Correct: Ms. Clemente says she will <u>try to</u> be here by three.

2. Use an infinitive after the word *ought*. *Should* means the same thing but does not need an infinitive.

    Incorrect: The team <u>ought try</u> to recruit a really tall center.

    Correct: The team <u>ought to try</u> to recruit a really tall center.

    Correct: The team <u>should try</u> to recruit a really tall center.

Comparisons

Comparing is telling how two or more things are alike and different. When you compare two things, you use words such as *more*, *less*, and words that end in *-er*. There are several mistakes that writers can make when they are making comparisons.

1. Be sure you are comparing similar things.

    Dep's bowling score was better than his partner.

This sentence is comparing a *bowling score* with a *partner*. Here is what the writer means:

Dep's bowling score was better than his partner's [bowling score].

2. Don't confuse *any* with *any other*.

    Katie is a better swimmer than <u>any</u> girl in her class.

Katie is a girl, so she cannot be a better swimmer than any girl. The writer means she is better than any *other* girl.

    Katie is a better swimmer than <u>any other</u> girl in her class.

THINK ABOUT **WRITING**

Directions: Read each sentence and look for incorrect usage. Rewrite the sentence correctly.

Example: Julie's dog is very different than my dog.

Julie's dog is very different from my dog.

1. Lee told us that Greg should of received the package by now.

    _____

2. Like I've said before, most people never know how well off they are.

    _____

3. Sarah divided the remaining cake between the three of us.

    _____

4. Phan will certainly be to the game Saturday to see her brother play.

    _____

5. When she got up off of the ground the last time, Yoko gave up skating.

    _____

6. Tina's got a sharper memory than any person I know.

    _____

7. The actors in that movie were worse than the movie I saw last week.

    _____

8. Sid said he knew someone who would try and get us tickets.

    _____

Vocabulary Review

Directions: Complete the sentences below using one of the following words:

concise   diction   encounter   idioms   style

1. Luisa wondered if she would _____ her old boyfriend at the reunion.

2. Silvio is always in a rush, so I have learned to be _____ when I speak with him.

3. That author has a _____ of writing that I enjoy reading.

4. I avoid using _____ because their meanings are often misunderstood.

5. The guest speaker's _____ was perfect. Every word was clear and grabbed the audience's attention.

Skill Review

Directions: Read each sentence below and evaluate it for word choice. Then revise the sentence to make it clearer.

1. Going to the movies is equally as entertaining as watching television.

_____

2. Jabrille's clothes got wet when he went out in the rain without an umbrella.

_____

3. That apple looks good.

_____

4. The actor was very scared that she would forget her lines.

_____

5. Strong winds knocked over the large tree.

_____

6. When I dropped the dish, it broke into many pieces.

_____

Skill Practice

Directions: Choose the <u>one best answer</u> to each question.

1. In my opinion, it seems to me as if the amount of traffic in this town has increased rapidly over the past ten years.

   Which is the most effective rewrite of this sentence?

   A. The amount of traffic in this town has increased rapidly over the past ten years.
   B. In my opinion, it seems to me as if the amount of traffic in this town had increased rapidly over the past ten years.
   C. It seems to me, in my opinion, that the amount of traffic in this town has increased rapidly over the past ten years.
   D. Over the past ten years, it seems to me as if the amount of traffic in this town has increased rapidly in my opinion.

2. The new baby was brought home from the hospital by the parents.

   Which is the most effective rewrite of this sentence?

   A. Brought home from the hospital was the new baby by the parents.
   B. The parents brought the new baby home from the hospital.
   C. By the parents, the new baby was brought home from the hospital.
   D. From the hospital, the new baby was brung home by her parents.

3. The first candidate's speech was much better than the second.

   Which correction should be made to the sentence?

   A. change <u>much better</u> to <u>much more good</u>
   B. move <u>was much better</u> to the beginning of the sentence
   C. insert <u>candidate's speech</u> after <u>second</u>
   D. change <u>much better</u> to <u>most best</u>

4. I decided to borrow the car <u>off of my best friend.</u>

   Which is the best way to write the underlined portion of the sentence? If the original is the best way, choose option (A).

   A. off of my best friend
   B. from my best friend
   C. off my best friend
   D. off of my better friend

5. The mother divided the chocolates between her four children.

   Which correction should be made to the sentence?

   A. change <u>divided</u> to <u>could of divided</u>
   B. replace <u>between</u> with <u>to</u>
   C. change <u>her</u> to <u>those</u>
   D. replace <u>between</u> with <u>among</u>

Writing Practice

Directions: Think about two different places that you have lived or would like to live. How are they different? How are they the same? On another sheet of paper, write an essay comparing the two places. Be sure to use formal style and avoid common errors in diction.

Directions: Choose the one best answer to each question.

1. Taro is different from Tamara because he would of been nervous speaking before a large group.

   Which is the best way to write the underlined portion of the sentence? If the original is the best way, choose option (A).

   A. different from Tamara because he would of been
   B. different from Tamara because he would have been
   C. different than Tamara because he would of been
   D. different from Tamara because they would of been

2. If you pay that fine, you will lose your driver's license.

   Which correction should be made to this sentence?

   A. replace If with Unless
   B. remove the comma after fine
   C. change will to would
   D. replace If with However

3. Cheryl did the laundry, made the bed, and is walking the dog.

   Which correction should be made to this sentence?

   A. change made to will make
   B. change is walking to will walk
   C. change is walking to walked
   D. change did to is doing

4. Rhode Island not only is the smallest state but also near the ocean.

   Which is the best way to write the underlined portion of the sentence? If the original is the best way, choose option (A).

   A. not only is the smallest state but also near the ocean
   B. is both the smallest state but also near the ocean
   C. not only is the smaller state but also is near the ocean
   D. not only is the smallest state but also is near the ocean

5. Like Mr. Murray said, about 200 people applied for this job.

   Which correction should be made to this sentence?

   A. change said to will say
   B. remove the comma after said
   C. replace Like with As
   D. replace about with around

6. The climate in the Caribbean is considered tropical even though it has lots of sun and rainfall.

   Which correction should be made to this sentence?

   A. insert a comma after tropical
   B. insert a semicolon after tropical
   C. replace even though with however
   D. replace even though with since

Review

7. John's brother and his mother took his injured dog to the veterinarian.

   Which correction should be made to this sentence?

   A. replace his mother with John's mother
   B. insert a comma after brother and mother
   C. replace his injured dog with John's injured dog
   D. replace his injured dog with his or her injured dog

8. The trio is singing tonight in spite of the fact that the lead singer has a bad cold.

   Which correction should be made to this sentence?

   A. insert a comma after tonight
   B. replace in spite of the fact that with because
   C. replace in spite of the fact that with since
   D. insert a comma after tonight and that

9. In the future time before us, world leaders around the globe must make tough decisions.

   Which is the best way to write the underlined portion of the sentence? If the original is the best way, choose option (A).

   A. In the future time before us, world leaders around the globe
   B. In the future, world leaders
   C. In the future time, world leaders
   D. In the time before us, world leaders around the globe

10. If Marie Rosello were mayor, this city would not have been in debt.

    Which correction should be made to this sentence?

    A. change were mayor to is mayor
    B. replace If with Because
    C. remove the comma after mayor
    D. change would not have been to would not be

11. After months of work on the construction project, at last it was finally completed by Jim.

    Which is the best way to write the underlined portion of the sentence? If the original is the best way, choose option (A).

    A. at last it was finally completed by Jim
    B. at last Jim finally completed it
    C. Jim finally completed it at last
    D. Jim finally completed it

12. Murray Mugford bought a used car at an auto dealership that was on sale for $2,000.

    Which is the best way to write the underlined portion of the sentence? If the original is the best way, choose option (A).

    A. used car at an auto dealership that was on sale for $2,000
    B. used car at an auto dealership selling for $2,000
    C. used car, that was at an auto dealership for $2,000
    D. used car that was on sale for $2,000 at an auto dealership

13. Wanting to leave the country to own a sheep farm in Australia, Ted and his wife Sonia packed up their things and left the country.

Which is the best way to write the underlined portion of the sentence? If the original is the best way, choose option (A).

A. Wanting to leave the country to own a sheep farm in Australia,
B. Because they wanted to own a sheep farm in Australia,
C. Although they wanted to own a sheep farm in Australia,
D. Their want of a sheep farm in Australia was great, so

14. The bitter disagreement among Dr. Freud and Dr. Jung developed gradually over many years.

Which is the best way to write the underlined portion of the sentence? If the original is the best way, choose option (A).

A. The bitter disagreement among Dr. Freud and Dr. Jung
B. The bitter disagreement, which among Dr. Freud and Dr. Jung
C. The bitter disagreement between Dr. Freud and Dr. Jung
D. As a result of the bitter disagreement among Dr. Freud and Dr. Jung

15. Calmed by the doctor and because he was under medication, Manuel finally was able to sleep.

Which is the best way to write the underlined portion of the sentence? If the original is the best way, choose option (A).

A. Calmed by the doctor and because he was under medication,
B. Calmed by the doctor, because he was under medication,
C. The doctor having arrived, and because he was under medication,
D. Calmed by the doctor and quieted by the medication,

16. Imagine you work for a company that makes computers. On a separate piece of paper, write a memo to your boss. Explain a problem you see at work, and how you propose solving the problem. Make sure to use correct capitalization, spelling, and punctuation.

Review

Check Your Understanding

On the following chart, circle the number of any item you answered incorrectly in the Chapter 5 Review on pages 166–168. Next to each group of item numbers, you will see the pages you can review to learn how to answer the items correctly. Pay particular attention to reviewing skill areas in which you missed half or more of the questions.

Chapter 5 Review

Skill Area	Item Number	Review Pages
Combine Ideas in Sentences	2, 4, 16	136–145
Write Effective Sentences	3, 7, 10, 12, 13, 15, 16	146–155
Style and Diction	1, 5, 6, 8, 9, 11, 14, 16	156–165

Text Structure

When you talk to a friend, do you think of one idea, develop it fully, and go on to the next? Usually not. In conversation, most people move quickly from idea to idea. However, this doesn't usually work in writing.

Read this paragraph. Does it have a single main idea? Does it develop it fully?

I lost my cell phone last week, but I got it back. Once I lost my favorite necklace and never found it. I looked all over my house and even called a few friends. I was luckier with the cell phone. A woman found it and used my address book to call my home.

The paragraph seems to be about a lost cell phone but also tells about a lost necklace. We don't find out where the cell phone was found or what happened when the woman called.

A stronger paragraph would have a clear beginning and ending. It would focus on the cell phone only. It would also give more details about what happened.

In this chapter you will learn about the different parts of a paragraph and how they work together to convey a single main idea.

Lesson 6.1: Paragraph Structure and Topic Sentences
Anything you build has a structure. Learn about the parts, or structure, of a well-built paragraph. Also learn how topic sentences make the subject of a text clear.

Lesson 6.2: Tone and Diction
What tone of voice do you use to show that you are upset? Learn how your choice of words also helps convey tone when you write.

Lesson 6.3: Order of Importance and Time Order
Two ways to organize ideas in a paragraph are order of importance and time order. Learn how to choose the appropriate organization and use it to put your ideas together effectively.

Lesson 6.4: Cause-and-Effect Order and Comparison-and-Contrast Order
You can organize ideas in a paragraph to tell the causes, or reasons something happens and the effects, or results. You can also organize to show how subjects, events, or ideas are similar and different.

Goal Setting

Think about how being organized helps you in your daily life. When you are organized, you know where to find the things you need quickly, and you get to the places you need to be on time. Writing well-organized sentences and paragraphs has the same benefits. When your writing is organized, the most important ideas are easy to find and the reader can easily follow your thinking without getting lost. Use the checklist to keep your learning organized! Check off each element or topic after you learn about it.

Paragraph Structure and Topic Sentences

_____ main idea

_____ topic sentence

_____ supporting sentences

_____ concluding sentence

Tone and Diction

_____ tone

_____ informal language

_____ formal language

Order of Importance and Time Order

_____ organize ideas in order of importance

_____ organize details in time order

_____ use transitions

Cause-and-Effect Order and Comparison-and-Contrast Order

_____ organize by effect with multiple causes

_____ organize by cause with multiple effects

_____ whole-to-whole pattern

_____ point-by-point pattern

What do you already know about paragraph organization?

_____

_____

_____

Which of the above topics do you want to learn more about?

_____

_____

_____

Paragraph Structure and Topic Sentences

Lesson Objectives

You will be able to
- Recognize effective paragraphs
- Identify and add topic sentences

Skills

- **Core Skill:** Summarize Text
- **Reading Skill:** Understand the Main Idea

Vocabulary

concluding sentence
convey
effective
main idea
paragraph
summarize
supporting sentence
topic sentence

KEY CONCEPT: A paragraph usually includes a topic sentence and other sentences that give more information.

Identify the complete sentence. Then add the missing end mark and comma.

A. Hundreds of scholars at the popular conference

B. At the end of the season the winning team

C. Reading their favorite magazines at the beach

D. When Amber left the house her dog ran after her

Paragraph Structure

A **paragraph** is a group of sentences that work together to **convey**, or communicate, a single main idea. A paragraph can stand alone or be part of a longer composition.

To write a paragraph, you need a topic sentence that clearly states the main idea. You also need additional sentences with enough details to support the main idea. The underlined sentence of this paragraph is the topic sentence that states the main idea. The other sentences tell more about the main idea.

> Buying a used car can be a sound investment if you take certain precautions. First, find out whether the car has ever been in an accident. Next, ask to see all maintenance records. You will also want to check the tires and examine the body of the car for rust. Most importantly, be sure to take the car for a test drive.

Every paragraph should have an audience, or potential reader, and a purpose. The paragraph you just read was written for someone who's interested in buying a car. The purpose was to share information.

These are the basic purposes for writing a paragraph:

- To inform or explain by sharing facts or other information

- To explain an idea, belief, or viewpoint

- To persuade someone to agree with a position or take action

- To entertain, often by narrating an event

Look at the following paragraph from a memo. Who is the audience?

> It is critical to the survival of our video store that you properly scan in returned DVDs. For one thing, if a DVD is not scanned in, our inventory will not be accurate. A customer calling about a movie may be told that we do not have it. Even more of a problem, customers may be unfairly accused of not returning a disk and charged for it. As a result, our reputation will be hurt, and customers will stop using our store.

Audience: Employees

Purpose: To persuade employees to follow an important procedure

Main idea: It is important to carefully scan returned DVDs.

UNDERSTAND THE MAIN IDEA

The topic is the subject of a passage, and the **main idea** is the most important point. The sentence that tells you the main idea is called the **topic sentence,** and it is often the first sentence in the passage. The rest of the passage usually supports, or gives more information about, the main idea. Identifying the topic sentence and finding the main idea will help you better understand what you read.

To find the main idea, ask yourself: *What is the topic? What is the main point the author is making about the topic?*

Read the following paragraph and identify the main idea.

> (1) Mountain climbing can provide you with a fresh look at yourself and the world. (2) As you climb, your attention moves away from everyday concerns to the challenges of the trail. (3) Pushed beyond your usual limits, you discover the power of determination and positive thinking. (4) As you hold onto trees and rocks for balance, you see tiny insects and plants up close. (5) Then, when you reach the top, you see mountains and valleys—the bigger world of which you are just a part.

Sentence 1 makes a general statement about the positive effect of mountain climbing on your views. Sentences 2 through 5 provide examples of ways your view changes. Only sentence 1 is general enough to include the ideas of the other sentences. Sentence 1 is the topic sentence that states the main idea.

The structure of a paragraph may differ depending on your purpose for writing it. When you write informative or explanatory paragraph, you should clearly state the main idea in the first sentence. The rest of the sentences should contain facts that build on each other to support the main idea.

When you write a persuasive paragraph, you need to state your position clearly in the first sentence. The remaining sentences will be a combination of facts and opinions that support your main idea.

Your placement of the main idea in a narrative paragraph may vary. You want to make sure to include it, but you may want to start with some interesting details, and state the main idea later on in the paragraph.

In a notebook, write a topic sentence for an informative paragraph and a topic sentence for a persuasive paragraph. How are they different?

An **effective**, or successful, paragraph has a topic sentence with a clear main idea and additional sentences with supporting details. When you write a paragraph, remain focused on the main idea. What is the main idea of the paragraph below? Where is the topic sentence?

> You can take a few simple steps to prepare your car for the harsh conditions of winter. First, change the antifreeze to prevent the water that cools your engine from freezing. Then check your heater, defroster, and the treads on your tires. Finally, make sure you have enough windshield-wiper fluid to keep your windshield clean, and check it often. In winter, the dirty slush ends up on your windshield whenever a truck passes. It also splashes your clothes when you walk. I might move to Florida to avoid the hassle.

The main idea is that a few simple steps will prepare your car for the harsh winter. The fist sentence is the topic sentence. The last three sentences do not support the main idea, so they should not be included.

THINK ABOUT **WRITING**

Directions: Read each paragraph below. If all sentences support the main idea, write *effective*. If not, tell which sentences do not support the main idea.

1. (1) Starting next Monday, there will be a new procedure for signing in for the restaurant staff. (2) For both the lunch and dinner shifts, all servers will need to sign in at least thirty minutes before we open. (3) They must already be in uniform when they sign in. (4) Speaking of uniforms, could servers please make sure their uniforms are clean at the beginning of their shifts? (5) That's why we provide machine-washable clothing. (6) Fabrics are easy to care for now.

2. (1) Liang bought an answering machine for his telephone and had no difficulty setting it up. (2) He plugged the AC adapter into an electrical outlet on the wall. (3) Then he inserted the small plug into the adapter jack on the base of the machine. (4) He also attached the phone jack to the answering machine and the answering machine's jack to the wall jack. (5) Finally, he set the date/time stamp.

3. (1) Marta did not expect her puppy to fail at obedience school. (2) The instructor began by teaching the "stay" command. (3) Most of the dogs responded appropriately, but Fluffy was a sweet border collie who wanted to play, not stay. (4) Marta got the puppy for her children. (5) Fluffy had been abandoned. (6) Marta was happy to give her a good home, but her husband liked cats better than dogs.

Topic Sentences

Most paragraphs consist of a **topic sentence** and **supporting sentences**. The topic sentence presents the main idea, and the supporting sentences explain, prove, or expand upon the main idea. Some paragraphs also end with a **concluding sentence**, which restates the main point, connects to the next paragraph, or ends in a lively way.

The advantage of using a topic sentence is that it can direct your writing and help you stay focused. The topic sentence usually comes at the beginning of a paragraph, but it can go anywhere in the paragraph. When it comes at the beginning, it tells the reader what to expect. What kind of information would you expect to see after reading the topic sentence below?

> Tomas has a wonderful recipe for a fruit tart.

You are correct if you thought the rest of the paragraph would give the recipe for a fruit tart.

> Tomas's delicious fruit tart is surprisingly easy to make. He starts with a sheet of ready-made puff pastry. Then he spreads fruit-flavored yogurt on the pastry. He cuts kiwi, cantaloupe, apples, and bananas into slices. He soaks the apple and banana slices in orange juice for a few minutes so they won't turn brown. Then he arranges all the fruit slices on the pastry in rows. The delicious dessert is ready to eat!

The topic sentence of a paragraph should engage the reader. It can be a statement or a question. A question at the beginning makes the reader want to find out more. Here is another way to start the paragraph about Tomas's fruit tart.

> Have you ever watched Tomas prepare his elegant fruit tart?

When the topic sentence comes at the end of the paragraph, it often summarizes or emphasizes what came before. Notice how the last sentence of this memo to a manager refers back to points made throughout the paragraph.

> Suppose that one of your best employees is not performing well. Instead of rushing to judge or criticize, consider the possibility that he or she has a back problem, sick family member, or some other personal difficulty. Set up a meeting in which you can express your concerns and listen to your employee's point of view. You may very well be able to solve the problem together. At the very least, you will both feel that you have been heard. If you treat an unsatisfactory employee with compassion, honesty, and respect, you have a good chance of improving the situation.

Reading Skill
Understand the Main Idea

Remember that the main idea is the most important point that a writer is trying to make. It is supported by all the sentences in a paragraph. The main idea of a paragraph may be stated directly or it may be implied.

Read the example about Tomas on this page. What is the most important idea in the paragraph? Is that idea stated directly? Is that idea supported by the sentences in this paragraph?

WRITE TO LEARN

Write a paragraph about an activity. Choose the activity, and list a purpose and audience. Then write a topic sentence. For example:

Topic (activity): soccer

Purpose: To explain the excitement of the game

Audience: Someone who doesn't play or watch the game

Topic Sentences: There is more to the game of soccer than running fast and kicking well.

A good topic sentence should be neither too general nor too specific. Compare the topic sentences below this descriptive paragraph.

> Pleasure boats and a now modest fishing fleet make Gloucester's harbor lively and picturesque. You can wander into the many artist galleries that line the streets and buy art or simply browse. If you're hungry, you'll find all kinds of restaurants. On a beautiful day, you can sit on a park bench and watch the water. You can also sunbathe and swim at one of the beaches.

Too general: Gloucester is a nice town in Massachusetts.

Too specific: Gloucester has many artists.

Strong: Once the center of the fishing industry in Massachusetts, Gloucester is now a great destination for a summer day.

The first sentence is too general because it doesn't indicate anything about why the town is nice or the writer's purpose (to persuade someone to visit). The second sentence is too specific because it refers to only one of the supporting details in the paragraph. The last sentence covers the main idea, indicates the purpose, and makes the reader want to find out why Gloucester is a great destination.

Suppose you had to add a topic sentence for the following paragraph of supporting details. Could you choose the most effective topic sentence to add to it?

> You can give the books to the children of your friends. You can donate them to a library. You can take them to the children's unit at your local hospital and read them aloud to the young patients. Whatever you do, don't throw out old books.

Which sentence below would be most effective at the beginning of the paragraph?

A. It's time to clean house.

B. Reading is one of the most important skills that a child can learn.

C. There are many things you can do with books when your children outgrow them.

D. Children's books get more expensive every year.

To answer this question, you need to read the paragraph and understand what the main idea is. Each of the first three sentences in the paragraph gives a use for old children's books, and the final sentence tells what not to do with them. The sentence that best describes the main idea is option (C).

Remember, a sentence is not necessarily an effective topic sentence just because it relates to the other sentences. For example, option (D) relates to children's books, just as the rest of the paragraph does. Children's books, however, is too general to be the main idea of the other sentences. Instead, what to do with old children's books is the main idea.

What topic sentence could you add to this paragraph about the writer's first day as a waiter? Look at all the details to figure out the main idea.

> The restaurant was overflowing with customers. I didn't know the menu yet and had even less understanding of the timing involved in serving food. I was scared that I would drop things, forget all my orders, and make everyone angry with me. I wanted to run away, but I decided to let my customers know it was my first day. To my relief, they were patient with me. My fellow waiters were also supportive. They told me when food was ready to be served or when a customer needed some water.

The writer begins by describing the challenge and ends by telling how it all worked out. Here is a possible topic sentence:

My first day as a waiter was scary, but everything worked out fine.

THINK ABOUT **WRITING**

Directions: Make each group of supporting sentences below into a complete paragraph by adding a topic sentence. Make sure your topic sentence states the main idea of the paragraph and is a complete sentence.

1. _____

First, we recommend conducting a survey of current customers. Find out what they like about the company's products and what they don't like. Then management must decide which customer complaints can be addressed cost effectively. Studies show that 20 percent of your customers buy 80 percent of your products. Our goal is to identify that 20 percent and provide excellent service to those customers. The end result will be an increase in sales and therefore an increase in profits.

2. _____

Andrea picked up several chairs and tables in various sizes for a few dollars each at flea markets. She bought irregular sheets for far less than the material would have cost at a fabric store. She used one of the sheets, in a green and blue paisley pattern, as a slipcover to cover the rather beat-up sofa in her living room. She draped part of another over a coffee table and used the scraps to make pillows.

3. _____

You can stack books on the shelves or help organize the periodicals. You can also assist the staff at the circulation desk when there are long lines of people. Schedule a regular time slot, or call whenever you have time to volunteer. Because of all the budget cuts, the staff is much smaller these days. The librarians will be grateful for any help you can give.

Vocabulary Review

Directions: Complete the sentences below using one of the following words:

concluding sentence   **effective**   **main idea**   **paragraph**

supporting sentence   **topic sentence**

1. Writing is _____ when it is clear and easy to follow.

2. A(n) _____ states the main idea of a paragraph.

3. A(n) _____ gives details about the main idea.

4. The _____ is the writer's most important point.

5. A group of sentences that work together is called a(n) _____.

6. A(n) _____ restates the main points of a paragraph.

Skill Review

Directions: Find and underline the main idea in each passage below.

1. (1) You can create an exciting collage even if you cannot draw well. (2) Start with a few small photos or magazine pictures. (3) Place the images on a large piece of paper, and try different arrangements. (4) When you are satisfied, glue the images to the paper. (5) Then add watercolors to connect the images or create a colorful background. (6) You can also add ribbons, feathers, and other objects.

2. (1) A mockingbird was living in a large tree outside my brother's bedroom. (2) From morning to night, the bird mimicked the songs of other birds. (3) It became impossible for my brother to study or even think. (4) Finally, he set up a tape recorder next to the window to record the mockingbird. (5) When he played back the recording, the confused bird started to mimic itself. (6) Within a very short time, the confused bird flew away, never to be heard from again. (7) My brother had found a solution to the problem of the noisy bird!

Directions: Read the passage below. Then write a summary of it.

> Wild animals are now finding their way to urban areas. In some cities, numerous deer and coyote are spotted each week. Recently, two deer somehow ended up in an empty city lot. They were happily munching on grass and shrubs when someone noticed them. Animal control officers arrived and used special darts to put the animals to sleep. Then they used a truck to carry the deer away from the city. The officers say the animals are doing well in their new area.

_____

_____

Skill Practice

Directions: Choose the <u>one best answer</u> to each question.

1. Some people use a manual to learn about new software. A manual allows them to absorb information at their own pace. Others like to listen to explanations. Still others prefer to learn by using the new software. They might read instructions but mostly learn through experience.

   Which sentence would be the most effective if inserted at the beginning of this paragraph?

   A. People often need to learn new things.
   B. People have different ways of learning.
   C. Some people are visual learners.
   D. Experience is a good teacher.

2. It was written by Jonathan Swift nearly 300 years ago. Gulliver gets shipwrecked and stranded several times. He finds himself in a place called Lilliput, where the people are so tiny they can stand on his hand. Then he lands in a country called Brobdingnag, where the people are as tall as church steeples. Last, he winds up in a land where horses are rulers and humans are slaves.

   Which sentence would be the most effective if inserted at the beginning of this paragraph?

   A. *Gulliver's Travels* was a bestseller.
   B. *Gulliver's Travels* is long.
   C. *Gulliver's Travels* was one of the first science fiction novels.
   D. *Gulliver's Travels* features a wide range of characters.

3. CGI creates realistic-looking characters and locations that are not real at all. Artists use computer software to "paint" them onto film. The characters look like they are interacting with the live actors. The dinosaurs in the *Jurassic Park* series are CGI. The same is true of the monsters in *The Mummy* and elements of hundreds of other movies. With the widespread use of CGI, audiences today can feel as though they are in the middle of a totally alien landscape.

   Which sentence would be the most effective if inserted at the beginning of this paragraph?

   A. More and more movies are using computer-generated graphics, or CGI.
   B. The velociraptors were the best thing in Jurassic Park.
   C. CGI stands for computer-generated graphics.
   D. With CGI, the movie business will soon not need live actors at all.

Writing Practice

Directions: Think of a place where you have spent a lot of time. Write two paragraphs about it. In the first paragraph, make the first sentence the topic sentence. In the second paragraph, place the topic sentence in the middle or end of the paragraph.

KEY CONCEPT: Tone and diction should be appropriate to an author's purpose and audience.

Rewrite each sentence correctly.

1. I should of known her telephone number.

2. Please try and be here by noon.

3. Like you know, Wei is never late for a meeting.

Tone and Diction

A person's tone of voice might be friendly or hostile, serious or playful, irritated or relaxed. Tone of voice shows the speaker's attitude, or feeling, toward the topic and audience. In the same way, a piece of writing has a **tone**, or an overall attitude.

Writers convey tone through **diction**, or word choice. A note to a friend might have a playful tone and contain **informal**, or casual, language. A letter asking a possible employer about a job would have a serious tone and use **formal**, or businesslike, language.

When writing a paragraph or composition, you need to use a tone and diction that are **appropriate**—that fit your purpose and audience. You might use a slang expression, or nonstandard language, in an e-mail to a friend. Slang, however, would not be appropriate in a business letter or in a formal essay.

> **Slang:** I am so into applying for that awesome job.
>
> **Formal:** I am greatly interested in applying for the job.

UNDERSTAND AUTHOR'S PURPOSE

Everything you read is written for a reason. This reason is called the **author's purpose**. The basic reasons for writing are to inform, to entertain, or to persuade. Identifying the author's purpose will help you better understand the meaning of the passage.

When the author's purpose is to inform, the author gives information or teaches you about something. If the author's main purpose is to entertain, the author might use humor to present ideas or tell a funny or scary story. Finally, if the author's purpose is to persuade, the author might present only one side of an argument in order to convince you to agree with his or her opinion or to take some action.

To identify the author's purpose, ask yourself: *What is the author writing about? Is the author giving information? Is the author writing to entertain? Is the author trying to persuade me to think a certain way or to take some action?*

Read the following paragraph and identify the author's purpose.

> Your daily responsibilities as our receptionist are quite straightforward. First, when you arrive, check your voice mail for messages. If a staff member has called in sick, let our office manager know right away. Your second priority is to check e-mail and pass on any questions. Throughout the day, you will be receiving phone calls and e-mails. In between, you may have to deal with minor emergencies. For example, if a machine breaks, you will need to call someone to repair it. At the end of each day, check supplies and list whatever is needed on an order sheet. If a staff member needs something important, fax the order sheet to Office Works right away. Otherwise, wait until Friday.

This passage attempts to inform a new receptionist about his or her responsibilities.

Core Skill
Paraphrase

When reading, it is helpful to stop periodically to check your understanding. One way to do this is to summarize. Another way is to paraphrase. When you **paraphrase** a sentence or paragraph, you state it again in your own words. While a summary is often shorter than the original text, a paraphrase is usually longer. A paraphrase should have the same tone and diction as the original text. Read the first paragraph in the Tone and Diction section and restate it in your own words. Make sure you use the same tone, and follow the same style of diction as in the original paragraph.

Everything is written for
a purpose. The basic
purposes are to inform,
persuade, and entertain.

Read the first example
paragraph on this page.
It is from a letter to
a local newspaper.
What was the author's
purpose?

Look at this paragraph that was taken from a letter sent to a newspaper. Which sentence should be removed?

> (1) I believe that the wind turbine project would be good for our area. (2) Our energy needs have grown, and wind turbines are an excellent way to produce energy. (3) Wind is clean, free, and renewable. (4) Also, unlike solar power, wind is available both day and night. (5) While even light winds will generate some electricity, stronger winds can create much more. (6) The strong winds coming from the mountain ranges in this area are, therefore, especially suitable for wind turbines. (7) I'd be bummed out if this project goes nowhere.

Sentence 7 does not match the rest of the paragraph in tone and diction. The tone of sentence 7 is much more casual and emotional than that of the rest of the paragraph. It also contains slang and informal language. The sentence should be removed.

Now look at the following e-mail message from a teenager to friends. Which sentence does not belong?

> (1) Hey, what are you guys doing Friday night? (2) Do you want to go to the new Will Smith movie? (3) I hear it's way cool. (4) Then we could go hang out at the diner. (5) I'll be wearing a funky purple sweater I just bought. (6) I can't wait to show it to you. (7) I look forward to hearing your response to my suggestion.

Sentence 7 does not fit in the paragraph. Sentence 7 has a formal tone and businesslike diction, while the rest of the paragraph has a casual tone and informal language. If the writer wants to include the idea that she looks forward to a response, she should revise the wording to fit her audience, which is her friends who will read the e-mail.

THINK ABOUT WRITING

Directions: Find and underline the sentence in each paragraph that does not match the rest of the paragraph in tone and diction.

1. (1) This letter is in regard to my year 2012 income tax return. (2) I received a letter from your office of the Internal Revenue Service claiming that I under-reported my income last year. (3) I sent my W2 forms when I filed my tax return but am now submitting copies for your convenience. (4) Can't you guys get anything right? (5) As the enclosed information clearly shows, my figures were correct. (6) I would appreciate it if you would check your records.

2. (1) Hey, did you watch the baseball game last night? (2) Our whole family went to see it. (3) I believe that, if one analyzes it, baseball is a sport that reflects the great American values of teamwork and sportsmanship. (4) It was the season opener, so the kids were all excited. (5) This was the first game Sarah's ever seen live. (6) The game was really close, but finally the Pirates beat the Dodgers by one run. (7) That new pitcher has a great arm.

3. (1) For a long time, most people believed that disease was caused by evil spirits. (2) Then about 400 years ago, a Dutch janitor named Antony van Leeuwenhoek began experimenting with lenses as a hobby. (3) In the process, he invented the microscope. (4) He was the first person to see the tiny bacteria and viruses that cause disease. (5) He thought it was so cool to look at a drop of water and see a bunch of tiny animals living in it.

4. (1) In 1630 a Spanish countess named Ana de Osorio and her husband moved to Peru. (2) After only a few months there, they both became sick with malaria. (3) They felt so sick they wanted to scream. (4) None of Ana's home remedies worked, but she heard that the local people used the bark of a tree as medicine. (5) That tree contained quinine, which fought off the disease. (6) In 1638 the de Osorios were called back to Spain. (7) Ana put some quinine bark into her luggage. (8) When they arrived in Spain, the country was in the middle of a malaria epidemic—and no cure was known. (9) Her medicine ended the epidemic.

Vocabulary Review

Directions: Complete the sentences using one of the following words:

appropriate   **author's purpose**   **formal**   **informal**   **tone**

1. I relaxed when I heard the friendly _____ of her voice.

2. In a casual conversation, slang might be _____.

3. *Hi* is a more _____ greeting than *Hello*.

4. The _____ for writing the article was to explain the causes of the problem.

5. Follow the rules of standard English when you write _____ essays.

Skill Review

Directions: Identify the author's purpose for each paragraph below.

1. Knowing your product is important in selling, but you also need to have an understanding of people. As a first-time salesperson in a children's clothing department, I was lucky to have a great supervisor. She taught me to examine cloth for its lightness, warmth, and strength of fibers. She also helped me understand that parents usually look for warmth in jackets, while people giving gifts care more about cuteness. Because of her training, I could be helpful to customers and, of course, successful in making sales.

_____

2. Extending the bike path would greatly benefit the environment, people in the community, and our local economy. First, a landscaped path would improve air quality since plants remove carbon dioxide from the atmosphere. Second, a path would make it easier for children and adults to exercise. They could also ride more safely. Finally, new stores might open up along the path to provide food and cold drinks. Please help us raise funds for this important project.

_____

3. "This is a very easy trek," I kept reassuring my hiking companion. Was I ever wrong! The path just got muddier and muddier. Just ahead, though, I could see wooden logs lining the trail. As usual, I went first as we walked in single file. "Be sure to watch your step," I shouted back to my friend with my typical overconfidence. Then turning my head to make sure she had heard, I slipped off a log in what felt like slow motion. Now, when I think I have all the answers, I like to remember my companion's wry smile and my day in the mud.

_____

Skill Practice

Directions: Choose the <u>one best answer</u> to each question.

Delivering a Presentation

(A)

(1) Much of the impact of a presentation is based on delivery style—what the audience sees and hears. (2) Only a small part of the impact is based on the content of the speech. (3) Therefore, even if you have an excellent message, you need to perfect your delivery style. (4) Otherwise, it will get in the way of your communication. (5) You don't want to look all stupid. (6) So, what can you do to strengthen your delivery?

(B)

(7) First, you need to make a personal connection with your audience. (8) Try sustaining eye contact with someone for your first point. (9) Then turn to a different person for each new point. (10) As you look at the person, turn your whole body and not just your head. (11) That way the person will feel acknowledged. (12) Using a conversational tone is also important. (13) You want people to feel as though you are talking to them and not at them.

(C)

(14) You also need to think of your voice as an instrument. (15) If you speak in a low, quiet voice, you might lull the audience to sleep. (16) That would be a real bummer. (17) To hold your audience's attention, vary the volume, but do not whisper or shout. (18) Also, vary the highs and lows of your voice. (19) Allow your sentences to flow, but pause before each important point. (20) That will allow your listeners to be ready. (21) Then pause after the point to let your listeners absorb the meaning.

---

1. Which revision would improve the effectiveness of paragraph A?

   A. Remove sentence 3.
   B. Move sentence 5 to follow sentence 6.
   C. Remove sentence 5.
   D. Move sentence 6 to the beginning of the paragraph.

2. Which revision would improve the effectiveness of the article?

   A. Move sentence 13 to the beginning of paragraph C.
   B. Remove sentence 16.
   C. Remove sentence 20.
   D. Remove sentence 13.

Writing Practice

Directions: Paraphrase the following paragraph. Use a dictionary to look up unfamiliar words.

With just a few adjustments in your lifestyle, you can reduce your water bill and help conserve this important resource. Remember to turn off the faucet when you brush teeth, shave, or wash dishes. Incorporate a basin as part of these activities. Run the water only for the last step. In addition, purchase a special showerhead that releases a limited amount of water.

Order of Importance and Time Order

Lesson Objectives

You will be able to

- Use order of importance
- Use time order

Skills

- **Core Skill:** Understand the Relationships among Ideas
- **Reading Skill:** Sequence Events

Vocabulary

cluster map
elaborate
order of importance
organize
time order

KEY CONCEPT: Two ways to organize ideas in a paragraph are order of importance and time order.

Rewrite each sentence using the correct form of the underlined verb.

1. I missed the bus even though I run for it.

2. Be sure to wash the fruit before you ate it.

Order of Importance

Every paragraph should have a purpose and an audience. You might write a paragraph to tell your best friend about something funny that happened, or you might want to persuade your employer to assign a special project to you.

Every paragraph you write should also have unity and coherence. In a unified paragraph, all sentences connect to the main idea. In a coherent paragraph, all sentences logically flow from one to another. The best way to create a coherent paragraph is to use a pattern of organization, such as order of importance, to help make the order clear.

When you **organize** [arrange] ideas in **order of importance**, you rank your ideas from most important to least important or from least important to most important. If you want to grab your reader's attention right away, you might present your strongest point first. Alternatively, you might want to build up to the most important point and thus save it for last.

When to Use Order of Importance

You might use order of importance to convey information or to persuade someone of your opinion.

Purpose	Sample Topic
To convey information	Activities that take place in the community center
To persuade	Why we need a new community center

Organize Ideas in Order of Importance

You can use a **cluster map**, or web, to organize ideas in order of importance. Think of a topic for a paragraph. On a sheet of paper, draw a map like the one below. Write the topic in the center. Then write three or more details about the topic in the boxes around it. Next, choose the most important detail, and write *1* next to it. Rank and number the other ideas by importance.

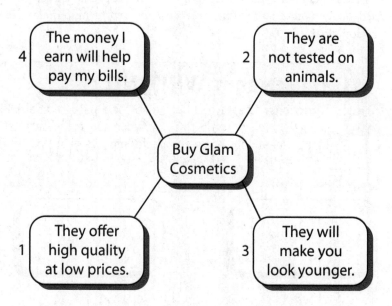

Look at the following paragraph created from the ideas in the cluster map. Notice that the writer adds details to **elaborate** on, or more fully explain, the ideas. Think about whether the writer orders the ideas from most important to least important or from least important to most important.

> I want to introduce you to my cosmetic line, Glam Products, and urge you to try some of the products. First, as a friend, you can support my efforts to pay all my bills and stay out of debt. Second, the products really do work and will make you look younger. Even more important, I know how much you care about animal rights, so you can feel good that these cosmetics were not tested on animals. Most important, the products offer high quality at low prices. Though inexpensive, they are made from the best ingredients. People who have allergies can use them without a problem. I know you will be pleased with them, so I hope you will buy some.

The paragraph is organized from the least important reason to the most important.

Use Transitions

Good writers use transitions in paragraphs and essays to make the pattern of organization clear. Here are some useful transitions for the order of importance pattern.

Transitions for Order of Importance				
first	second	mainly	more important	most important

Now look at the paragraph you just read on page 187. Which transitions did the writer include to make the organization clear? The transitions *first, second, even more important,* and *most important* help make the organization clear.

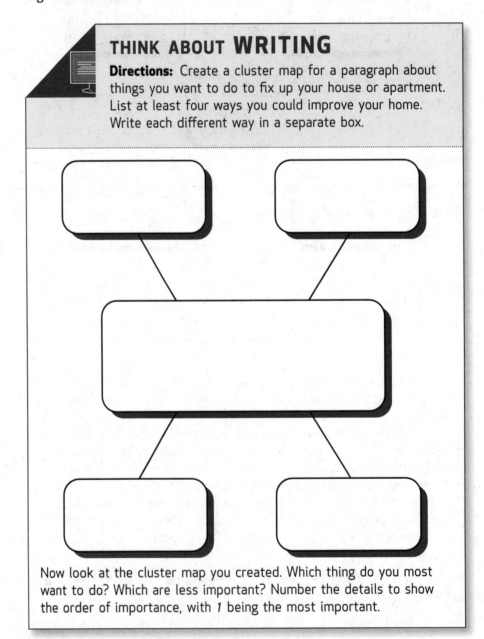

THINK ABOUT WRITING

Directions: Create a cluster map for a paragraph about things you want to do to fix up your house or apartment. List at least four ways you could improve your home. Write each different way in a separate box.

Now look at the cluster map you created. Which thing do you most want to do? Which are less important? Number the details to show the order of importance, with *1* being the most important.

USE NARRATIVE TECHNIQUES

Writers use narrative techniques to tell a story. This type of writing needs to have a clear story line that is told in a well-organized order. An effective writer uses words that guide the reader through the sequence of events in the story.

When you read, look for transitions and specific words that help you identify the sequence of the events.

Read the paragraph below. Identify the narrative techniques that express sequence.

Patty's annual review was coming up soon, and she felt that she deserved a raise. On the day before the review, she prepared her case. First, she created a spreadsheet describing her projects. Second, she recorded the time she spent on each project. Next, she added compliments she had received about her work. Then, she entered the current status of each project. That evening after work, she practiced her request for a raise with a friend. Finally, she approached her review with confidence.

The word *soon* lets the reader know when the main event will take place. The writer then uses the specific words *the day before* to signify time order. The word *first* clues the reader to the start of a sequence of events. The words *second, next, then,* and *after* help the reader follow the sequence. The word *finally* signals the end of the sequence.

Core Skill
Understand the Relationships among Ideas

A pattern of organization is a way of putting ideas together so that each one transitions, or connects, to another. You can organize ideas in a paragraph or composition in several different ways. One option is to put them in order of importance, either from most important to least important or from least important to most important. Another option is to use time order, or tell what happens first, next, and last. Using a clear pattern of organization will help your reader understand the relationships among ideas.

Choose a favorite book or movie and make a list of the reasons you enjoy it. Then rearrange your reasons so they appear in order from the least important to the most important.

Remember that the use of transitions help the reader understand when events occur.

The charts on this page give examples of when writers use time order and what transitions they use.

Read the following example.

Jacob went to the park. He packed a picnic. He called Lin. They ate near the oak tree.

The paragraph above is confusing. The reader does not know what order events happened in, and the events do not make sense in the order they are presented.

In a notebook, rewrite the paragraph. Add time order transitions to make the order of events clear for readers.

WRITE TO LEARN

Think of something that you know how to do. Create a list of the steps. Then write a paragraph telling your reader how to do it. Include transition words and phrases to help make the order clear for the reader.

Time Order

When you organize ideas in **time order**, you tell about them in the order in which they occur.

When to Use Time Order

Time order is one of the easiest organization patterns to use. Simply tell about events in the order in which they happen. Time order is very useful for telling a story or explaining to someone how to do something, such as make a pizza.

WHEN TO USE TIME ORDER

Purpose	Sample Topic
To explain steps in a process	How to make pizza
To explain how something works	How an electric switch works
To describe a routine	How you get ready in the morning
To tell about an event or experience	A funny thing that happened on the first day of your job

Use Transitions

Transitions can help readers follow the sequence of steps and the order of events. Transitions, such as *first* and *next,* often begin a sentence and are followed by a comma. Words, such as *when* and *during,* begin a phrase or a clause.

Transitions for Time Order				
first	second	next	then	finally
before	after	during	while	at the same time
soon	later	when	until	afterward

Organize Details in Time Order

To organize details in time order, follow these steps. First, make a list of all the details you need to include. Then go back and number the details in the order they should happen. Here is an example of a list of steps that have been numbered to show the correct order.

Research It
Use Time Order

Use reliable Internet sites to research a news story that has taken place over a long span of time. Then write a summary of the story. Tell the events in the correct time order. Use transition words to help your readers follow the sequence of events in the story.

How to Make a Pizza

2. Spread out the pizza dough on the baking sheet.
1. Grease the baking sheet.
7. Bake the pizza at 350°F for about 12–15 minutes.
5. Add the cheese.
3. Pour on tomato sauce.
4. Spread the tomato sauce around.
6. Add your favorite ingredients.

Using the ordered list as a guide, the paragraph might be written like this.

You can buy good pizzas, but the ones you make at home can be even better. Just follow these steps, and enjoy the process. First, grease a baking sheet and spread out the pizza dough on it. The dough should be about $\frac{1}{2}$ inch thick throughout. Then pour on the tomato sauce and use a knife to spread it around. Next, put on some grated or sliced cheese. Now you can add as many favorite ingredients as you like. Finally, bake the pizza in the oven at 350°F for 12–15 minutes. When the cheese turns golden, you will know that the pizza is ready. You will be amazed at how good it is.

Notice that the writer added the transition words *first, next, then, now, finally,* and *when.* These words give the reader clues about the order of events and make the writing even clearer.

THINK ABOUT **WRITING**

Directions: Number the items in each list in time order.

1. Getting ready for work

   _____ I take a quick shower.

   _____ I eat breakfast.

   _____ I get dressed.

   _____ I leave the house.

   _____ The alarm goes off.

2. Making pancakes

   _____ Flip the pancakes.

   _____ Add $\frac{1}{3}$ cup of milk.

   _____ Measure the mix into a bowl.

   _____ Pour the mixture onto the griddle.

   _____ Mix well.

3. Planting a tree

   _____ Put the tree in the hole.

   _____ Give the newly planted tree plenty of water.

   _____ Holding the tree straight, fill the hole with dirt.

   _____ Dig a hole in the ground.

   _____ Spread the roots out in the hole.

4. Wars in American history

   _____ World War I

   _____ Vietnam War

   _____ American Revolution

   _____ Civil War

   _____ World War II

5. Giving a speech

   _____ Edit the speech.

   _____ Answer questions from the audience.

   _____ Present the speech.

   _____ Rehearse the speech.

   _____ Write the speech.

Vocabulary Review

Directions: Complete each sentence below using one of the following terms.

cluster map   elaborate   order of importance   time order

1. When you write a paragraph presenting key points, you might present your ideas in

   _____.

2. When you write a story, you usually tell the events in _____.

3. To _____ means "to describe or explain more fully."

4. A(n) _____ is a kind of graphic organizer.

Skill Review

Directions: Identify the transition words in the paragraph below.

1. We are excited to tell you, our most valued salespeople, about our new shaving gel and
   the upcoming ad campaign. First, dynamic ads will appear at the very same time on TV,
   radio, and the Internet. The TV and radio ads will appear during prime time. The Internet
   ads will also be highly visible. Second, the packaging is eye-catching and bold. Most
   important, we have changed the formula. The new gel has a fresher scent. It also allows for
   a closer, more comfortable shave. With all of these exciting innovations and plans, your job
   should be an easy one!

   _____

   _____

Directions: Identify the pattern of organization used in each paragraph. Write the type
of the pattern below the paragaph.

2. We are asking everyone to use computer files for record keeping and to stop making
   paper copies. The biggest reason is that everyone in the company can have access to the
   electronic files. Almost as important, the cost of paper has increased, and we need to cut
   down on these expenses. Finally, we are concerned about the environment. We feel that
   cutting back on paper use is one way to help care for our planet. Changing routines is hard,
   but we know we can count on your cooperation.

   _____

3. The company picnic took place last Saturday, and everyone seemed to enjoy the day. In the
   morning, employees and their families gathered in the parking lot and waited for the bus.
   During the bus ride, children and adults sang songs. When we arrived at the beach, we set
   up our blankets and sunbathed for a while. Then most people ran into the water to cool off.
   At noon, we all came together for a picnic lunch. Afterward, the children played volleyball,
   while the adults talked. At the end of the day, we were all tired but content.

   _____

Skill Review (continued)

4. To ask for time off, you need to send a written request to the human resources department. There is no form to use, but you should follow these steps. First, write your name at the top. Next, write the date or dates that you will need to be out of the office. Then explain whether this is a vacation day or a personal day. You can take a personal day for medical purposes, a religious holiday, or other personal reason. Finally, bring your request to the human resources office. Most of the time, your request will be granted by the end of the day.

_____

5. Reorder the sentences in this paragraph so that all the steps are in the correct order. Add some transitions to make the order clearer.

> (1) If you don't have much time to cook dinner for yourself, make some scrambled eggs. (2) Add a tablespoon of milk to the eggs, and stir some more. (3) Crack open two eggs and mix them in a bowl with salt and pepper. (4) Heat up a small amount of butter or oil in a pan, and add the eggs. (5) When the eggs are no longer runny but still moist, they are ready to eat. (6) Use a spatula to occasionally stir the egg mixture so it cooks evenly.

_____

_____

_____

_____

_____

6. Write your own persuasive paragraph based on the home improvements cluster map you made for the Think about Writing on page 188. Write to a friend, persuading him or her to help you with your renovations, or you can write to a building manager, convincing him or her to pay for the changes you need. Include transitions that show order of importance.

_____

_____

_____

_____

7. Write a paragraph using one of the lists in the Think about Writing on page 192. Include transitions to show the time order relationships among the items in the list.

_____

_____

_____

_____

Skill Practice

Directions: Choose the <u>one best answer</u> to each question.

How to Increase the Sales Force

(A)

(1) Because our company is growing, you will need to fill some new positions. (2) Your success will depend upon your ability to evaluate resumes, ask good interview questions, and assess people skills. (3) Here are some guidelines that will help you.

(B)

(4) First, look through all the resumes to find possible candidates. (5) Consider only the applicants with basic sales experience. (6) If a resume is full of mistakes, do not consider the applicant for the position. (7) The people you hire must also be able to send well-written e-mails to customers.

(C)

(9) Many of your questions will come from a need to clarify something on the resume. (10) For example, you might want to find out more about the software an applicant used to sell. (11) List all your questions and bring them to the interview. (12) Finally, interview the best candidates and ask your questions.

(D)

(13) Be sure to listen carefully to the answers and take notes. (14) Just as important, notice how the applicant behaves during the interview process. (15) Does he or she seem approachable and confident? (16) These are some of the qualities we look for in a salesperson.

---

1. Which sentence below would be the most effective if inserted at the beginning of paragraph C?

   A. Second, interview candidates that you like.
   B. Second, eliminate candidates you don't like.
   C. Second, choose candidates that are possible for the job.
   D. Second, prepare interview questions to ask potential candidates.

2. Which revision would improve the effectiveness of the article?

   A. Begin a new paragraph with sentence 11.
   B. Begin a new paragraph with sentence 12.
   C. Begin a new paragraph with sentence 14.
   D. Begin a new paragraph with sentence 15.

Writing Practice

Directions: What is something you've always wanted to do but have never done? Choose an activity and write about it. Decide if you will write about it in sequence or in order of importance. Be sure to use transitions to help the reader.

Cause-and-Effect Order and Comparison-and-Contrast Order

Lesson Objectives

You will be able to

- Use cause-and-effect order
- Use comparison-and-contrast order

Skills

- **Core Skill:** Solve Problems
- **Core Skill:** Use a Graphic Organizer

Vocabulary

cause
effect
compare
contrast
multiple
Venn diagram

KEY CONCEPT: You can organize the ideas in a paragraph in cause-and-effect order or comparison-and-contrast order.

Combine the two sentences. Use the conjunction or conjunctive adverb in parentheses and a comma or a semicolon.

1. Carlos sold more cars than anyone else. He will be honored at the meeting next month. (therefore,)

2. Lisa lives in Utah. Her sister lives in Florida. (but)

Cause-and-Effect Order

When you organize a paragraph in **cause-and-effect** order, you tell the **cause** of an event, or the reason something happens. Also you tell the **effect** of an event, or what happens as a result of that event.

When to Use Cause-and-Effect Order

You can use cause-and-effect order when you want to explain what happened. You might choose cause-and-effect order, for example, to explain what happened to you one day when 12 inches of snow fell in two hours. Where were you at the time? What happened to you as a result of all that snow? You also might use cause-and-effect order to **predict**, or figure out in advance, what might happen. For example, what will happen as the result of an injury to the star of your favorite team. What caused the injury? What will be the effect of the injury on the player and team?

Purpose	Sample Topics
To explain the cause	Why a local business had to close
To explain the effect	What happened because the river overflowed
To predict the effect	What might happen as a result of a new industry in town

Organize Ideas by Effect with Multiple Causes

There are two ways to organize ideas in cause-and-effect order. The first way is to start with the effect and then explain what caused it. Suppose you were late for work this morning and you want to write an e-mail to your boss to explain why you were late. You start with the effect: You were late for work. Then you explain a cause: The subway broke down, and you were stuck on the broken train. One effect may have **multiple**, or several, causes. If more than one event caused you to be late, you would include all the causes in your e-mail.

The following paragraph is an example of an e-mail you might send to your boss. The ideas are organized in cause-and-effect order. Look at the paragraph, and think about the effect (I was late for work) and its two causes (I was stuck on the broken train. I had to gather up my papers.).

> This morning I was late for work. That is because there was an electrical problem on the subway, and the subway train stopped. As a result, I was stuck on the train for almost an hour. Finally, the train started again, and I was able to get off at my stop. Because I was in such a hurry, I tripped on the curb. Consequently, all my papers went flying, and I had to run around gathering them up. For these reasons, it took me an extra hour to get to work and I was late.

Often cause-and-effect order follows time order. That is, you tell about the events in the order they happened. Telling when events happened is often helpful in explaining how one event caused another. Think about what happened first in the paragraph. Then think about what that caused to happen next.

Sometimes there are a string of cause-and-effect events. One cause will have an effect. In the paragraph about being late for work, for example, the electrical problem (cause) caused the train to break down (effect). That effect becomes a cause, and it causes something else to happen. The train broke down (cause), and that caused you to be stuck on the train (effect).

> cause (electrical problem) ⟶ effect (train stops)
> cause (train stops) ⟶ effect (you are stuck)
> cause (you trip) ⟶ effect (papers fly)
> cause (papers fly) ⟶ effect (you pick them up)

Identifying cause and effect is a critical step in problem solving. Once you identify the problem, you can figure out the cause. Then you can determine the effects. Understanding the causes and effects will help you find the best solution for the problem.

Think of a problem you have experienced, such as *I'm always tired at work*. Identify the cause, for example, *I go to bed too late*. After identifying the cause of the problem, come up with a solution: *I should go to bed earlier*.

Organize Ideas by Cause with Multiple Effects

Another way to organize ideas in cause-and-effect order is to start with the cause and then to explain its effects. In the same way that one effect may have multiple causes, one cause may have multiple effects. The following paragraph gives one cause and describes two effects. As you read the paragraph, think about the cause and the effects.

> The hospital built a new wing. As a result, jobs were created. First, the hospital hired a construction firm to design and build the wing. Consequently, previously unemployed workers got jobs. In addition, the hospital hired staff. Because the hospital was larger, more doctors, nurses, and other staff were hired. Since the hospital was bigger and there was more staff, the hospital could admit more patients. Thus, the new wing created jobs and allowed more patients to be treated.

Use Transitions

As you know, good writers use transitions to help make the pattern of organization clear. Here are some transitions you can use when you organize ideas in cause-and-effect order.

Transitions for Cause and Effect			
as a result	because	consequently	due to
for this reason	since	therefore	thus

Now look at the paragraph about the hospital. Which transitions did the writer include to make the organization clear? The transitions *As a result, Consequently, Because, Since*, and *Thus* are clues to cause-and-effect order. What do the transitions *First* and *In addition* help you understand?

Recognize Cause-and-Effect Relationships

Not every event is a cause or an effect. Just because one event happens first does not mean it causes the next event. Only use cause-and-effect transitions to relate events that have a cause-and-effect relationship. Read the following passage:

> The hockey team won the game, and the star player scored seven goals. For this reason, the player broke his leg in practice. As a result, he will be out for the season.

This passage contains one cause-and-effect relationship: the player broke his leg, and as a result, he will be out for the season. The star player did not break his leg because he scored seven goals. The transition *For this reason* should not be used because there is no cause-and-effect relationship. A transition showing time order, such as *The next day*, could be used instead.

Now look at this list of some effects of higher prices for new cars. Which is not an effect of new cars being too expensive?

1. People keep their old cars and accumulate more mileage.

2. New cars get better gas mileage.

3. Mechanics get more business fixing people's old cars.

4. Customers want to save money, so they purchase used cars rather than new cars.

Number 2 is not an effect. It may be true that new cars get better mileage, but it is not an effect of higher-priced cars.

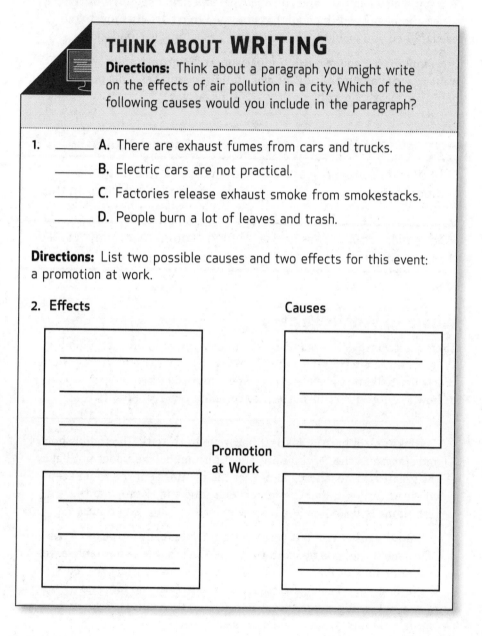

THINK ABOUT WRITING

Directions: Think about a paragraph you might write on the effects of air pollution in a city. Which of the following causes would you include in the paragraph?

1. _____ **A.** There are exhaust fumes from cars and trucks.

   _____ **B.** Electric cars are not practical.

   _____ **C.** Factories release exhaust smoke from smokestacks.

   _____ **D.** People burn a lot of leaves and trash.

Directions: List two possible causes and two effects for this event: a promotion at work.

2. **Effects**   **Causes**

Promotion at Work

Comparison-and-Contrast Order

When you use **comparison-and-contrast order**, you show how subjects, events, or items are similar **(compare)** and different **(contrast)**.

When to Use Comparison-and-Contrast Order

You compare and contrast when you want to tell how two things are alike or different. If you were choosing between two different jobs, for example, you might compare and contrast the jobs to help you decide. You would think about different aspects of the jobs. Are the job locations different? Which location is better for you? Do you want to work near home, or can you commute?

You could also compare and contrast the experience required or the pay scales and benefits. Which job pays more? Which benefits meet your needs? Then you would make a decision based on the comparison.

In a similar way, you can use comparison-and-contrast order when you want to write about the advantages and disadvantages. This organization helps you clearly describe positives and negatives.

Purpose	Sample Topics
To describe similarities and differences	How was this year's vacation similar to and different from the one you took last year?
To explain advantages and disadvantages	Which candidate for mayor will do the most for the city?

Whole-to-Whole Pattern

There are two ways to organize ideas in comparison-contrast order. When you use a **whole-to-whole pattern**, you write everything about one subject. Then you write everything about the other subject. Look at how a writer used this pattern to compare two restaurants.

> Jake's Grill has the tastiest barbecue in the city. The food is hot and spicy, and the servings are huge! Although Jake's does not have the greatest atmosphere, do not let the plainness of the room keep you from dining there. The food is delicious and cheap, and the restaurant is clean. You'll have a wonderful dining experience.
>
> On the other hand, if you want atmosphere, dine at Chez Paris. Like Jake's, the food is delicious. Unlike Jake's, the restaurant serves small portions of French food, not barbecue. In contrast to Jake's, the dining room is elegant. If you want both atmosphere and a wonderful dining experience, Chez Paris is the choice for you. Be warned, though. Unlike Jake's, it is expensive!

Point-by-Point Pattern

When you use a **point-by-point pattern**, you tell one thing about one subject and then compare it with the same point for the other subject. After that, you tell about the next point, and so on. Here's how the writer compared the restaurants, using this pattern.

> Both Jake's Grill and Chez Paris serve delicious food, but each restaurant serves a different kind of food. Jake's is the best barbecue in town. On the other hand, Chez Paris serves the best French food. At Jake's, the food is hot and spicy, and the servings are huge. In contrast, Chez Paris does not serve hot and spicy food, and the portions are small. In addition, the atmosphere at the two restaurants is different. Jake's is plain and simple, but the dining room at Chez Paris is elegant. The cost of meals is different, too. Dinner at Jake's is cheap, while dinner at Chez Paris is expensive! Both restaurants are wonderful dining experiences.

Use Transitions

You can use transitions to make the comparison-and-contrast organization in your writing clear. Look for some of these transitions in the paragraphs about Jake's Grill and Chez Paris.

Transitions for Comparison and Contrast				
also	besides	in addition	likewise	similarly
although	but	in contrast	on the other hand	unlike

Plan a Comparison-and-Contrast Paragraph

A graphic organizer can help you organize your ideas before you write in comparison-and-contrast order. A Venn diagram and a chart are both helpful graphic organizers for comparison-and-contrast order. If you use a chart, set it up in columns like the ones in the chart below.

Items to Discuss	Jake's Grill	Chez Paris
Type of food	barbecue	French
Quality of food	hot and spicy, large servings	not hot and spicy, small servings
Atmosphere	plain and simple	elegant
Price	cheap	expensive

Core Skill
Use a Graphic Organizer

You can use a graphic organizer to help organize ideas before you write. A cluster map shows a main idea and details. You used a cluster map to organize ideas in order of importance. Diagrams and charts are graphic organizers. You can use a cause-effect diagram to show one effect with several causes or one cause with several effects.

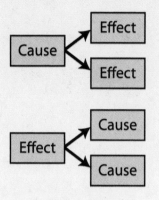

Use a **Venn diagram** to show how two things are alike and different. The similarities go in the space where the two circles overlap.

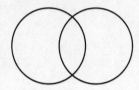

Look at the paragraph about the two restaurants. Now make a Venn diagram to compare the two restaurants.

Think about two different places where you have lived or would like to live. How would you compare and contrast them? First, make a Venn diagram to organize your ideas. Then use either the whole-to-whole pattern or the point-by-point pattern to write a paragraph about the two places.

THINK ABOUT **WRITING**

Directions: Complete the comparison-and-contrast charts below.

1.

Items to Discuss	**Dogs**	**Cats**
Care	_____	_____
	_____	_____
	_____	_____
Behavior	_____	_____
	_____	_____
	_____	_____
	_____	_____

2.

Items to Discuss	**Ocean**	**Pond**
Qualities	_____	_____
	_____	_____
	_____	_____
Appearance	_____	_____
	_____	_____
	_____	_____
	_____	_____

Directions: Compare and contrast two possible career choices. Tell how they are alike and how they are different. Then, in a notebook, write a summary using one of the compare-and-contrast patterns.

Career Choice 1: _____ Career Choice 2: _____

How are they alike?

_____

_____

_____

_____

_____

_____

_____

_____

How are they different?

_____	**Skills Needed**	_____
_____		_____
_____	**Educational Background Needed**	_____
_____		_____
_____	**Potential Job Availability**	_____
_____		_____
_____	**Possible Salary**	_____
_____		_____
_____	**Potential for Advancement**	_____
_____		_____

Vocabulary Review

Directions: Match each item in the first column with an item from the second column to best complete each sentence.

1. A **cause**

2. When you **compare**, you

3. A **Venn diagram**

4. **Multiple** causes

5. An **effect**

6. When you **contrast**, you

A. is one kind of graphic organizer.

B. tell how things are different.

C. tells why something happened.

D. is what happens as a result of something else.

E. tell how things are alike.

F. mean that an event has more than one cause.

Skill Review

Directions: Imagine that you are going to write about each situation described below. Complete each graphic organizer to help you organize your thoughts.

1. How being in a traffic jam affects your day

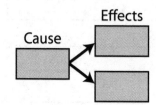

2. Similarities and differences between two activities you enjoy

Activity 1: _____   Activity 2: _____

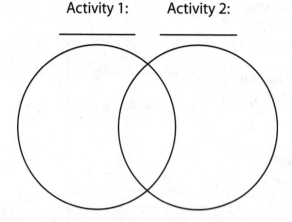

Skill Practice

Directions: Choose the <u>one best answer</u> to each question.

To: All Employees
Date: March 16
Re: Changes to Workweek

(A)

(1) Our company needs to lower energy costs. (2) Likewise, the administration has decided to change the workweek. (3) We believe that the schedule changes will help both the company and the employees. (4) This memo explains all these changes in detail.

(B)

(5) Right now, all employees work a five-day, forty-hour week. (6) They work 80 hours over a two-week period. (7) Since employees work from 8:30 to 5:00 and get one-half hour for lunch, they are paid for an eight-hour day. (8) Because we are open five days a week, we must heat the building for five days. (9) That adds to our energy costs. (10) In addition, employees must commute to work five days each week. (11) That adds to commuting costs.

(C)

(12) As in the original schedule, employees will work 80 hours over a two-week period. (13) Unlike the original schedule, employees will work only nine days over that two-week period. (14) The company will close every other Friday. (15) With the new schedule, employees will work from 8:30 to 6:00 Monday through Thursday and 8:30 to 5:00 every other Friday.

(D)

(16) This will reduce the company's energy costs. (17) In addition, it will reduce employees' commuting costs but not their wages.

---

1. Which sentence would be most effective if inserted at the beginning of paragraph C?

   A. The new workweek is like the old workweek.

   B. While based on the old plan, the new workweek has significant differences.

   C. On most days, you will be working from 8:30 to 6:00.

   D. There are many ways to organize workweeks.

2. Sentence 2: <u>Likewise,</u> the administration has decided to change the workweek.

   Which is the best way to write the underlined part of sentence 2? If the original is the best, choose option (A).

   A. Likewise,

   B. As a result,

   C. Similarly,

   D. On the other hand,

Writing Practice

Directions: Write one or two paragraphs comparing and contrasting two characters from a movie you have seen. Use either a whole-to-whole pattern or a point-by-point pattern. Include transitions that make the comparison-and-contrast order clear.

Directions: Choose the <u>one best answer</u> to each question. <u>Questions 1 through 6</u> refer to the following article.

The Five Functions of Management

(A)

(1) The five basic functions of management are planning, organizing, staffing, directing, and controlling. (2) Managers have these functions in all businesses, but the scope of each function and the time it takes vary. (3) For example, all managers need to plan, but top managers spend the most time planning. (4) That can be hard to believe when you consider the thick-headed plans they so often come up with. (5) Usually, lower-level supervisors spend most of their time directing and controlling.

(B)

(6) Planning means figuring out what should be done in the future. (7) It involves setting goals, objectives, and procedures. (8) It includes collecting and sorting information from many sources.

(C)

(9) Even when there are daily crises, managers must be careful to leave time for planning.

(D)

(10) The organizing function answers the question "How will the work be divided?" (11) Part of a supervisor's job is to group activities and job duties into sections or teams. (12) Organizing involves assigning these activities and jobs. (13) Staffing is the task of selecting and training employees. (14) The manager must evaluate the performance of employees and make promotion decisions. (15) He or she must also decide how much people should be paid.

(E)

(16) No matter what name it is given, directing is important for job satisfaction, productivity, and communication. (17) In the directing function, the supervisor tries to keep employees happy while meeting the department's objectives. (18) Directing is the day-to-day process of guiding, coaching, and supervising employees. (19) It is what supervisors spend most of their time doing. (20) Coaching your child's sports team can be very rewarding.

(F)

(21) Controlling means deciding whether plans are being met and progress is being made. (22) It also involves correcting any problems along the way. (23) Without planning, none of the other four functions of management could be done. (24) Supervisors would be unable to control if there were not a plan to check against.

Review

1. Which revision would improve the effectiveness of paragraph A?

   A. Move sentence 2 to follow sentence 3.
   B. Move sentence 4 to follow sentence 5.
   C. Move sentence 5 to the beginning of paragraph B.
   D. Remove sentence 4.

2. Sentence 9: Even when there are daily crises, managers must be careful to leave time for planning.

   Which revision should be made to the placement of sentence 9?

   A. Move sentence 9 to follow sentence 7.
   B. Move sentence 9 to follow sentence 10.
   C. Move sentence 9 to the end of paragraph B.
   D. Remove sentence 9.

3. Which revision would improve the effectiveness of the article?

   A. Begin a new paragraph with sentence 11.
   B. Begin a new paragraph with sentence 12.
   C. Begin a new paragraph with sentence 13.
   D. Begin a new paragraph with sentence 14.

4. Which sentence below would be the most effective if inserted at the beginning of paragraph E?

   A. Directing is also called leading or motivating.
   B. A satisfied employee is a productive employee.
   C. Supervisors must know how to direct.
   D. Communication is so important in the business world.

5. Which revision would improve the effectiveness of paragraph E?

   A. Move sentence 17 to follow sentence 19.
   B. Move sentence 19 to follow sentence 20.
   C. Move sentence 20 to the beginning of paragraph F.
   D. Remove sentence 20.

6. Sentence 23: Without planning, none of the other four functions of management could be done.

   Which revision should be made to the placement of sentence 23?

   A. Move sentence 23 to the end of paragraph E.
   B. Move sentence 23 to the beginning of paragraph F.
   C. Move sentence 23 to follow sentence 21.
   D. Move sentence 23 to follow sentence 24.

Directions: Choose the <u>one best answer</u> to each question. <u>Questions 7 through 12</u> refer to the following article.

An English Teacher at the Court of Siam

(A)

(1) Anna Crawford was born in Wales, Great Britain, in 1845. (2) She attended school in Wales while her mother and stepfather were living in India. (3) As soon as Anna graduated, she traveled to India to join them. (4) It was a long and difficult journey by ship. (5) Now a jet can carry you that far in a matter of hours.

(B)

(6) Before she was 20, Anna had already traveled widely and learned several Eastern languages. (7) She had also married a British major named Thomas Leonowens. (8) Their first child died and Anna grew ill. (9) Doctors prescribed a change of climate, common advice in a time when medical knowledge was limited. (10) Anna and Thomas moved to Australia. (11) Unfortunately, their ship was wrecked on the way there. (12) They were so bummed by their bad luck that they scoped out another place to live. (13) They moved to London, England, next. (14) Then they tried Singapore in the Far East.

(C)

(15) After two years in Singapore, Anna's husband died. (16) She was 28 now and had two surviving children. (17) She opened a school to support them and herself. (18) The king of Siam (the country now called Thailand) heard about her work and summoned her. (19) That might sound easy, but the king had 67 children. (20) He wanted her to give a European education to his children.

(D)

(21) He wanted Anna to teach Western knowledge to the children's mothers as well.

(E)

(22) Anna stayed in Siam for six years. (23) She taught her pupils English, math, and science. (24) Anna also tried to teach them that slavery, which was then a part of life in Siam, was wrong. (25) In 1867 she became ill again and went to America to live. (26) She corresponded with her Siamese students for the rest of her life. (27) When one of them became king at his father's death, she watched proudly as he abolished slavery. (28) Seventy-five years later, in 1945, the publication of *Anna and the King of Siam* made Anna famous. (29) The book was based on Anna's memoirs, which were called *The English Governess at the Siamese Court*. (30) A hit musical followed, and then the movie *The King and I* was made.

---

7. Which revision would improve the effectiveness of paragraph A?

   A. Move sentence 4 to follow sentence 5.

   B. Move sentence 3 to follow sentence 4.

   C. Move sentence 5 to the beginning of paragraph B.

   D. Remove sentence 5.

8. Sentence 12: They were so bummed by their bad luck that they scoped out another place to live.

Which revision should be made to the placement of sentence 12?

   A. Move sentence 12 to follow sentence 7.

   B. Move sentence 12 to follow sentence 13.

   C. Move sentence 12 to the beginning of paragraph C.

   D. Remove sentence 12.

9. Which revision would improve the effectiveness of paragraph C?

   A. Move sentence 15 to the end of paragraph B.

   B. Move sentence 17 to follow sentence 18.

   C. Move sentence 19 to follow sentence 20.

   D. Move sentence 20 to the beginning of paragraph D.

10. Sentence 21: He wanted Anna to teach Western knowledge to the children's mothers as well.

Which revision should be made to the placement of sentence 21?

   A. Move sentence 21 to the end of paragraph C.

   B. Move sentence 21 to the beginning of paragraph E.

   C. Move sentence 21 to follow sentence 17.

   D. Remove sentence 21.

11. Which sentence would be most effective if inserted at the beginning of paragraph E?

   A. Anna remained sickly.

   B. Anna was a dedicated letter writer all her life.

   C. Anna had a very productive time at the king's court.

   D. Anna believed children should learn about the importance of justice.

12. Which revision would improve the effectiveness of paragraph E?

   A. Begin a new paragraph with sentence 26.

   B. Begin a new paragraph with sentence 27.

   C. Begin a new paragraph with sentence 28.

   D. Begin a new paragraph with sentence 29.

Directions: Choose the one best answer to each question.

13. (1) There are several reasons to participate in community activities. (2) It's a good way to meet your neighbors. (3) Most importantly, you get a good feeling when you give back. (4) Studies indicate that doing good works may help people live longer. (5) Also, you find out what's going on in your neighborhood.

    Which revision would improve the organization of the paragraph?

    A. Move sentence 4 to follow sentence 2.
    B. Move sentence 3 to follow sentence 1.
    C. Move sentence 5 to the beginning of the paragraph.
    D. Remove sentence 1.

14. The auroras light up the night sky with dazzling colors. They form (_____) the sun sends flares of particles into space.

    Which word best completes the sentence to indicate a cause-and-effect order?

    A. when
    B. before
    C. so
    D. finally

15. Some of the particles loop around Earth's magnetic fields and hit air molecules, (_____) them to glow.

    Which word best completes the sentence to indicate a cause-and-effect order?

    A. due to
    B. as a result
    C. causing
    D. consequently

16. (_____) the sun is especially active or the solar wind especially strong, the Northern Lights can be seen further south than usual.

    Which word best completes the sentence to indicate a cause-and-effect order?

    A. Before
    B. Because
    C. Following
    D. When

17. (1) Chris and Gary competed in the neighborhood chili cook-off. (2) Chris made his chili with beef and two kinds of beans. (3) _____, Gary made a version with beans, vegetables, and tofu.

    Which word or phrase should be added to the beginning of sentence 3?

    A. On the other hand
    B. Similarly
    C. As a result
    D. Because

18. Both Janet and Pria are bloggers, (_____) Janet's blog has a larger following.

    Which word or phrase should be added to the sentence?

    A. consequently
    B. likewise
    C. besides
    D. but

Review

19. (1) Hi, can you meet me for lunch today?
(2) Sure, what time and where?
(3) How about Vinny's Pizza at 12:30?
(4) Certainly, that restaurant and time are quite acceptable.
(5) Awesome! See you soon.

Which sentence should be revised for tone?

A. Sentence 2
B. Sentence 3
C. Sentence 4
D. Sentence 5

20. (1) A week of camping was good for my family. (2) We took hikes and identified local plants. (3) Another way it was good was that we did all of the cooking over a campfire. (4) Our fitness improved with all of the kayaking and swimming.

Which sentence should be added after sentence 1?

A. The best part was relying on each other for company and entertainment.
B. We also had to talk to each other since we didn't bring any electronic devices.
C. Because of this, I want to go again next year.
D. Most of the time, we go to amusement parks.

21. (1) Having a plan makes you an efficient shopper. (2) At home, make a list of what you need and collect any coupons you are going to use. (3) Don't forget to look for store specials. (4) Start on one side of the store and go aisle-by-aisle. (5) Bring cloth bags with you to be environmentally friendly. (6) Have your method of payment ready for the cashier.

Which correction should be made to the paragraph?

A. Move sentence 3 to the beginning of the paragraph.
B. Move sentence 4 to the end of the paragraph.
C. Move sentence 5 to follow sentence 2.
D. Remove sentence 6.

22. Which sentence should be included in a formal job evaluation?

A. Ted's lazy work recently may find him on the street.
B. Ted is a nice guy, but his speed sure doesn't wow me.
C. I won't break my arm patting Ted on the back for that kind of work.
D. Ted could improve his production by adhering to his department's schedule.

23. Begin by writing down your current daily routine. Next, identify open blocks of time. Also, figure out if any activities can be moved or deleted. After that, decide on the best time for your exercise. Write it on your calendar to make sure you remember it.

What topic sentence could be added to the paragraph?

A. Having a calendar to plan activities is essential.
B. Exercise will improve your life.
C. Everyone should join a gym.
D. Fitting daily exercise into your schedule is possible.

24. I'm so psyched about the great gas mileage on my new set of wheels.

What is the best way to revise the above sentence to give it a formal tone?

A. I am pleased that the gas mileage for my latest car is in the economical range.
B. Whoa, I'm spending so much less time at the pump with this buggy.
C. My wallet is so much fatter with this gas tank.
D. I'm thrilled that this new vehicle delivers at the pump.

25. (1) Check your schedule and put the meeting on it. (2) There will be several topics of discussion. (3) The historic Myers building needs some renovations. (4) We need to organize a team to work at the high school post-prom party. (5) We need volunteers to staff the annual bike repair fair. (6) The next meeting of the Community Association will be held on April 24.

Which correction should be made to the paragraph?

A. Move sentence 6 to the beginning of the paragraph.
B. Move sentence 3 to follow sentence 5.
C. Move sentence 1 to follow sentence 2.
D. Delete sentence 4.

26. When you clean a fish tank, start by putting the fish in another tank or container with some of the water from the original tank. Next, remove the remaining water and any plastic decorations. After that, wipe down the inside walls with a clean, damp cloth. Refill the tank.

Which sentence should be added to the end of the paragraph?

A. Put the fish back after the water warms to about 75 degrees.
B. Wipe down the bottom of the tank with a new cloth.
C. Your fish will enjoy swimming in their newly cleaned habitat.
D. Work quickly because some fish don't like to be out of their home tank.

27. Everyone should visit at least one of our national parks. They teach us about our cultural heritage. The beautiful vistas and stunning scenery help us appreciate nature. Also, visiting a local national park provides an economical way to have a vacation.

What is the author's purpose in writing this paragraph?

A. to inform
B. to persuade
C. to explain
D. to entertain

28. (1) Richard's General Store is going to shut its doors at the beginning of next month. (2) Business has been steadily declining since a new mall was built in town last year. (3) Many of the older people who knew Richard have moved, and the younger folks shop at the new stores. (4) Therefore, Richard has no choice but to close. (5) The inventory clearance sale will start on the 15th of this month.

Which sentence should be added between sentences 3 and 4?

A. I have always enjoyed his selection of greeting cards.
B. As a result, his profits have declined while his expenses stayed high.
C. Sadly, the young people do not recognize the value of a local store.
D. It's a shame, because Richard knew all of those kids.

29. (1) There are two main types of trees, coniferous and deciduous. (2) Coniferous trees have needle-like leaves that don't fall off. (3) These trees have the same appearance all year. (4) (_____), deciduous trees have broad leaves that do fall off in autumn, and regrow in the spring. (5) Deciduous trees look different at different times throughout the year.

Which phrase should be added to the beginning of sentence 4?

A. Similarly
B. In contrast
C. Therefore
D. Interestingly

30. Choose an issue that your community is facing and that you feel strongly about. Write an essay about it. Include causes of the issue and possible effects if the issue is not resolved. Be sure to use transitions to help your reader understand how ideas are related.

Check Your Understanding

On the following chart, circle the number of any question you answered incorrectly. Next to each group of item numbers, you will see the pages you can review to learn the content covered in the question. Pay particular attention to review those lessons in which you missed half or more of the questions.

Chapter 6 Review

Skill Area	Item Number	Review Pages
Paragraph Structure and Topic Sentences	2, 3, 4, 5, 7, 10, 11, 25, 27	172–179
Tone and Diction	1, 8, 19, 22, 24	180–185
Order of Importance and Time Order	9, 12, 13, 20, 21, 23	186–195
Cause-and Effect Order and Comparison-and-Contrast Order	6, 14, 15, 16, 17, 18, 26, 28, 29, 30	196–205

ESSAY WRITING PRACTICE

Text Structure

Directions: Write an essay that uses one of the text structures described below. Use one of the suggested prompts or one of your own ideas. Make sure to use the correct paragraph structure. Establish a clear main idea and include enough details to support it. Present the main idea in a topic sentence. Use the tone and diction that are appropriate for your audience.

If necessary, review Lesson 6.1, 6.2, 6.3, or 6.4 for help with paragraph structure, tone and diction, order of importance, time order, cause-and-effect order, and comparison-and-contrast order.

ORDER OF IMPORTANCE AND TIME ORDER

- Explain how to do something, such as make a quilt, create a scrapbook, build a bird feeder, or cook a favorite recipe.

- Explain how something works, such as a computer, cell phone, electric appliance, or automobile.

- Describe a routine, such as how you study for a test, prepare for a large family gathering, or pay your bills.

- Tell about an event or experience, such as a favorite family holiday, a vacation, a sports outing, or the first day on a new job.

CAUSE AND EFFECT

Use cause-and-effect order tell about:

- establishing a neighborhood leash law for pets

- the destruction of local wetlands or other natural area to build condominiums

- changing the driving age from your state's current age to a lower one

- having a weekly farmer's market in the local area

COMPARISON AND CONTRAST

Compare and contrast the qualities and merits of any two:

- automobiles

- financial planners

- medical offices

- banks

- brands of jeans

- airports

Review

ESSAY WRITING PRACTICE

_____

_____

_____

_____

_____

_____

_____

_____

_____

_____

_____

_____

_____

_____

_____

_____

_____

_____

_____

_____

_____

_____

_____

_____

_____

_____

_____

The Writing Process

If you could write about anything at all, what would you choose as your topic? That seems like a simple enough question, but writers often find that the hardest part of writing is getting started. There are several factors to consider when getting ready to write:

- Who is my audience?

- What is my purpose?

- Where should I begin?

In this chapter you will learn about the steps involved in the writing process. By breaking down the process, the task of writing will feel more manageable.

Lesson 7.1: Prewriting
Learn the three steps of prewriting and how they will help you get started.

Lesson 7.2: Writing
Learn how to create a rough draft with an introduction, body paragraphs, and a conclusion.

Lesson 7.3: Revising and Editing
It's time to add the finishing touches to your writing. This lesson will guide you to change your writing to make it better.

Goal Setting

Writing opportunities present themselves to you every day. It could be a report that you prepare for your boss or a simple note that you write to your child's teacher. We all have reasons for wanting to be good writers. Think about your reasons as you respond to the checklist below.

I want to learn more about the writing process so I can

_____ write clear reports at work.

_____ communicate effectively when I e-mail co-workers.

_____ be more creative in my journal writing.

_____ send postcards that clearly tell about my vacation.

_____ send thank-you notes that clearly express my feelings.

_____ send in well-written editorials to my local newspaper.

What other reasons do you have for wanting to learn about the writing process?

_____

_____

_____

_____

_____

Prewriting

KEY CONCEPT: The prewriting process helps you develop ideas, organize them, and prepare to write.

Rewrite the following sentences in correct time order.

Finally, I took my shiny car for a ride. Once it dried, I buffed off the wax until the hood sparkled. Next, I soaked the car with soapy water and gave it a good rub. After drying off the water, it was time to apply the wax. First, I gathered all the necessary equipment: sponges, rags, a bucket of soapy water, and wax. I decided to clean my car.

The Prewriting Process

Often, the hardest part of writing is getting started. You may know what your topic is. You may even know what information to include. Nevertheless, putting the first words down on paper can seem impossible. What do you say first? What's most important? How can you get your reader interested? How can you make your reader understand?

Fortunately, there is a way to get past these first problems in writing. It is the **prewriting** process. This **process** is a series of steps that will help you develop and organize ideas and prepare to write.

Steps in Prewriting
1. Thinking about what you are writing
2. Brainstorming (listing ideas)
3. Organizing ideas

Think about the Topic

Answer the following questions about your writing. Your answers will help you see more clearly what you are trying to do and how to go about doing it.

- *What am I writing about?*
- *Who is going to read my writing?*
- *What is my purpose for writing?*

For example, imagine that a writer wants to write about how her neighborhood turned a vacant lot into a playground. The lot was overgrown with weeds. There was trash, broken glass, and an abandoned car in the lot. Neighborhood kids played in the lot because there wasn't a park nearby. People in the neighborhood worked together to make it into a playground. Here's how the writer might answer the questions about her topic.

- *What am I writing about?*

  a neighborhood project to turn a vacant lot into a playground

- *Who is going to read my writing?*

  the editor and readers of our local newspaper

- *What is my purpose for writing?*

  to tell how my neighborhood turned an ugly lot into a place for kids to play

The writer did not do research to answer these questions. She simply thought about why she was writing. Answering the questions made the writing process more concrete. She knew what she had to do.

Brainstorm

Brainstorming is a way of gathering ideas to write about. When you brainstorm, you jot down every idea that comes to mind about your topic. Don't worry about spelling or writing in complete sentences. Don't even think about whether an idea is good or bad. All you're trying to do is to **generate**, or come up with, ideas.

Reading Skill
Understand the Topic

The first step in the prewriting process is to ask yourself what you will write about. When choosing a topic, be careful that you don't try to cover too much information. When that happens, it is easy for the topic of your writing to get lost.

After you brainstorm a list of ideas for your topic, go back and review it. Cross out any ideas that are too broad. Another way to narrow your focus is to choose one of the ideas from your list and brainstorm again.

Read the following topic and list of ideas:

Making Movies

- rehearsal
- thrillers
- dramas
- selecting actors
- comedies
- how movies are made
- role of the producer and director
- filming

Which ideas are too broad and should be crossed off the list?

If you are writing about a topic that is very familiar, you will be able to generate many ideas for your brainstorm list. But if your topic is less familiar, or if you just need more ideas, then doing some research will give you the boost you need.

Your local public library has books, magazines, newspapers, and videos. The reference librarians are there to help you, so make sure to talk with them.

A university library will usually have more scholarly books than a public library. Often, you will be able to borrow books from distant university libraries through your local one.

The Internet can be a valuable resource. Since there is so much information available, and some is inaccurate, you need to be careful. Use websites that end with .edu, .gov, or .org.

A personal interview can provide information that you simply can't get any other way. If you do conduct personal interviews, make sure to take notes and photos. If possible, audio or video record the interviews.

Make a list of places and people that can help you with your research.

Below is a list of ideas the writer came up with by brainstorming about the vacant lot.

> The Vacant Lot
>
> city donated lot
> kids played in lot
> my nephew suggested the park
> kids needed playground
> neighbors volunteered to clean it up
> lot was an eyesore—weeds, broken glass, and cans
> collected money to buy equipment

THINK ABOUT **WRITING**

Directions: In a notebook, brainstorm a list of ideas about each of the following topics. Spend a few minutes on each. You will be using one of these lists later for a piece of writing, so save your work.

1. My best vacation
2. My oldest friendship
3. What I'll be doing five years from today
4. An exciting sports event
5. Someone I admire
6. My favorite restaurant
7. A dream come true

Organize Ideas

The third step in prewriting is **organizing** information. When you organize, you look at the list of ideas you brainstormed and decide which ideas you want to include. Then you add any new ideas that you think of.

Next decide on a pattern of organization. You might choose order of importance, time order, cause-and-effect, or comparison-and-contrast. If you need a review of patterns of organization, turn to Chapter 6. When you have chosen a pattern, number your ideas in the order in which you will write about them.

Look how the person writing about the vacant lot organized her list.

> The Vacant Lot
>
> 4. city donated lot
>
> 2. kids played in lot full of glass and trash
>
> ~~my nephew suggested the park~~
>
> 3. kids needed playground
>
> 5. neighbors volunteered to clean it up—city provided trash truck
>
> 1. lot was an eyesore—weeds, broken glass, and cans
>
> 6. collected money from local businesses to buy equipment
>
> 7. put in basketball court, playground equipment

Notice the changes the writer made. She crossed out one idea and added to some new ideas. Then she numbered them in a time order. She wanted to tell about the park in the order in which events happened.

You learned about the importance of organizing your ideas during the prewriting process.

To practice organizing ideas, number the items in the following list to show a logical pattern of organization.

What I Did on Sunday

_____ stayed up late reading

_____ before bed, ironed clothes needed for work

_____ met friend for breakfast

_____ went for long bike ride

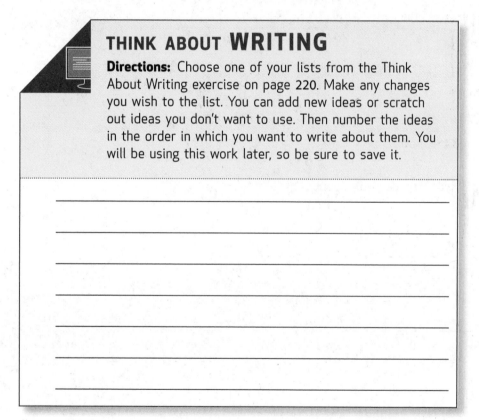

THINK ABOUT **WRITING**

Directions: Choose one of your lists from the Think About Writing exercise on page 220. Make any changes you wish to the list. You can add new ideas or scratch out ideas you don't want to use. Then number the ideas in the order in which you want to write about them. You will be using this work later, so be sure to save it.

Vocabulary Review

Directions: Complete each sentence below using one of the following words.

brainstorming   **generate**   **prewriting**   **process**

1. The steps taken to carry out a plan is called a _____.

2. When someone is _____, they are coming up with ideas.

3. The work done to prepare for writing is called _____.

4. Before you write, you must _____, or come up with, ideas.

Skill Review

Directions: Read the topic and list of ideas. Put an X next to any idea that is too broad for the topic.

Topic: Why Thanksgiving is my favorite holiday

_____ roasting the perfect turkey

_____ preparations

_____ the history of Thanksgiving

_____ family traditions

_____ different traditions around the world

Directions: Write your own topic. List five ideas that support the topic.

Topic

_____

Ideas

_____

_____

_____

_____

_____

Skill Practice

Directions: Organize ideas and outline a paragraph.

1. Read the topic and list of ideas. Place an X next to any ideas that don't fit the topic. Then number the remaining ideas in the order that makes the most sense.

   My First Job
   _____ 16 years old
   _____ needed money
   _____ first day on job
   _____ my first grade teacher
   _____ length of employment
   _____ interview for job
   _____ what I learned
   _____ computers have taken over
   many jobs

2. Using the topic and two of the selected ideas above, create an outline for a paragraph.

I. Topic Sentence

   _____

   _____

   A. Supporting Idea 1

   _____

   B. Supporting Idea 2

   _____

   C. Supporting Idea 3

   _____

   D. Concluding Sentence

   _____

   _____

Writing

KEY CONCEPT: A piece of writing consists of an introduction, a body, and a conclusion.

List the three steps that make up the prewriting process.

1. _____

2. _____

3. _____

Lesson Objectives

You will be able to

- Understand the three parts of a piece of writing: introduction, body, and conclusion

- Write a rough draft that includes an introduction, a body, and a conclusion

Skills

- **Core Skill:** Produce Coherent Writing

- **Core Skill:** Apply Knowledge of Language

Vocabulary

incorporate
rough draft
stages

Write a Rough Draft

Now that you have completed prewriting, you are ready to put your ideas down on paper. This is done most easily if you do it in **stages**, or steps, just like prewriting. The first step in actually writing is to create a **rough draft**, a first version of a piece of writing.

The purpose of the rough draft is to turn your list of ideas into sentences and paragraphs. Don't worry too much about grammar or spelling. You can fix those mistakes later. Just try to get your ideas down in the proper order. Use your list as a guide, but if you think of new ideas or want to change the order of ideas, go ahead.

Your writing will have an introduction, a body, and a conclusion.

Introduction

The **introduction** does three things:

- introduces the topic

- gives the main idea or states the claim of the writing

- gives the reader some idea of what will be discussed

When the writer began creating the draft for the story of the vacant lot, she wrote this introduction. Notice how she achieved the three goals of an introduction.

> There used to be a vacant lot down the street. It was filled with trash, broken glass, and cans. Besides being an eyesore, it was dangerous. Kids played there. They often cut themselves on broken glass and rusty cans. Finally, people got together and did something. Now it's a park and playground for neighborhood kids.

Here are some hints that will help you write a good introduction.

1. **State your main idea or claim clearly.** When you introduce your topic, state your main idea or claim, clearly. If your readers know what to expect, they will understand your ideas better. Also, if you clearly state your main idea or claim, you can look back at it as you write. You can make sure that what you say in the body supports your main idea or claim.

2. **Give your readers an idea of the content and organization.** If you provide readers with an idea of what to expect, then they won't become confused by how you present your ideas. If you can't explain the content and organization, you may not be quite ready to begin writing. Go back to Step 1 of prewriting.

3. **Get your readers interested so they will keep reading.** Establish a context for your writing so your readers have a focus. You could begin with an odd or interesting fact. You could explain why your information is important. You could begin with a question. Here's how a question could be used to introduce "The Vacant Lot."

> *What do you do with a vacant lot? Our neighborhood had that problem. One lot was empty and ugly. Everyone talked about it. No one knew what to do with it. Then one day, we found the answer. We would turn the lot into a playground.*

THINK ABOUT WRITING

Directions: Write an introduction on a separate sheet of paper. Use your list of ideas from the Think about Writing exercises on pages 220 and 221. Write on every other line so you will have room to revise later. When you're finished, check your writing. Make sure it states the topic and main idea or claim. It should also give your readers an idea of the content and organization and establish a context that will get them interested.

You have learned that the paragraphs that make up the body of your writing should support your main idea. To be coherent, or understandable, each new idea should begin a new paragraph. If information does not relate to the main idea, it should not be included in the body.

Read the body paragraph below. It is about different ways that people can help the environment. Decide where a new paragraph should begin.

Taking public transportation is one way that many people help the environment. Most cities have systems that offer several departure times, making it easy to get to and from work every day. Reusable cloth grocery bags are another way to help the environment. Simply leave the bags in the trunk of your car. Then take the bags out whenever you go to the grocery store. After shopping, hand the bags to the bagger and feel good knowing that you are helping to protect the environment.

Body

In the introduction, you told what your main idea was. In the **body** of your writing, you **incorporate**, or include, details and facts that explain the main idea.

Use your numbered list of ideas as a guide while writing the body. If new ideas occur to you, add them as you go. Start a new paragraph for each big idea or subtopic you want to explain.

Compare the development of ideas in "The Vacant Lot" to the original list. Also notice how the ideas are divided into paragraphs. The first paragraph tells about the lot the way it was. The second paragraph is about how the neighborhood changed it.

> Just a year ago, the lot was covered with weeds. Kids played in the lot. It was dangerous, though, because of the trash. Broken glass and cans were lying around. However, kids didn't have any other place to play except in the street.
>
> We turned the lot into a playground. A group met with people from the city. They talked the city into donating the land. Other people talked local businesses into donating playground equipment and money. We put in a basketball court and some playground equipment. Then everyone in the neighborhood pitched in to clean up the lot. The city provided a trash truck to haul the junk away.

As you write, look back at your introduction from time to time. Be sure that you are giving the information you said you wanted to include.

THINK ABOUT WRITING

Directions: Now begin the body of your writing. Continue to use the list of ideas as your guide in writing. Add details as you think of them. Create new paragraphs for each big idea. Write on every other line so you will have room to revise later.

Conclusion

Your **conclusion** is the ending for your writing. It's not new information. It is a wrap-up of what you have already said. The length of your conclusion depends on the length of the whole piece of writing. It might be one or two sentences or one or more paragraphs.

There are many ways to write a conclusion. One way is to summarize what you have said. Your conclusion will be a reminder for your reader. It says again, in a different way, the main idea you gave in your introduction. Here is how the writer of "The Vacant Lot" might have used a summary as her conclusion.

> Working together, our neighborhood got rid of an eyesore. In the process, we've given kids a safe place to play.

Another way to end your writing is to tell your reader the broader truth of what you've said. "The Vacant Lot" might have been ended like this:

> The vacant lot had been a problem in our neighborhood for years. No one knew what to do with it. We found the answer when we stopped looking at the lot only as a problem. Instead, we looked at it as an opportunity. Now we have a great new park for our kids.

This conclusion says the story is not just about getting rid of a vacant lot or building a playground. It's also about turning problems into opportunities.

THINK ABOUT **WRITING**

Directions: Complete the draft you worked on earlier by writing a conclusion. Write on every other line so you will have room to revise later. Before you start, read the introduction and body you have already completed to refresh your memory.

Directions: Complete each sentence below using one of the following words.

incorporate   **rough draft**   **stages**

1. Breaking a project into smaller _____ can make it easier to complete.

2. When a writer puts ideas down on paper without worrying about mistakes, he or she is creating a _____.

3. When you _____ details into your writing, you add information.

Directions: Read the following article. Decide where to divide the body of the article into paragraphs.

We've all been feeling the need to keep an eye on our spending. The same holds true for those in charge of overseeing our town's budget. It is an awesome responsibility and one not taken lightly. After hours and hours of discussion, the budget committee has come up with a list of budget cuts. The first cut affects trash pickup. We are instituting a pay-as-you-throw program. What that means for you is that you will now have to purchase specially marked trash bags. Your trash will still be picked up every week, but it must be put into these designated trash bags. The cost to you is less than $1 a bag. The school budget will also be affected by budget cuts. Beginning with the upcoming school year, cuts will be made to the extended-day programs. Bus service will no longer be provided for students who stay at school until 5:00. Families affected by this cut will need to make other transportation arrangements. Finally, library hours will be scaled back. The library will be closed on Mondays and will open an hour later during the week. Fees for overdue books will increase to 10 cents a day.

1. What sentence should begin the second paragraph?

_____

_____

2. What sentence should begin the third paragraph?

_____

_____

3. What sentence should begin the fourth paragraph?

_____

_____

Skill Practice

Directions: Read the topic ideas below. Choose one, or create one of your own, and write an introduction. Be sure to include the topic and main idea in your introduction. You should also let your readers know about the content and organization of your writing.

A valuable lesson I have learned
Renting movies versus going to the cinema
The perfect way to spend a weekend
How to choose the right computer

_____

_____

_____

_____

_____

_____

_____

_____

_____

_____

_____

_____

_____

_____

_____

_____

_____

_____

_____

Lesson Objectives

You will be able to

• Understand revising

• Understand editing

• Revise and edit a rough draft

Skills

• **Reading Skill:** Understand Organization

• **Core Skill:** Create Concluding Paragraphs

Vocabulary

editing
pertinent
revising

KEY CONCEPT: During revision, writers make changes to improve their writing.

Write *T* if the statement is true. Write *F* if it is false.

_____ There should be no errors in a rough draft.

_____ Transition words add links between paragraphs.

_____ The body of a piece of writing should include details and examples to make your writing clearer.

_____ It is okay to change the order of ideas during revision.

Revise

The next step in the writing process is **revising**. When revising, you can change the order of ideas, rewrite sentences or paragraphs, make different word choices, or cut out ideas that you no longer think are **pertinent**, or important. Here are a few specific things to look for.

Improve Word Choices

Read each sentence carefully. Have you chosen the best words to say exactly what you mean? Precise words will make your writing clearer and more interesting.

Improve Links Between Paragraphs

One way to improve the links between paragraphs is by starting paragraphs with transition words. These are words such as *furthermore, then, on the other hand, as a result, in addition,* and *another advantage is.* Transition words show how ideas are connected. They help your writing to be coherent.

Add Details and Examples

Check to see if your ideas are clear. If not, your writing might need more details or examples. Use facts, descriptive words, or examples to **support**, or help prove or illustrate, what you are saying.

The following is a revised draft of "The Vacant Lot." Notice how the writer has improved word choices, added details, and made the links between paragraphs stronger.

> ### The Vacant Lot
>
> What do you do with a vacant lot? Our neighborhood had that problem. One lot was empty and ugly. Everyone talked about it. No one knew what to do with it.

Then one day, we found the answer. We would turn the lot into a playground. The lot was covered with weeds, but children still played in it. It was dangerous, though, because broken glass and cans were lying around. Sadly, children didn't have any other place to play except for in the street.

A group met with people from the city. They talked the city into donating the land. Other people talked local businesses into donating playground equipment and money. Then everyone in the neighborhood pitched in to clean up the lot. The city provided a trash truck to haul the junk away. We put in a basketball court and some playground equipment.

As a result of people working together, our neighborhood got rid of an eyesore. In the process, we've given children a safe place to play.

THINK ABOUT WRITING

Directions: Revise your draft. Look for ways to make your ideas clearer. You might want to change words, put ideas in a different order, or add transition words.

UNDERSTAND ORGANIZATION

When you read, it is often helpful to notice the way the writer has organized his or her ideas. Being aware of how one idea leads to another can help you understand the relationship among the ideas. Ideas might be organized in order of importance, from most important to least important or from least important to most important. Another way ideas are often organized is by time order, or by what happens first, next, and last. Still another way is by cause and effect. Finally, information can be organized by comparing and contrasting. Being aware of organization will help you understand the relationship among ideas as you read.

Read the following paragraph and identify the way it is organized.

> Delia had a lot to accomplish before the guests arrived for the party that afternoon. First, she prepared the food. Next, she wrapped the presents. Then, she picked flowers from her garden and arranged a beautiful bouquet as a centerpiece for the table. Finally, she got dressed and prepared to welcome her guests.

This paragraph is organized by time order. The words *first*, *next*, *then*, and *finally* help readers identify the organization.

WRITE TO LEARN

When revising, look for ways to improve word choices and add details. Using precise, descriptive words makes your writing clearer and more interesting to read.

Read the following passage.

> Sanouk walked through the woods alone. It was quiet. He needed time to think about what he should do next—go back to school or take the job he was offered. Sanouk loved spending time at the beach.

Revise the passage by improving word choices and adding descriptive details. Cut out any ideas that don't belong.

Reading Skill
Understand
Organization

As you read, it is helpful to notice how a writer has organized a piece of writing. Did he or she organize according to order of importance, time order, cause and effect, or by comparison and contrast?

Reread "The Vacant Lot." How it is organized?

A concluding paragraph wraps up what you have already told your readers in the introduction and body of your writing. Without a concluding paragraph, your writing would end abruptly.

Read the concluding paragraph below. It summarizes what the writer did to prepare for a job interview.

Having a plan in place is important when looking for a job. If you allow time to research the company, practice answering interview questions, and get your clothes cleaned and ironed, you can feel assured that you are ready for any interview.

Choose a favorite book or movie. Write a concluding paragraph that summarizes why you enjoyed it.

Edit

Editing is correcting mistakes in grammar, punctuation, capitalization, and spelling. Follow these steps:

1. **Read your writing out loud.** Listen for words or sentences that sound wrong or awkward. Mark these places. You can come back and figure out what is wrong after you have finished reading aloud.

2. **Look at each sentence by itself.** Look for anything that is wrong. Be especially alert for fragments and run-ons.

3. **Read your writing several times.** Each time, look for a certain kind of mistake you sometimes make. For example, if you have trouble with using commas, look closely at all the commas.

THINK ABOUT **WRITING**

Directions: Edit your draft. Look for and correct errors in spelling, grammar, capitalization, and punctuation. Then make a clean copy.

Peer Review

Having someone else review your work can be a great way to improve your writing. You can ask a classmate, friend, or family member. This is called peer review. The reviewer can help you find typos, errors, inconsistencies, and things that don't make sense.

1. **Ask your peer to read your finished writing.** Revise and edit your work before the peer review. This will help you get the most benefit from the review.

2. **Tell the peer if you are looking for help revising, editing, or both.** Let your friend know what help you are looking for. You may want help organizing your content. You may want someone to check for spelling and grammar errors. You may want someone to ensure your content makes sense.

3. **Read or listen to the critique thoughtfully.** Read or listen to all of your peer's thoughts before responding. If your peer has questions, address them by revising your text.

4. **Ask question.** If you do not understand a comment or question, ask your peer for more information.

Publish

Publishing is your final step. When you publish your work, you make it available for people to read and respond to. Depending on your goals, you could publish for a select few or for a large audience.

Here are a few ways you could publish your work.

- Start your own blog.
- Post on someone else's blog.
- Print copies and mail them.
- Attach a copy of your writing to an e-mail.
- Submit your writing to a local newspaper.
- Submit your writing to a workplace newsletter.
- Submit your writing for publication in a national magazine.

Just remember—don't publish until your writing is as clear and error-free as you can get it.

Write on a Regular Basis

The more you write, the more comfortable you will feel writing. Writing skills, like many other skills, become better with time.

Try different types of writing, including narrative writing, persuasive writing, and informational writing. You may find that you prefer one type to another.

Whatever you enjoy, all of your writing will improve with regular practice.

Vocabulary Review

Directions: Match each word in column 1 with its definition in column 2.

Column 1

1. _____ editing
2. _____ pertinent
3. _____ revising

Column 2

A. important
B. correcting errors in a piece of writing
C. changing a piece of writing to make it better

Directions: Read each writing prompt. Then decide which pattern of organization would be best to use in writing about it.

1. Write about how you would teach someone to make a peanut butter-and-jelly sandwich.

   A. comparison and contrast
   B. order of importance
   C. time order
   D. cause and effect

2. Write about the importance of getting an education.

   A. comparison and contrast
   B. order of importance
   C. time order
   D. cause and effect

3. Write about a time when you were not prepared for something. What happened and why?

   A. comparison and contrast
   B. order of importance
   C. time order
   D. cause and effect

Directions: Read the following editorial passage. Then, on a separate piece of paper, write a concluding paragraph.

> It has come to my attention that our town is considering cutting the school budget. The biggest cut would be to after-school programs. This is a big mistake. The benefits of after-school programs far outweigh the cost to keep them running.
>
> The reality is that most families are either single-parent households or have both parents working full time. That means that without an after-school program, students would be returning to empty homes. If a parent isn't home until 6:00 and children are dismissed from school at 2:30; there are three and a half hours of unsupervised time. After-school programs keep our children off the streets and out of trouble.
>
> The social interaction that after-school programs provide is also beneficial to students. Sports teams, debate clubs, and theater groups allow students to spend time together to pursue non-academic interests. Students involved in extracurricular activities become more social and learn how to negotiate other areas of their lives.
>
> Finally, after-school programs provide structure for students who need homework support and would otherwise be on their own. Students are more likely to complete homework assignments if there is time carved out of each day for this. It simply becomes part of their daily routine.

Skill Practice

Directions: Read the passage below. Revise and edit it to make the writing clearer, more interesting, and correct.

It is important to find time every day to unwind, de-stress, and relax. This is good not only for your physical body, but for your mind as well. There are lots of different ways to slow down and relax. If you can find just 30 minutes a day to relax, you will start to notice a difference in many areas of your life.

One way to acomplish this is to meditate. Some people are intimidated by the idea of meditation. Dont be. Meditation is simply finding a quiet place to sit, close your eyes, and let your mind let go of all the stresses in your life. It takes practice. If this happens to you, remind yourself that you're worth 30 minutes a day and that taking the time to meditate will help you get more done during the rest of the day. Many people say they can't stop thinking about everything else they need to do and feel antsy sitting still when there's so much to get done. That's not a lot of time.

Many people find it helpful to practice yoga there are many forms of yoga, so you need to find the form that suits you. The latter option allows you to get learn yoga in your own home. You can learn yoga by taking classes or by renting yoga DVDs. Whatever method you choose, it is important to find time to de-stress every day. Meditation and yoga are just two options.

The key is to find something you enjoy that helps you relax. Go for a walk, ride a bike, or take a cooking class. Are you feeling stressed? Does it seem like there's not enough time in the day to accomplish everything you need to do? Do you find yourself running out of patience?

_____

_____

_____

_____

_____

_____

_____

_____

_____

_____

ESSAY WRITING PRACTICE

The Writing Process

Directions: Write an essay on a topic of your choice. Be sure to follow all of the steps in the writing process.

- **Prewriting:** Develop your ideas in the prewriting process. Choose a topic, audience, and purpose. Brainstorm ideas related to the topic. Organize the ideas in a meaningful order.

- **Writing:** Write a rough draft. Start with an introduction that tells the main idea and provides an overview of what you will discuss. Next develop the body with facts and details that support the main idea. Finally, write a conclusion that wraps up or summarizes your essay. Remember, don't include new information in the conclusion.

- **Revising and Editing:** Revise your essay to change the order of ideas, rewrite sentences, or replace words or phrases. Edit for mistakes in grammar, usage, and punctuation. Write your final draft once you have made all necessary revisions and completed the editing.

If necessary, review Lessons 7.1, 7.2, or 7.3 for help with prewriting, writing, revising, and editing.

_____

_____

_____

_____

_____

_____

_____

_____

_____

_____

_____

_____

_____

_____

_____

Review

ESSAY SCORING CHECKLIST

A. Does your essay have a clear main idea and stay on topic?

☐ **1.** No, my essay has a weak main idea and does not stay on topic.

☐ **2.** My essay has a clear main idea, but it also includes some points that are not directly related to the main idea.

☐ **3.** Yes, my essay has a clear main idea and all subtopics connect to the main idea.

☐ **4.** Yes, my essay has a strong main idea and subtopics that reveal thoughtful connections to the main idea.

B. Are the ideas in your essay well organized, with enough subtopics and transitions?

☐ **1.** No, the ideas in my essay are not in any order, and there are no subtopics or transitions.

☐ **2.** My essay shows some planning, but it does not contain enough subtopics and transitions.

☐ **3.** Yes, the ideas in my essay are logically connected with more than one subtopic and a few transitions.

☐ **4.** Yes, my essay is well organized with multiple subtopics and effective transitions.

C. Do the paragraphs in your essay contain details that support the main idea, and are connections between details and main idea stated clearly?

☐ **1.** No, many of the paragraphs in my essay contain details that don't support the main idea, or many of the paragraphs don't have any details at all.

☐ **2.** Many of the paragraphs contain sufficient supporting details, but the connections between details and main idea are not stated.

☐ **3.** Yes, the paragraphs in my essay contain relevant and concrete details, and the connections between details and main idea are stated but simple.

☐ **4.** Yes, the paragraphs in my essay contain excellent relevant details, and the connections between details and main idea are fully explained.

D. Do the sentences in your essay display variety in word choice and structure as well as correct usage, punctuation, and spelling?

☐ **1.** No, the sentences in my essay are not worded correctly or varied in structure, and most of them contain errors in usage, punctuation, and spelling.

☐ **2.** The sentences in my essay contain appropriate but vague words, basic sentence structure, some errors in punctuation and spelling, and many errors in usage.

☐ **3.** Yes, the sentences in my essay vary somewhat in structure, include appropriate and specific words, and contain only a few small errors in usage, punctuation, and spelling.

☐ **4.** Yes, the sentences in my essay display excellent word choice, great variety in structure, and almost no errors in usage.

Text Types and Purposes

Have you ever wanted to write a letter to the editor of your local newspaper, or express your opinion on a blog? If a friend asks for the recipe for your excellent chili, can you provide it in an organized way? Do you have an idea for story, but you don't know where to begin writing?

In order to write well, you have to know the type of writing you are doing, how to approach your task, and how to structure your text.

In this chapter you will learn about the different text types and purposes, and how to use each one effectively.

Lesson 8.1: Arguments

When you write an argument to persuade your readers, you have to support your claims with clear reasons and relevant evidence.

Lesson 8.2: Informative/Explanatory Texts

When you write an informative/explanatory text, you need to examine a topic and convey ideas, concepts, and information through the selection, organization, and analysis of relevant content.

Lesson 8.3: Narrative Texts

When you write a narrative text, you develop real or imagined experiences or events. You should use effective techniques, engaging descriptive details, and well-structured event sequences.

Goal Setting

Writing for a specific purpose involves first defining your purpose and then using the appropriate text structure. When you know the components and steps involved in each type of writing, your own writing will be more effective. Use the checklist to keep your learning organized! Check off each topic after you learn about it.

Arguments

_____ introduce a claim

_____ write an argument to support your claim

_____ assess accuracy of source

_____ respond to counterclaims

_____ provide a conclusion

Informative/Explanatory

_____ introduce a topic

_____ develop a topic

_____ organize ideas, concepts, and information

_____ use appropriate and varied transitions

_____ provide a concluding statement or section

Narrative

_____ establish a point of view

_____ introduce characters and establish a context

_____ organize an event sequence

_____ use sensory language

What do you already know about text types and purposes?

_____

_____

_____

Which of the above topics do you want to learn more about?

_____

_____

_____

Arguments

KEY CONCEPT: An argument is an essay in which the writer takes a position on an issue and presents reasons and evidence to convince readers to change their thoughts or actions regarding the issue.

Have you ever argued about an issue such as immigration or the death penalty? If so, you are not alone. Such issues may affect your actions and voting choices. However, to win an argument, you must provide more than your **opinion***, or belief. You need reasons and facts to support your point of view.*

Suppose your city council proposes raising parking fees in order to fund local parks and recreation. Would you be in favor of this increase? Make a list of sources you could use for facts to support an argument for or against the proposed parking fee increase.

Arguments

Persuasive arguments must be logical. To create a convincing argument, focus on the parts of your essay, from start to finish.

Introduce a Claim

A **claim** is a statement of the writer's opinion. To develop a claim, begin with issues in local or national news. Consider these topics:

- Outsourcing of jobs
- School uniforms

Which of these issues do you feel more strongly about? About which issue are you more knowledgeable? Try phrasing an issue in the form of a question to capture the different opinions:

- Is job outsourcing hurting or helping the American economy?

- Should public schools require students to wear uniforms?

Then answer the question you formed:

- Job outsourcing is hurting/helping the American economy.

- Public schools should (not) require students to wear uniforms.

This answer is your claim, and it should appear in the first paragraph of your essay. You can begin your argument by using one of the following strategies:

Action: Is there an event—a protest, or public meeting—you can describe?

Quotation: What does a relevant person have to say?

Reaction: Using verbs such as *think* or *wonder,* what are your thoughts on the issue?

Rhetorical Question: What question should you ask readers? Remember, a **rhetorical question** is a statement phrased in the form of a question. When you ask a rhetorical question, you do not expect an answer.

Write an Argument to Support Your Claim

Although a claim is an opinion, you can support it with facts from reliable sources. First, list three to five reasons you think others should agree with your claim.

Claim: Public schools should require students to wear uniforms.

- **Reason 1:** Uniforms lower the cost of clothing for students.

- **Reason 2:** Uniforms help protect low-income students from being bullied.

- **Reason 3:** Uniforms keep distractions from learning to a minimum.

These reasons will be **topic sentences**, or introductions to the main idea, for each paragraph. Next, provide **evidence**, or grounds for belief, for each reason. Evidence comes in various forms:

- **Anecdotes:** short stories about real people or events

- **Descriptions:** observations of items, people, or events

- **Facts:** information that can be proven; **statistics** are number-based facts

- **Graphics:** charts, graphs, diagrams, or photographs

- **Quotations:** exact words from an expert or affected person

Complete each paragraph by stating and explaining one or more pieces of evidence. Consider the following anecdote regarding Reason 2:

Uniforms help protect low-income students from being bullied. Appearance is a common reason that students bully others. Student harassment may focus on weight, eyeglasses, hair styles—and clothes. If uniforms are required for everyone, low-income students may no longer be bullied because their parents cannot afford to dress them in expensive clothes. Ana, a student bullied for her clothing, says, "Kids used to tease me for wearing the same outfit two or three days a week. Now that we all wear uniforms, I don't stand out so much, and that's a good thing."

THINK ABOUT WRITING

Directions: Create an outline for an argument. Complete the outline below. You will use the outline to write an argument at the end of this lesson. Note the type of evidence you believe will support your reasons. Add specific evidence later.

Argument Outline

I. **Introduction**
   Circle One: *Action, Dialogue or Quotation, Reaction, Rhetorical Question*

II. **Claim:**

III. **Reasons and Evidence**
   A. Reason 1 and Evidence:
   B. Reason 2 and Evidence:
   C. Reason 3 and Evidence:

WRITE TO LEARN

Select a print or digital source that relates to the claim you developed in your argument outline. You may choose a book, a magazine or newspaper article, or a journal article, for example. Using this source, respond in writing to the bulleted evaluation questions listed on this page.

When your responses are complete, finish this sentence starter: *This source is credible/not credible because . . . .*

Assess Accuracy of Source

When it comes to research, not all sources are equal. Some sources are written and reviewed by experts in related fields. These sources are accurate and **credible**, or deserving of belief or trust. However, other sources may not be accurate. How can you tell the difference? Use key questions to assess, or evaluate, each source:

- Who is the author, publisher, or reviewer of the source? What degrees, credentials, or experience does this person or organization have? Is the person or organization regarded by others as an expert or authority in the field?

- What is the purpose of the source: to inform, to persuade, to entertain, or to explain? Remember that an author's purpose affects choices about what information to include in a source and how to present the information.

- When was the source published or revised? Is it current or is it out-of-date?

- Where is the source located: on the public, easily accessible World Wide Web, or in an academically reviewed library database?

- Why do you want to use this source? Which reason does it support?

Respond to Counterclaims

Because you are expressing an opinion in an argument, there are other possible opinions or claims that go against your point of view. These opposing views are called **counterclaims** because they run counter to, or against, your claim.

When writing an argument, it is important to acknowledge counterclaims:

- Uniforms limit student self-expression.

- Uniforms are cheaply made.

- Uniforms do not fit everyone well.

After you acknowledge each counterclaim, you can respond to it.

> Some may argue that uniforms limit student self-expression. However, what uniforms do, in fact, is take emphasis away from superficial expression. Without this outlet, students must focus on more meaningful forms of expression, such as speaking and writing. Mr. Jones, a teacher at a school that recently adopted a uniform policy, says, "Students are being forced to find new ways of expressing themselves that are not dictated by external fashion trends."

When determining how you will respond to a particular counterclaim, consider these issues:

- Is there any part of a counterclaim with which you agree? If so, it is acceptable to acknowledge this.

- For what reasons do you disagree with all or parts of a counterclaim?

- What evidence are you able to offer that shows that a counterclaim is not as strong as your claim?

THINK ABOUT WRITING

Directions: In your notebook, continue creating the outline for the argument you will write at the end of this lesson. There is no required number of counterclaims to which you must respond, but you should acknowledge the most common ones.

Outline (continued)

IV. **Counterclaims**
  A. Counterclaim 1:
    a. Response + Evidence:
  B. Counterclaim 2:
    b. Response + Evidence:
  C. Counterclaim 3:
    c. Response + Evidence:

To find accurate sources for your evidence, your public library is a good place to start. Many libraries have sizable **databases**, or online listings of reliable, published reference materials. Using the library's database is one way to locate and assess accurate sources. You may also rely on material from government or educational websites whose Internet addresses, or URLs, end in .gov, or .edu. You can search for information using keywords, a subject, an author's name, and other search options. You can also find the publication information to create a **citation**, or reference to your source document.

Locate the topic you focused on in your claim and find at least one example of each of the following types of supporting evidence:

_____ Fact
_____ Graphic
_____ Quotation
_____ Statistic

Add the evidence you collect to your argument outline. Include the citation data with each entry.

If you need help using a database or obtaining source citations, ask a librarian to help you.

Read the sample conclusion on this page. Mark the text as follows:

- Underline the claim restatement.

- Draw a box around the summary of important reasons and/or evidence.

- Label the type of final insight the writer provides as Connection to Reader, Quotation, Fact/Statistic, or Anecdote.

With a partner, discuss the effectiveness of this conclusion. Use these discussion questions:

- What does the writer leave you thinking about?

- Is this a satisfying ending for this essay? Why or why not?

- Are you persuaded to consider the writer's argument? Why or why not?

- What does the writer do well in the conclusion?

- What suggestions do you have to improve the conclusion?

Provide a Conclusion

Now that you have stated your claim, supported it with reasons and evidence, and acknowledged and responded to counterclaims, it is time to write the **conclusion**, or the end of your essay.

Generally, a conclusion has two purposes. First, it must reinforce your argument. Secondly, it must leave the readers with something to think about.

To reinforce your argument, use these strategies:

- Restate your claim.

- Summarize the most important reasons or evidence.

To provide a final insight that will leave readers thinking, use one or more of these strategies:

- Explain why readers should care about your argument. How does it affect them personally?

- Provide a provocative or thoughtful quotation.

- Deliver a stunning fact or statistic.

- Offer a particularly moving anecdote or short story.

Combine both purposes as you write your conclusion.

American public schools should move to adopt uniform policies for students because school hallways should lead students to classrooms where they can develop their minds; school halls should not serve as fashion runways. In short, the public school is the last great center of democracy in American society—a place where all students are created equal and should have equal opportunities to think and grow. Ana, a student once bullied for her clothing, has a final thought on the subject: "Since our school adopted uniforms, I find it easier to study. It's great to be able to concentrate on my classes instead of worrying about being teased."

THINK ABOUT **WRITING**

Directions: In your notebook, complete the outline for the argument you will write at the end of this lesson.

....

Outline (continued)

V. **Conclusion**
   A. Restatement of claim:
   B. Summary of most important reasons and evidence:
   C. Final Insight: Circle One: *Connection to Reader, Quotation, Fact/Statistic, Anecdote*
   Description:

Use Cohesive Language

Arguments are written using **formal** and **cohesive** language. Formal language refers to the use of words and phrases that are appropriate for school and business settings. The following words or expressions—which are appropriate for spoken language or writing among friends—are generally not used in formal writing. It is, however, acceptable for informal words or expressions to appear within quoted material a writer is using as evidence.

| Avoid | Use Instead |

- **Abbreviations:** Use *for example* in place of *e.g.,* or use *and so on* in place of *etc.*

- **Contractions:** For instance, write out *could not* instead of using *couldn't.*

- **Vague Language:** For instance, use *evidence* or *reasons* in place of *things.*

- **Personal Pronouns:** Generally, avoid using first- and second-person pronouns (*I, we, you*) in favor of third-person pronouns (*he, she, they*).

- **Slang or Idioms:** For instance, use *popular* instead of *cool,* or use *laughing* instead of *rolling in the aisles.*

Cohesive language refers to transition words and phrases that make the relationships among claims, reasons, evidence, and counterclaims clear for readers.

Relationship	Transition Words or Phrases
acknowledgment	*granted, agreed, of course* Granted, some believe that uniforms limit students' self-expression.
example	*for example, for instance, in fact, specifically* What uniforms do, in fact, is to take emphasis away from superficial expression.
summary	*finally, in conclusion, in other words, in short* In other words, without the distraction of external fashion trends, students express themselves through speaking and writing.
supplement	*also, in addition, besides, too, moreover* With superficial distractions out of the way, students also have more time to devote to their studies.

Directions: Match each vocabulary word with its definition.

1. _____ argument   **A.** able to be trusted or believed

2. _____ citation   **B.** statement of opinion

3. _____ claim   **C.** publication information

4. _____ counterclaims   **D.** written opinion supported by reasons and evidence

5. _____ credible   **E.** collection of searchable information

6. _____ database   **F.** statements in opposition to an opinion

Skill Review

Directions: Read the argument below. Then answer the questions that follow.

- **Introduction of Claim:**

Public school students should be required to wear school uniforms.

- **Reason 1:** Uniforms lower the cost of clothing for students.

Although families must buy uniforms at the beginning of the school year, most of the cost of outfitting students is then finished. When students no longer face peer pressure to wear the latest fashionable outfits to class, it makes a difference in the family budget. Buying new clothing throughout the year is far more costly than purchasing a few uniforms.

- **Reason 2:** Uniforms help protect low-income students from bullying.

Uniforms help protect low-income students from being bullied. Appearance is a common reason that students bully others. Student harassment may focus on weight, eyeglasses, hair styles—and clothes. If uniforms are required for everyone, low-income students may no longer be bullied because their parents cannot afford to dress them in expensive clothes. Ana, a student bullied for her clothing, says, "Kids used to tease me for wearing the same outfit two or three days a week. Now that we all wear uniforms, I don't stand out so much, and that's a good thing."

- **Reason 3:** Uniforms keep distractions from learning to a minimum.

Some may argue that uniforms limit student self-expression. However, what uniforms do, in fact, is take emphasis away from superficial expression. Without this outlet, students must focus on more meaningful forms of expression, such as speaking and writing. Mr. Jones, a teacher at a school that recently adopted a uniform policy, says, "Students are being forced to find new ways of expressing themselves that are not dictated by external fashion trends."

In conclusion, American public schools should move to adopt uniform policies for students because school hallways should lead students to classrooms where they can develop their minds; school halls should not serve as fashion runways. In short, the public school is the last great center of democracy in American society—a place where all students are created equal and should have equal opportunities to think and grow. Americans should not sacrifice this grand ideal to support a culture of superficial judgment and materialism.

Skill Review (continued)

1. Which passage below <u>best</u> begins an introduction for the argument?

   A. The dictionary defines a uniform as "a suit of clothing worn by a particular group." Many people wear uniforms, including nurses, firefighters, and waiters.

   B. For many years, students in private schools have worn uniforms. Today, many public schools are considering the benefits of uniforms.

   C. Should public school students wear uniforms if uniforms reduce social friction, help focus students' attention on their studies, and relieve a financial burden for parents?

   D. A typical school uniform consists of a cotton shirt and khaki or navy colored pants, skirt, or shorts. The cost is about $30.00.

2. Which evidence below <u>best</u> supports Reason 1?

   A. description of a busy mall setting in early August

   B. statistics contrasting the cost of regular clothing with uniforms

   C. photographs from back-to-school clothing advertisements

   D. quotations from a school dress code policy

3. From which credible source might the writer find evidence to support Reason 2?

   A. government website

   B. teen magazine

   C. letter to the editor

   D. parenting blog

4. Which evidence below best supports Reason 3?

   A. anecdote about a parent and student shopping for clothes

   B. facts from research about school learning objectives

   C. statistic about the number of schools with uniform policies

   D. quotation from a teacher about causes of conduct problems

5. From which credible source might the writer find evidence to support Reason 3?

   A. *.com* uniform website

   B. YouTube video about classroom management

   C. Web forum about school uniforms

   D. interview with a school principal

Skill Practice

Directions: Using the completed outline in your notebook, write an argument in the space below.

Make sure to use one of the strategies discussed in the lesson for introducing a claim. Then state your claim.

For each paragraph, state a reason the reader should agree with your claim. Then state and explain supporting evidence. Make sure to vary the types of evidence you cite. If you use outside sources to supply evidence, make sure your sources are credible. Provide source citations at the end of your essay.

Next, research some counterclaims to your argument. Acknowledge and respond to common counterclaims. You may include further evidence in this section.

Finally, conclude by restating your claim, summarizing important reasons and evidence, and leaving readers with a final insight. Use one of the final insight strategies discussed in the lesson.

Reread your argument and make necessary corrections to ensure that you have used formal and cohesive language throughout the essay.

Skill Practice (continued)

Informative/Explanatory Texts

Lesson Objectives

You will be able to

- Organize ideas, concepts, and information in informative or explanatory text

- Use appropriate and varied transitions

- Provide a concluding statement or section

Skills

- **Core Skill:** Use Formatting, Graphics, and Multimedia

- **Core Skill:** Use Domain-specific Vocabulary and Precise Language

Vocabulary

bias
domain-specific vocabulary
explanatory
informative
multimedia
transitions

KEY CONCEPT: In an informative or explanatory text, the writer examines a topic for the purpose of informing the reader or explaining the steps in a process.

When you need information about topics such as creating a Web page or doing your taxes, do you ask for help from friends or coworkers? Have you given information to others? To provide information, approach the task in the same way as you would an argument: state the topic clearly and support it with evidence. Make a list of topics about which you have given others information. Did you provide the information verbally? Did you write out the information for others to keep for reference?

Informative or Explanatory Texts

When writing to inform or to explain, choose a topic that is not too broad or too narrow. The topic must be suitable for the task and for the audience. For example, if your boss asks you to create a flyer about the company's recycling program, do not focus on city-wide recycling. That topic is too broad for the task and for your audience of coworkers. Similarly, do not focus on recycling in just one department. This topic is too narrow for the task and the audience. Your flyer must apply to all departments and employees.

Introduce a Topic

To develop a topic for an **informative** text (text that adds to the knowledge of the reader) or **explanatory** text (text that clarifies or explains), identify the purpose of the text, the format, the audience, and the audience's needs. Consider graphics and **multimedia**, or additional sound and video elements, you can use to aid comprehension.

Purpose	Are you writing to inform readers about a process, similarities and differences, causes and effects, or problems and solutions?
Format	Are you writing an e-mail, an office memo, or a report?
Audience	Who is the audience for this information—the public, your coworkers, or your supervisor?
Needs	What does your audience know about this topic? What do they need to know?

State your topic and say what will follow in your text. Present this information in topics sentences like this:

> Everyone wants to do well in school, but for many, the process for achieving good grades is a mystery. Luckily, there are some clear and easy strategies students can use to solve this mystery.

Begin your text with one of the strategies for structuring an argument:

Action: Describe an event, such as a student receiving a report card.

Quotation: Use a quote about the topic from someone affected by the topic, such as a student, parent, or teacher.

Reaction: Use verbs such as *analyze* to relay thoughts about the topic.

Rhetorical Question: Ask readers to consider a topic-related question.

Develop a Topic

Select and analyze relevant facts, definitions, concrete details, quotations, and examples to help you develop your topic.

Focus on what your readers already *know* about the topic, *what they need to know*, and what they will *learn* from your text. You can use a *KWL* Chart such as the one that follows:

K *What do my readers already **know**?*	W ***What** do my readers need to know?*	L *What will my readers **learn** by reading my text?*
• Teachers use homework, projects, and tests to assess student learning. These assessments are graded.	• They need to know how to get good grades.	• Study skills • Organizational skills • Test-taking skills

Add information such as the following to the *L* (Learn) column in order to develop each idea:

- **Facts:** information that can be proven true through credible sources

- **Definitions:** meanings of words that may be unfamiliar to the reader

- **Concrete Details:** specific descriptions that help readers understand the writer's meaning

- **Quotations:** exact words from an expert or affected person

- **Examples:** anecdotes, graphics, or statistics

When using information such as facts, quotations, and examples to inform or to explain, it is important for writers not only to report the information to readers, but to analyze or evaluate it as well. For each piece of information, ask yourself these questions:

- Does the information come from a credible author or publisher?

- Is it factual and accurate? Does it show **bias**, or favoritism toward one point of view?

- How does this information relate to the topic?

- How does this information relate to other information? Does it show the next step in a sequence? Is it the cause of a particular effect? Does it show a similarity or a difference with another piece of information? Is it a possible solution to a stated problem?

Use these questions to analyze, make connections among, and revise if necessary the information in the third column of your *KWL* chart.

Examine the following example.

- Study Skills

Create a schedule for regular study sessions. <u>Research shows that the brain needs time to process information.</u> (*fact*) Therefore, it is often ineffective to study the night before a test. Students should study for ten to fifteen minutes at a time for several days prior to a test. Yolanda, a student whose grades in science have recently improved, says, "<u>Each night, I read over the day's science notes two or three times. By the time the teacher announces a test, I feel as if I don't really have to study because I already know the material so well.</u>" (*quotation*)

THINK ABOUT WRITING

Directions: In a notebook, copy this *KWL* chart and take notes for an informative or explanatory text you will write at the end of this lesson. As a topic, choose something that others often ask you to explain, such as how to make a favorite recipe, use a cell phone feature, or change a flat tire. Then fill in each column.

K	W	L

Organize Ideas, Concepts, and Information

After gathering and analyzing information that supports your topic, identify broader categories into which your information will fit—such as the ones that follow.

Category	Identification
Cause-and-Effect	Are you telling about the reasons an event took place, or about the results of the event?
Comparison-and-Contrast	Are you telling about the similarities or differences of subjects within your topic?
Problem-and-Solution	Are you describing a problem and suggesting a solution?
Sequence	Are you telling about events in time order or describing the steps in a process?

Before you begin writing, plan your introduction and topic sentences:

Introduction: Anecdote—student receiving report card
Topic Sentence: Everyone wants to do well in school, but for many, the process for achieving good grades is a mystery. Luckily, there are some clear and easy strategies students can use to solve this mystery.

Then determine how your ideas can be organized in a graphic organizer. To compare and contrast, use a Venn diagram. Use boxes and arrows to organize the other categories.

Compare and Contrast:

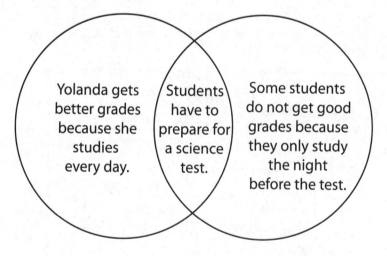

Yolanda gets better grades because she studies every day.

Students have to prepare for a science test.

Some students do not get good grades because they only study the night before the test.

Cause and Effect:

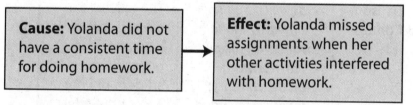

Cause: Yolanda did not have a consistent time for doing homework.

Effect: Yolanda missed assignments when her other activities interfered with homework.

Problem and Solution:

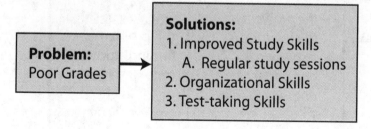

Problem: Poor Grades

Solutions:
1. Improved Study Skills
   A. Regular study sessions
2. Organizational Skills
3. Test-taking Skills

Sequence:

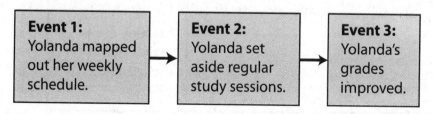

Event 1: Yolanda mapped out her weekly schedule.

Event 2: Yolanda set aside regular study sessions.

Event 3: Yolanda's grades improved.

Core Skill
Use Formatting, Graphics, and Multimedia

If your text contains complex information, you may want to use some of the following strategies to guide your readers.

- **Formatting:** Add headings, bold-faced words, or phrases that come before particular sections of text.

- **Graphics:** Use visual elements, such as charts, graphs, tables, diagrams, photographs, or illustrations.

- **Multimedia:** Include sound and video elements in computer applications.

Review the graphic organizers on this page. Identify any places where there is complex information presented. Would special formatting or, a graphic, help clarify this information? Make a note of it in your notebook. If the information was presented in a computer presentation, would a multimedia element help clarify this information? If so, make a note of it.

WRITE TO LEARN

For each category in the chart on this page, use transition words and phrases to write two to three sentences that illustrate the relationship. Label the relationship in each passage. For example:

<u>Because</u> the student did not study for the test, she failed. <u>Consequently</u>, her course grade dropped. (*Cause-and-Effect*)

You may use a variety of topics for these passages, or you may choose to write passages based on the topic you are developing in your notebook for the text you will write at the end of this lesson.

THINK ABOUT WRITING

Directions: In your notebook, plan your introduction and topic sentence. Then select a piece of information from the *L* section of your *KWL* chart and an organization category. Use one of the graphic organizers shown on the previous page to show the organization you chose.

Use Appropriate and Varied Transitions

Transitions are words and phrases that make the relationships among ideas and concepts clear for readers. Look at the chart of relationships and transitions below. When drafting and revising, use appropriate transitions from the chart as you move from sentence to sentence and paragraph to paragraph. Make sure to use a variety of transitions so that your writing does not become repetitive.

Relationship	Transition Words and Phrases	Example
Cause-and-Effect	• *because; due to; for this reason; if . . . then; since* • *as a result; consequently; so; therefore; thus*	She was not prepared for the test; <u>as a result</u>, her grade was low.
Comparison-and-Contrast	• *as well as; equally; similarly; in the same way; likewise* • *but; however; on the contrary; on the other hand; rather*	The teacher offered special help after class; <u>however</u>, the student did not accept the offer.
Problem-and-Solution	• *the problem is; the question is* • *a solution is; one answer is; one way to solve*	<u>One way to solve</u> the problem of finding study time is to move or eliminate another activity.
Sequence	• *after; finally; first; next; then*	<u>First</u> Yolanda found it hard to study each night; <u>then</u> she made it a habit.

A paragraph might use more than one type of transition words and phrases; for example:

One solution (*Problem-and-Solution*) for poor grades is to create a schedule for regular study sessions. Research shows that the brain needs time to process information. Therefore, (*Cause-and-Effect*) it is often ineffective to study the night before a test. Students should study for ten to fifteen minutes at a time for several days prior to a test. Yolanda, a student whose grades in science have recently improved, says, "Each night, I read over the day's science notes two or three times. By the time the teacher announces a test, I feel as if I don't really have to study because I already know the material so well."

THINK ABOUT **WRITING**

Directions: In a notebook, copy the following paragraph and add appropriate, varied transitions. Label the relationship clarified by each transition you add.

_____ is to organize course materials. Students who earn poor grades are often the ones whose folders have papers spilling from them. _____ a student is unable to find his or her things, _____ it is difficult to study or complete assignments. _____, get a three-ring binder and a set of dividers. Create a section for each course. _____ as the instructor gives assignments and notes, date them and place them in the appropriate section in chronological order. This system enables a student to find what he or she needs quickly and efficiently.

Provide a Concluding Statement or Section

Now that you have introduced your topic and developed and organized your information, it's time to write the **conclusion**, or end of your text.

Generally, a conclusion has two purposes. First, it must reinforce the main idea and important details. Secondly, it must leave the readers with something to think about.

To reinforce your main idea, use these strategies:

- Restate your topic.

- Summarize the main ideas and important details.

To provide a final insight that will leave readers thinking, use one of these strategies:

- Explain why the readers should care about your topic. How does it benefit readers to know about this topic?

- Provide a meaningful quotation.

- Deliver a particularly interesting fact.

- Offer an interesting anecdote or short story.

Combine both purposes as you write your conclusion:

> Many students perform poorly in school, not because they want to, but because they do not know how to perform differently. (*restate the topic*) The key to changing the outcome is changing the behaviors that come before it. Students can reform their study skills, organizational strategies, and test-taking skills with specific tactics that will yield improved grades. (*summarize main ideas and details*) Malcolm remembers the first *A* he earned in a reading class in this way: "For the first time, I felt smart." (*meaningful quotation*)

THINK ABOUT **WRITING**

Directions: In your notebook, copy the graphic organizer shown below and make notes for the conclusion of the informative or explanatory text you will write at the end of this lesson.

> **Restate the topic:** _____
>
> **Summarize main ideas and important details:**
>
> _____
>
> **Final insight:** *Circle One—Connection to Reader, Quotation, Fact, Anecdote*
>
> _____

USE DOMAIN-SPECIFIC VOCABULARY AND PRECISE LANGUAGE

Domain-specific vocabulary refers to words that belong to a particular area of knowledge. For example, terms such as *search engine* and *hard drive* belong to the area of computer science. People who are informed about a particular area of knowledge are also familiar with domain-specific vocabulary. However, when writing about a particular area of knowledge, you may need to define the domain-specific vocabulary for your readers. You should also define words that have other meanings when used in everyday language.

Domain	Vocabulary Examples
Mathematics	*factor, multiple, inverse*
Science	*amino acid, carbon compound, fission*
Social Studies	*capitalism, federalism, feudalism*
Technology	*application, download, firewall*

Precise language refers to words that are specific rather than vague. These words help readers understand information. For example, use *download* in place of *get* to describe accessing an application from the Internet.

Vague Word	Precise Words
lots	a specific quantity or specific examples
good	*cost-effective, useful, error-free*
bad	*erroneous, corrupt, inefficient*
thing	a specific item, object, task

Core Skill
Use Domain-Specific Vocabulary and Precise Language

Review the graphic organizers in your notebook. Circle any domain-specific vocabulary you have used. Will you need to define any of these terms for your readers? If so, make a note of them.

Draw a box around any vague language. Cross out this language and replace it with precise language. Consult a thesaurus, if necessary.

Vocabulary Review

Directions: Match each vocabulary word with its definition.

1. _____ bias

2. _____ explanatory

3. _____ informative

4. _____ multimedia

5. _____ transitions

A. adding to one's knowledge or understanding

B. sound or video elements in a computer application

C. preference that influences judgment

D. words or phrases used to clarify relationships among ideas

E. serving to clarify or explain

Directions: Read the explanatory text below. Then answer the questions that follow.

- **Introduction of Topic:**

1. A student opens a report card with trembling hands. Will the grades be good or bad? Everyone wants to do well in school, but for many, the process for achieving good grades is a mystery. Luckily, there are some clear and easy strategies students can use to solve this mystery.

- **First Supporting Idea, with Heading:**

Improved Study Skills

2. One solution for poor grades is to create a schedule for regular study sessions. Research shows that the brain needs time to process information. Therefore, it is often ineffective to study the night before a test. Students should study for ten to fifteen minutes at a time for several days prior to a test. Yolanda, a student whose grades in science have recently improved, says, "Each night, I read over the day's science notes two or three times. By the time the teacher announces a test, I feel as if I don't really have to study because I already know the material so well."

- **Second Supporting Idea, with Heading:**

Organizational Skills

3. Another solution is to organize course materials. Students who earn poor grades are often the ones whose folders have papers spilling from them. If a student is unable to find his or her things, then it's difficult to study or complete assignments. First, get a three-ring binder and a set of dividers. Create a section for each course. As the instructor gives assignments and notes, date them and place them in the appropriate section in chronological order. This system enables a student to find what he or she needs quickly and efficiently.

- **Third Supporting Idea, with Heading:**

Test-taking Skills

4. Review all quizzes, homework, and class notes to understand the types of questions that are likely to be on the test. Make sure you can identify the purpose of a question. Identifying the purpose will help you to respond correctly.

- **Conclusion:**

5. Many students perform poorly in school, not because they want to, but because they do not know how to perform differently. The key to changing the outcome is changing the behaviors that come before it. Students can reform their study skills, organizational strategies, and test-taking skills with specific tactics that will yield improved grades. Malcolm remembers the first *A* he earned in a reading class in this way: "For the first time, I felt smart."

Skill Review (continued)

1. Which strategy is used to introduce the topic—action, dialogue or quotation, reaction, or rhetorical question? Explain your reasoning.

_____

_____

_____

_____

_____

2. Which strategy could the writer use to develop the main idea of the fourth paragraph—fact, definition, concrete detail, quotation, or other example? Explain your reasoning.

_____

_____

_____

_____

_____

3. Read the following sentence from the text. Consider how you would replace the underlined word with a more precise word.

   If a student is unable to find his or her <u>things</u>, then it's difficult to study or complete assignments.

   Which word BEST replaces the underlined word?

   A. objects
   B. materials
   C. stuff
   D. gadgets

4. Read the following sentence from the text:

   Many students perform poorly in school, not because they want to, but because they do not know how to perform differently.

   Which word shows a transition of contrast?

   A. many
   B. do
   C. because
   D. but

Skill Practice

1. Write a conclusion to an essay about a topic you know well using each of the following strategies: connection to reader, quotation, fact, and anecdote.

_____

_____

_____

_____

2. Organizational skills can benefit you in many areas of your life. Choose one area in which you think more organization would be helpful. Consider such areas as banking, shopping, housekeeping, social activities, or other activities. Write a paragraph about how your selected activity could benefit from organization, and be sure to use at least three transition words or phrases. Underline the transitions.

_____

_____

_____

_____

3. Describe the graphic organizer (e.g., Venn Diagram, boxes with arrows) you would select to organize information about each of the following ideas. Explain which type of relationship the organizer is showing.

   A. You want to compare a team approach to a project to an approach in which employees report to managers.
   B. You are describing the steps you took to save money over the course of a project.
   C. You want to show how you solved the problem of employees reporting late to work.
   D. You want to show why the copier keeps breaking down.

   A. _____

   B. _____

   C. _____

   D. _____

Writing Review

Directions: Using the completed KWL chart and graphic organizer in your notebook, write an informative or explanatory text in the space below (use an additional piece of paper, if needed).

Make sure to use one of the strategies discussed in the lesson for introducing your topic. Then state your topic and describe the information to come.

Use the broad categories to organize your body paragraphs. Will you use sequence to explain the steps in a process? Will you describe the causes and effects of an event? Will you describe similarities and differences among concepts within a topic? Will you introduce a problem and then propose a solution?

Finally, conclude by restating your topic, summarizing main ideas and important details, and leaving readers with a final insight. Use one of the final insight strategies discussed in the lesson.

Reread your text and make necessary corrections to ensure that you have used appropriate and varied transitions and precise language throughout the text. Also, make sure you have defined domain-specific vocabulary. Consider adding headings or graphics where appropriate.

_____

_____

_____

_____

_____

_____

_____

_____

_____

_____

_____

_____

_____

KEY CONCEPT: In a narrative text, the writer tells a real or imagined story.

When friends and family gather, they often pass the time telling stories about events that have taken place in their lives. These stories connect the tellers with the listeners through shared experiences. Unlike arguments and informative or explanatory texts, narrative texts are based on description and sequence rather than statements and evidence.

Read the following titles:
Our Summer Vacation in the Ozarks
The Case For and Against an Increased Sales Tax
How to Install Your New Model R2900 Dishwasher

Which of these texts do you think might be an argument (A)? Which might be an informative text (I)? Which might be a narrative text (N)? Write an A, I, or N next to the title you think it describes.

Narrative Texts

When telling a story, the writer must first establish the **point of view**, or the perspective from which the story will be told.

ESTABLISH A POINT OF VIEW

The teller of a story is called a **narrator**, and there are different types of narrators. Read the following explanations of different types of narrators and then consider the effect of varying narrative points of view on the familiar story of "The Hare and the Tortoise."

To read "The Hare and the Tortoise," go to the website below and scroll down to the heading List of Illustrations in Colour. Click on the link to "The Hare and the Tortoise" that follows that heading.

http://www.gutenberg.org/files/11339/11339-h/11339-h.htm

With a partner, discuss how each point of view would affect the story.

- A **first-person narrator** is a participant in the events described. Using first-person pronouns, such as *I*, *me*, and *my*, this narrator tells what he or she thinks, feels, does, says, or observes. However, this type of narrator cannot know or report what other characters think or feel about events unless he or she reports the **dialogue**, or speech, of other characters.

  I was boasting of my speed before the other animals.

ESTABLISH A POINT OF VIEW (continued)

- A **subjective first-person narrator** shows bias, or a preference that influences judgment, as a result of his or her characteristics, such as gender, age, ethnicity, values, or goals. This type of narrator may become **unreliable**, or untrustworthy, if he or she changes the truth for his or her own purposes.

Although I was a bit sleepy after a night of gathering food for my family, I was sharing stories of my speed with the other animals.

- An **objective first-person narrator** participates in events, but he or she tries to report these events without exercising judgment, allowing you, the reader, to make your own judgments.

I was telling of my speed before the other animals.

- A **third-person narrator**, who is not a participant in events and uses third-person pronouns, such as *they, she,* or *his,* is an **omniscient** or all-knowing voice that is knowledgeable about what every character thinks, feels, says, and does.

The Hare was once boasting of his speed before the other animals. The Tortoise, annoyed with the Hare's boasting, accepted a challenge to race.

- A **limited third-person narrator** focuses on the thoughts, feelings, and actions of one character.

The Hare was once boasting of his speed before the other animals. "I have never yet been beaten," said he, "when I put forth my full effort. I challenge any one here to race with me." When the Tortoise accepted, the Hare said, "That is a good joke. I could dance round you all the way."

Core Skill
Establish a Point of View

Select an event that happened to you recently that involved one or two other people.

Write a paragraph about that event from the point of view of a subjective first-person narrator.

Then rewrite the same paragraph, telling the same story this time using a limited third-person narrator.

Begin with a short exposition, or introduction, including the characters and setting. Then work through the conflict of the event, to the story's turning point, or climax, and its resolution.

Then respond in writing to the following questions:

- Which story clues in each paragraph reveal the paragraph's point of view?

- How did changing the point of view from first person to third person affect the story? Did the change have an effect on the conflict or on the resolution?

Share and discuss your responses with a partner.

Narrative Plot

A narrative is written as a sequence of events called the **plot**. The narrative plot begins with a section called the **exposition**. In the exposition, the writer introduces characters and establishes a context for the story. **Characters** are the people (or animals) who take part in the events of a story. The narrator is one type of character, but there are other types, as well.

- **Primary**—the main or most important character in a story
- **Secondary**—the characters who support the primary character
- **Round**—a character who changes over the course of the story
- **Flat**—a character who remains the same over the course of a story
- **Protagonist**—the primary character whose actions the story follows
- **Antagonist**—the character who stands in the way of the protagonist's goal

The **context** is the situation or set of circumstances or events in which the primary character is involved. Generally, the context includes a **setting**, or time and place of action, and a **conflict**, a problem the primary character faces with another character, nature, or fate. A character may also struggle with him- or herself over two or more choices.

Narrative writers often use planning charts, such as this one, to outline the characters and context.

Exposition
Narrative Point of View: limited third-person
Primary Character/Protagonist: Hare (round)
Important Secondary Character(s)/Antagonist(s): Tortoise (flat)
Context (setting and conflict): The setting is most likely a natural area, such as an open field, because there are many animals. Tortoise accepts boastful Hare's challenge to a race.

THINK ABOUT WRITING

Directions: Many stories in a person's life are worth repeating. Certainly the story of Hare and Tortoise has been repeated across cultures and generations. Choose a true story you find yourself telling and retelling frequently to friends and family or a story you have heard many times from a particular friend or family member. Then, in a notebook, copy the narrative planning chart above, copying the headings only. Begin taking notes for the narrative text you will write at the end of this lesson based on the story you chose.

Organize an Event Sequence

Events in a plot are generally organized in **chronological** or time order. However, writers sometimes choose to flash back to earlier events or preview future events. A plot can be divided into five parts:

- **Exposition**—the story background: characters and setting

- **Rising Action**—the events that make the primary character's conflict more challenging or complicated and builds to the climax

- **Climax**—the turning point of the story

- **Falling Action**—the events that lead toward an end to the conflict

- **Resolution**—the solution to the problem

THINK ABOUT WRITING

Directions: In the narrative planning chart that you copied into your notebook, make notes about examples of rising action, climax, and falling action you can use for the narrative text you will write at the end of this lesson.

USE NARRATIVE TECHNIQUES

To connect with readers and make them care about a story and its outcome, a narrative writer must make the characters and events seem real. Writers use a number of **techniques** or strategies to accomplish this goal.

Dialogue: the words spoken by a character and enclosed within quotation marks

- *The Tortoise said quietly, "I accept your challenge."*

Pacing: the speed of action

- *So a course was fixed and a start was made. The Hare darted almost out of sight at once, but soon stopped, and, to show his contempt for the Tortoise, lay down to have a nap. (The race is planned, begins, and progresses within two sentences. The pacing is quick, mimicking the subject—a race.)*

Transition Words and Phrases: words used to show the order of events, shifts in time or setting, or relationships among experiences and events

- *. . . when the Hare awoke from his nap, he saw the Tortoise just near the winning post . . . (order of events)*

Precise Language: words that create specific, rather than vague, images or feelings

- *The Hare was once boasting of his speed before the other animals.* (The writer uses the precise word *boasting* rather than a vague or neutral word such as *telling* or *speaking*.)

Core Skill
Use Narrative Techniques

Using the paragraph that you wrote earlier with the subjective first-person point of view (page 263), rewrite the same paragraph using an example of each of the following narrative techniques.

- Dialogue
- Quick Pacing
- Slow Pacing
- Sequence Transition
- Time or Setting Transition
- Precise Language

Share and discuss your examples with a partner.

Use Sensory Language

Perhaps one of the most important techniques narrative writers use is description. When describing characters, setting, or other story elements, narrative writers often use **sensory language**. Sensory language appeals to at least one of a reader's five senses. This appeal to the senses involves the reader in the action and experience of the story.

Sense	Example
Sight	"That is a good joke," said the Hare; "I could <u>dance round you</u> all the way."
Sound	The Tortoise said <u>quietly</u>, "I accept your challenge."

Here are some additional examples the writer might have used:

Sense	Example
Smell	Lulled by the <u>scent of fresh spring grass</u>, the Hare lay down to have a nap.
Touch/ Feeling	The Tortoise plodded on and plodded on, <u>lifting one heavy foot</u> after another.
Taste	To celebrate, the Tortoise munched on a <u>bitter, but crunchy</u>, leaf of cabbage.

THINK ABOUT WRITING

Directions: In your notebook, read the narrative planning chart you have been working on. Identify places where you will use narrative techniques. For each area you identify, make a note and write a few key phrases or sentences that you can use in your draft.

_____ Dialogue

_____ Pacing

_____ Transitional Words and Phrases

_____ Precise Language

_____ Description and Sensory Language

Provide a Conclusion

The final part of a narrative plot is the conclusion, or the **resolution**. It is the place where the primary character's conflict is settled. It is also the place where the character may learn a valuable lesson as a result of the story's events.

Resolution
The Hare loses the race. The Hare learns, "Slow and steady wins the race."

If a writer chooses to narrate a story in the first person, the narrator may **reflect** or think directly about the significance of the event in his or her life.

For example,

> *I couldn't believe what a fool I had been. Certainly, the Tortoise has taught me a valuable lesson. No amount of speed is of value during a nap. I wouldn't make this mistake again.*

Vocabulary Review

Directions: Match each vocabulary word with its definition.

1. _____ context
2. _____ narrative
3. _____ narrator
4. _____ point of view
5. _____ sensory language

A. teller of a story
B. words appealing to the five human senses
C. standpoint, perspective, or attitude
D. circumstances or situation
E. a real or imagined story

21st Century Skill
Think Creatively

Brainstorm three possible conclusions or resolutions to the narrative text you have been planning in your notebook.

- What are three possible outcomes of the conflict?

- What are three possible lessons the primary character might learn?

- If you plan to use a first-person point of view, what are three possible reflections the narrator might make?

Present your narrative planning chart to a partner. Then describe the three possible endings. Have your partner help you select the ending readers will find most satisfying.

Directions: Read the narrative text below. Then answer the questions that follow.

1 | That summer, my luck was so bad that finding one hundred shiny silver dollars under a big prairie sky would not have changed anything. I was finally old enough to spend my summer break from school at my uncle's cattle ranch, something my siblings had been doing for years. I heard Uncle Cos promise my mom, "I'll put Rachel to work." Now, in my mind, *work* meant sleeping late, riding horses, fishing, and swimming. However, Uncle Cos had something else in mind entirely.

2 | Sure, the first morning was slow, but by supper, my uncle received a worrisome call from one of the ranch hands. A neighbor had spotted some coyotes hovering near the cattle. When he hung up, his eyes jumped around the room, resting momentarily with each person until they landed on me. "It is time to put you to work. Get your pack," he said.

3 | Thinking we were going on an adventure, just the two of us, I hurried to get my gear—a coat, blanket, food, flashlight, and my phone. My nerves were buzzing with excitement as I climbed into my uncle's dusty pick-up truck, and we headed toward the herd, bumping along on the dirt trail.

4 | When we reached the top of the ridge, he put the truck in park and left the engine idling. "You make camp under that big oak tree and keep an eye out. If you see any coyotes, call me on your phone. I am going to drive around the perimeter of the ranch. I will be back in an hour or two."

5 | I stared at him in disbelief. Was he crazy? I could not believe he wanted me to sit alone in the dark with nothing but the rustling of the cattle to keep me company. I started to object, but then thought the better of it. I did not want to fail my first assignment before it even started. Slowly, I climbed down from the truck and headed toward the tree.

6 | The first fifteen minutes or so passed rather quickly. I busied myself making a small camp. Then, I ran out of tasks, and the boredom set in. I started checking my watch every thirty seconds it seemed, which was a terrible idea. Then I started counting cows, but that made me sleepy. If my uncle did not return soon, I feared madness would set in. A plan began to form in the far corners of my mind. I could force my uncle to return with one phone call. It would not be a lie exactly. It was dark out there, and a shadow could look like anything. I picked up my phone and dialed my uncle's number. "Yeah?" he answered.

7 | "I think I saw something near the cattle, and they seem a little spooked."

8 | "I'll be right there," he said.

9 | When he returned, he asked me to take him to the spot where I had seen the coyote. I chose a random spot to cement my story. My uncle squatted near the ground, looking for paw prints. "I don't see anything," he said, eyeing me skeptically.

10 | The next night proceeded in much the same way. By the third night, I had settled into the routine. My uncle dropped me off at the tree and left for his perimeter drive. I had just finished writing my name in the dirt with a stick, when my eye sensed movement at the far edge of the herd. The cattle lowed and shifted. I got up and crept along the edge of the herd. Soon, the full moon revealed the yellow eyes of a coyote staring hungrily through the darkness. I took off running toward the tree while trying to dial my uncle at the same time. He picked up, "Yeah?" I yelled, "Coyote!" After two nights of false alarms, my uncle did not react with concern. "I'm almost done with my drive. I'll be there in thirty or forty minutes. Sit tight." When he hung up, I fought hard to blink back tears for the calf that would reap the consequences of my lies.

Skill Review (continued)

1. What is the narrative point of view of the story?

   A. first person
   B. limited third person
   C. objective third person
   D. third person

2. Which character is primary?

   A. Rachel
   B. mom
   C. Uncle Cos
   D. sibling

3. Read the following sentence from the text:

   I had just finished writing my name in the dirt with a stick, when my eye sensed movement at the far edge of the herd.

   To which sense does it appeal?

   A. smell
   B. taste
   C. sight
   D. sound

4. Read the following sentence from the text:

   "I think I saw something near the cattle, and they seem a little spooked."

   Which word is the BEST example of precise language?

   A. something
   B. near
   C. cattle
   D. spooked

5. Read the following sentence from the text:

   After two nights of false alarms, my uncle did not react with concern.

   Which part of the sentence is an example of a time transition?

   A. After two nights
   B. of false alarms
   C. my uncle did not
   D. react with concern

6. In which paragraph does the narrator reflect on the significance of the story's events?

   A. 1
   B. 3
   C. 6
   D. 10

Skill Practice

Directions: Using the narrative planning chart that you completed in your notebook, write a narrative text in the space below.

Establish the exposition by defining the narrative point of view, introducing the primary character and important secondary characters, and describing the setting.

Organize the sequence of events naturally and logically through rising action, the climax, and falling action. Use appropriate transitions to convey sequence, show shifts in time or setting, or illustrate relationships among events.

Develop the characters and plot through narrative techniques such as dialogue, pacing, precise language, description, and sensory language.

Provide a conclusion that follows and reflects on the narrated events.

Skill Practice (continued)

WRITING PRACTICE

Text Types and Purposes

Directions: Write an argument, informative or explanatory text, or narrative in response to one of the prompts below. As needed, review Lesson 7.1, 7.2, 7.3, 8.1, 8.2, and 8.3 for help with planning, writing strategies, text structure, and revising and editing.

ARGUMENT

People often form strong opinions on various issues based on their personal experiences with those issues. For example, a person who has dealt with high medical costs may hold a strong opinion about health insurance. Choose a past personal experience that caused you to form a strong opinion. Using this experience to introduce your claim, write a formal argument in which you support your claim with logical reasons and evidence. Make sure to use clear transitions, address counterclaims, and provide a conclusion.

INFORMATIVE OR EXPLANATORY TEXT

Personal experiences often lead people to learn new information or skills. For example, if a child joins a soccer team, a parent may begin studying the game. If a driver has a flat tire, he or she may learn to change a tire in order to be prepared next time. Choose a personal experience you have had that led you to learn new information or develop a new skill. Using this experience to introduce your topic, write a formal informative or explanatory text in which you organize concepts into broader categories and support your ideas with relevant facts, details, and examples. Provide a conclusion and use clear transitions, precise language, domain-specific vocabulary, and headings, as needed.

NARRATIVE TEXT

A narrative text often ends with a reflection about the significance of the events in the story. Choose a personal experience from which you learned an important life lesson. For example, you may have learned a lesson about telling the truth after telling a lie. Using this experience, write a narrative text in which you establish a point of view, introduce characters, and organize a logical sequence of events. Include an exposition, rising action, a climax, falling action, and a resolution. Make sure to use narrative techniques such as dialogue, pacing, transitions, precise language, description, and sensory language. Provide a conclusion in which the narrator or primary character reflects on the meaning of the narrated events.

Review

WRITING PRACTICE

_____

_____

_____

_____

_____

_____

_____

_____

_____

_____

_____

_____

_____

_____

_____

_____

_____

_____

_____

_____

_____

_____

_____

_____

Writing, Part I

This Posttest will help you evaluate whether you are ready to move up to the next level of test preparation. It has two parts. Part I consists of 50 multiple-choice questions that test the grammar, usage, and organization skills covered in this book. Part II contains an essay writing activity.

Directions: Choose the <u>one best answer</u> to each question. Some of the sentences contain errors in organization, sentence structure, usage, or mechanics. A few sentences, however, may be correct as written. Read the sentences carefully and then answer the questions based on them. For each question, choose the answer that would result in the most effective writing of the sentence or sentences.

When you have completed the test, check your work with the answers and explanations on pages 288–289. Use the evaluation chart on page 290 to determine which areas you need to review.

Writing

1. Tim hosts unusual, interesting, and fun beach party's every summer.

   Which correction should be made to this sentence?

   A. change hosts to hosting
   B. change beach to beech
   C. change party's to parties
   D. change summer to Summer

2. Floyd's Furniture Store sold three chairs, a bookcase, and two couches today but Floyd says business is bad.

   Which is the best way to write the underlined portion of the sentence? If the original is the best way, choose option A.

   A. chairs, a bookcase, and two couches today but
   B. chairs a bookcase and two couches today but
   C. chairs, a bookcase, and two couches, today but
   D. chairs, a bookcase, and two couches today, but

3. The press release said that senator Salazar will, as usual, be in his home district in late summer.

   Which correction should be made to this sentence?

   A. change press release to Press Release
   B. change senator to Senator
   C. remove the commas before and after as usual
   D. insert a comma after said

4. Our supervisor asked whose responsible for the area east of Chatworth Lane.

   Which correction should be made to this sentence?

   A. replace Our with Are
   B. change supervisor to Supervisor
   C. replace whose with who's
   D. change east to East

5. The dog growled at Jo and me, then he rubbed his head against my hand.

   Which is the best way to write the underlined portion of the sentence? If the original is the best way, choose option A.

   A. growled at Jo and me, then he rubbed
   B. growled at Jo and I, then he rubbed
   C. growled at Jo and me. Then he rubbed
   D. growled at Jo and I. Then he rubbed

6. The cdc recommends that everyone get a flu shot.

   Which correction should be made to this sentence?

   A. change flu to Flu
   B. change cdc to CDC
   C. change the period to an exclamation point
   D. insert a comma after recommends

7. Either William or his <u>wife have taken care of Yoko's</u> baby more than I can remember.

Which is the best way to write the underlined portion of the sentence? If the original is the best way, choose option A.

A. wife have taken care of Yoko's
B. wife have took care of Yoko's
C. wife has taken care of Yokos
D. wife has taken care of Yoko's

8. Patricia felt angrily when she learned that Howard had quit his job.

Which correction should be made to this sentence?
A. replace <u>angrily</u> with <u>angry</u>
B. replace <u>she</u> with <u>her</u>
C. replace <u>his</u> with <u>their</u>
D. change <u>learned</u> to <u>learns</u>

9. My neighbors, who don't ever seem to sleep, have went on a vacation to Finland.

Which correction should be made to this sentence?
A. replace <u>My</u> with <u>Mine</u>
B. replace <u>who</u> with <u>whom</u>
C. change <u>have</u> to <u>has</u>
D. change <u>went</u> to <u>gone</u>

10. The rules state that <u>each runner must have their own number and</u> be at the starting line at noon.

Which is the best way to write the underlined portion of the sentence? If the original is the best way, choose option A.

A. each runner must have their own number and
B. each runner must have had their own number and
C. each runner must have his or her own number and
D. each runner must has his or her own number, and

11. Last week, <u>not only Marla and also John wrote</u> letters to the town's newspaper complaining about poor police protection.

Which is the best way to write the underlined portion of the sentence? If the original is the best way, choose option A.

A. not only Marla and also John wrote
B. not only Marla but also John wrote
C. not only Marla, and also John, wrote
D. not only Marla, but also John wrote

Writing

Directions: Questions 12 through 19 refer to the following memo.

To: All Metalcraft Employees
From: Teresa Rodriguez, CEO
Re: Environmental Issues

(A)

1   Now we are expanding our efforts even more. (2) As you know, Metalcraft has always been concerned about environmental issues. (3) I am pleased to announce the following ways in which Metalcraft will become even more friendly to the environment. (4) Partnering with several conservation groups, the Beechtree River will be cleaned up. (5) Those of you who like to fish will be happy to hear that the state has agreed to stock the river with trout as soon as the water quality improves. (6) Of course, fish is better for you than red meat. (7) We are also looking for volunteers to help work on the wetlands project. (8) We need people now to help build the ponds and to monitor water quality.

(B)

9   We will no longer provide disposable foam coffee cups, but we will provide coffee mugs for everyone. (10) You will no longer freeze in August because the air conditioner will be set to a warmer temperature! (11) Even though you will have to wash your cup each day, we will eliminate tons of landfill garbage. (12) We will use unbleached coffee filters and paper towels to avoid adding poisonous dioxin to the atmosphere. (13) We will also reduce the amount of energy we use for heating and air conditioning.

(C)

14   In conclusion, let me say thank you to everyone. (15) Who is ready to deal with a few small inconveniences for an important cause.

(D)

16   My goal is to see Metalcraft become one of the most environmentally friendly companies in the United States. (17) With your help, I know we can reach that goal.

---

12. Sentence 1: Now we are expanding our efforts even more.

    Which revision should be made to the placement of sentence 1?

    A. Move sentence 1 to follow sentence 2.
    B. Move sentence 1 to the end of paragraph B.
    C. Move sentence 1 to the beginning of paragraph D.
    D. Remove sentence 1.

13. Sentence 4: Partnering with several conservation groups, the Beechtree River will be cleaned up.

    Which is the best way to write the underlined portion of sentence 4? If the original is the best way, choose option (A).

    A. the Beechtree River will be cleaned up
    B. the Beechtree River will be cleaned up by us
    C. the cleanup of the Beechtree River will take place
    D. we will clean up the Beechtree River

14. Which revision would improve the effectiveness of the memo?

Begin a new paragraph with

A. sentence 3.
B. sentence 4.
C. sentence 7.
D. sentence 17.

15. Sentence 6: Of course, fish is better for you than red meat.

Which revision should be made to the placement of sentence 6?

A. Move sentence 6 to follow sentence 4.
B. Move sentence 6 to the beginning of paragraph B.
C. Move sentence 6 to the end of paragraph C.
D. Remove sentence 6.

16. Which sentence would be most effective if inserted at the beginning of paragraph B?

A. We advise you to cut back on the amount of coffee you drink.
B. We will also be making changes in the workplace to help the environment.
C. Do you know how bad foam cups are for the environment?
D. The process of bleaching paper creates deadly dioxin.

17. Sentence 10: You will no longer freeze in August because the air conditioner will be set to a warmer temperature!

Which revision should be made to the placement of sentence 10?

A. Move sentence 10 to follow sentence 11.
B. Move sentence 10 to the end of paragraph B.
C. Move sentence 10 to the beginning of paragraph C.
D. Remove sentence 10.

18. Sentences 14 and 15: In conclusion, <u>let me say thank you to everyone. Who is</u> ready to deal with a few small inconveniences for an important cause.

Which is the best way to write the underlined portion of sentences 14 and 15? If the original is the best way, choose option A.

A. let me say thank you to everyone. Who is
B. let I say thank you to everyone. Who is
C. let me say thank you to everyone, who are
D. let me say thank you to everyone who is

19. Which revision would improve the effectiveness of the memo?

A. Move paragraph A to follow paragraph B.
B. Move paragraph C to follow paragraph A.
C. Join paragraphs B and C.
D. Join paragraphs C and D.

Writing

Directions: Questions 20 through 27 refer to the following e-mail.

From: Personnel Department
Subject: Potential Applicants

(A)

1   We are a small company that is expanding quickly. (2) Thank you for your interest in Balthazar Robotics. (3)We design and manufacture robots for work and home use. (4) The robots we make will meet business and personal needs in a rapidly changing world.

(B)

5   We are looking for self-motivated applicants who were interested in growing with us. (6) Because we are a young company, there is a lot of room for promotion. (7) If you are an energetic worker who is looking to grow within a company, consider Balthazar Robotics. (8) Follow the directions below to apply.

(C)

9   Applications are available online or at our facility. (10) To find an application, go to www. balthazarrob.com. (11) Click on *Employment* to read job descriptions for open positions. (12) The application will pop up on your screen. (13) Complete the application, and attach a copy of your resume. (14) If you see a job you are interested in, click on *Apply Now*. (15) Hit *Send* to submit your application. (16) If you prefer, you can complete a paper application. (17) Print the online application, or pick up an application at the facility. (18) Then use black ink to complete the application. (19) Attach your resume. (20) Return your application by mail or in person.

(D)

21   We require interviews. (22) After we review your application, we will notify you to schedule an interview. (23) Some companies do not require interviews. (24) At that time, you should schedule an appointment with are personnel office.

---

20. Which revision would improve the effectiveness of paragraph A?

- **A.** Move sentence 2 to the beginning of paragraph A.
- **B.** Move sentence 2 to the end of paragraph A.
- **C.** Move sentence 4 to the end of paragraph B.
- **D.** Remove sentence 1.

21. Which sentence would be most effective if inserted at the beginning of paragraph B?

- **A.** Some of Balthazar's robots help around the house by doing chores.
- **B.** Balthazar Robotics has an exercise room for energetic employees who want a good workout.
- **C.** Right now, Balthazar Robotics is hiring personnel in the manufacturing division of our fast-growing company.
- **D.** In the future, most people will have robots at home and at work.

Writing

22. Sentence 5: We are looking for self-motivated applicants who were interested in growing with us.

Which revision should be made to sentence 5?

A. change <u>applicant</u> to <u>applicant's</u>
B. insert a comma after <u>who</u>
C. replace <u>were</u> with <u>are</u>
D. replace <u>growing</u> with <u>grew</u>

23. Which sentence would be most effective if inserted at the beginning of paragraph C?

A. You can submit a resume instead of a job application.
B. Everyone who wants to apply should have access to a computer.
C. Job descriptions are posted online.
D. First, you will need to complete an application.

24. Sentence 14: If you see a job you are interested in, click on *Apply Now*.

Which revision should be made to the placement of sentence 14?

A. Move sentence 14 to the beginning of paragraph C.
B. Move sentence 14 to follow sentence 11.
C. Move sentence 14 to follow sentence 17.
D. Remove sentence 14.

25. Which revision would improve the effectiveness of the e-mail?

Begin a new paragraph with

A. sentence 13.
B. sentence 16.
C. sentence 18.
D. sentence 22.

26. Sentence 23: Some companies do not require interviews.

Which revision should be made to the placement of sentence 23?

A. Move sentence 23 to follow sentence 15.
B. Move sentence 23 to follow sentence 21.
C. Move sentence 23 to the end of paragraph D.
D. Remove sentence 23.

27. Sentence 24: At that time, you should schedule an appointment with are personnel office.

Which correction should be made to sentence 23?

A. change <u>should schedule</u> to <u>should have scheduled</u>
B. remove the comma after <u>time</u>
C. replace <u>are</u> with <u>our</u>
D. change <u>personnel</u> to <u>personnels'</u>

Writing

28. In today's paper, there is several articles about community programs.

Which is the best way to write the underlined portion of the sentence? If the original is the best way, choose option A.

A. In today's paper, there is several article
B. In todays paper, there is several articles
C. In todays paper, there are several articles
D. In today's paper, there are several articles

29. The governor feels strongly that solutions to this city's serious problems must come from we citizens.

Which is the best way to write the underlined portion of the sentence? If the original is the best way, choose option A.

A. this city's serious problems must come from we citizens
B. this city's serious problems must come from us citizens
C. this citys serious problems must come from us citizens
D. this city's seriously problems must come from we citizens

30. Give those extra bags to Terry and I; we will recycle them.

Which correction should be made to this sentence?

A. replace those with that
B. replace I with me
C. replace we with us
D. replace them with they

31. An organized planner, Javier knows how many people have sent in their reservations.

Which is the best way to place an appositive the sentence? If the original is the best way, choose option A.

A. An organized planner, Javier knows
B. An organized planner, Javier, knows
C. An organized planner Javier, knows,
D. An organized planner Javier knows

32. Laura realized that she canceled her credit card before she could buy Toshio a birthday gift.

Which is the best way to write the underlined portion of the sentence? If the original is the best way, choose option A.

A. realized that she canceled her credit card
B. she realized that she canceled her credit card
C. realizes that she canceled her credit card
D. realized that she had canceled her credit card

33. Kathy can now having recovered from a bad cold enjoy life again.

The most effective revision of the sentence would begin with which group of words?

A. Enjoying life again, Kathy
B. Having recovered from a bad cold, Kathy
C. Kathy can now enjoy
D. Kathy, enjoying life again, can now

34. The efficiency expert said that the engine room should have more workers and fewer contraptions. The efficiency expert studies plant operation.

Which word does not fit with the tone of the paragraph?

A. expert
B. workers
C. contraptions
D. plant

36. The belief that many experts think is true is that California will suffer another earthquake within 10 years.

Which is the best way to write the underlined portion of the sentence? If the original is the best way, choose option A..

A. The belief that many experts think is true is
B. The belief held by a majority of distinguished experts is
C. Many experts believe
D. It is true

35. After Todd will announce his plans to marry Danita, he bought a ring and planned an engagement party.

Which is the best way to write the underlined portion of the sentence? If the original is the best way, choose option A.

A. Todd will announce his plans to marry Danita,
B. Todd had announced his plans to marry Danita,
C. Todd announces his plans to marry Danita,
D. Todd was announcing his plans to marry Danita,

37. Because we had planned to fly out today, our flight was canceled.

Which is the best way to write the underlined portion of the sentence? If the original is the best way, choose option A.

A. Because we had planned to fly out today,
B. Because we had planned to fly out today
C. Although we had planned to fly out today
D. Although we had planned to fly out today,

Writing

Directions: Questions 38 through 45 refer to the following letter.

Dear Coworkers,

(A)

1   I know how much you will have enjoyed the fettuccine Alfredo that I brought to the company potluck. (2) Since many of you wanted the recipe, I am including it in this letter. (3) It is fairly simple to make and also vegetarian.

(B)

4   I hope you will enjoy making and serving the fettuccine Alfredo as much as I do. (5) First, you need to gather all the ingredients. (6) You will need the following: 1 pound of fettuccine; 1 pint of heavy cream; 1 cup (1 stick) butter; 1 cup freshly grated Parmesan cheese (about 5 ounces); and 2 egg yolks. (7) After you gather the ingredients, you are ready to begin cooking. (8) Bring 3 or 4 quarts of water to a boil. (9) Add the fettuccine and cook, stirring occasionally, for about 8–10 minutes. (10) At the same time, heat the cream until it just begins to simmer. (11) Then stir in the cheese, a little at a time. (12) When all the butter is melted, remove the sauce from the heat. (13) Continue to stir the cheese and cream mixture over a low heat for about 10 minutes. (14) Then add the butter, little by little. (15) Beat a small amount of sauce into the egg yolks, pour the egg yolk mixture back into the sauce, and you can stir the sauce thoroughly. (16) Season the sauce with salt and pepper to taste. (17) Some people believe that salt should not be added to food because having too much salt is not healthy.

(C)

18   Serve your fettuccine Alfredo immediately and enjoy! (19) Drain the pasta, and transfer the hot noodles to a large pasta bowl. (20) Pour on the creamy sauce, and mix until all the noodles are coated.

Christina

---

38. Sentence 1: I know how much <u>you will have enjoyed the fettuccine Alfredo</u> that I brought to the company potluck.

Which is the best way to write the underlined portion of sentence 1? If the original is the best way, choose option (A).

- **A.** you will have enjoyed the fettuccine Alfredo
- **B.** you enjoy the fettuccine Alfredo
- **C.** you enjoyed the fettuccine Alfredo
- **D.** you had enjoyed the fettuccine Alfredo

39. Sentence 4: I hope you will enjoy making and serving the fettuccine Alfredo as much as I do.

Which revision should be made to the placement of sentence 4?

- **A.** Move sentence 4 to follow sentence 1.
- **B.** Move sentence 4 to the end of paragraph A.
- **C.** Move sentence 4 to follow sentence 5.
- **D.** Move sentence 4 to the end of paragraph B.

Writing

40. Which revision would improve the effectiveness of the letter?

Begin a new paragraph with

A. sentence 7.
B. sentence 11.
C. sentence 15.
D. sentence 16.

41. Sentence 12: When all the butter is melted, remove the sauce from the heat.

Which revision should be made to the placement of sentence 12?

A. Move sentence 12 to follow sentence 14.
B. Move sentence 12 to follow sentence 15.
C. Move sentence 12 to the beginning of paragraph C.
D. Remove sentence 12.

42. Sentence 15: Beat a small amount of sauce into the egg yolks, <u>pour the egg yolk mixture back into the sauce, and you can stir the sauce thoroughly.</u>

Which is the best way to write the underlined portion of sentence 1? If the original is the best way, choose option (A).

A. pour the egg yolk mixture back into the sauce, and you can stir the sauce thoroughly
B. pour the egg yolk mixture back into the sauce and stirring the sauce thoroughly
C. pour the egg yolk mixture back into the sauce, and stir the sauce thoroughly
D. pouring the egg yolk mixture back into the sauce, and you can stir the sauce thoroughly

43. Sentence 17: Some people believe that salt should not be added to food because having too much salt is not healthy.

Which revision should be made to the placement of sentence 17?

A. Move sentence 17 to follow sentence 9.
B. Move sentence 17 to follow sentence 15.
C. Move sentence 17 to the beginning of paragraph C.
D. Remove sentence 17.

44. Which sentence would be most effective if inserted at the beginning of paragraph C?

A. Once the sauce is done and the pasta is cooked, it is time to combine them.
B. Fettuccine Alfredo is a popular pasta dish.
C. Eating vegetarian food, like fettuccine Alfredo, is healthy.
D. Serve a fresh garden salad and garlic bread with your fettuccine Alfredo.

45. Sentence 18: Serve your fettuccine Alfredo immediately and enjoy!

Which revision should be made to the placement of sentence 18?

A. Move sentence 18 to follow sentence 19.
B. Move sentence 18 to the end of paragraph B.
C. Move sentence 18 to the end of paragraph C.
D. Remove sentence 18.

Writing

46. The apartment manager and the building owner both signed the letter; <u>he said that he was sorry</u> that the rent had to be raised.

    Which is the best way to write the underlined portion of the text? If the original is the best way, choose option (A).
    A. he said that he was sorry
    B. the letter said that he was sorry
    C. they said that he was sorry
    D. the letter said that the owner was sorry

47. When Christy learned about her raise she was thrilled.

    Which correction should be made to this sentence?
    A. change <u>learned</u> to <u>learns</u>
    B. insert a comma after <u>raise</u>
    C. replace <u>her</u> with <u>hers</u>
    D. change <u>was</u> to <u>is</u>

48. Dr. Sanford's theory is that it is better to deal with a problem than to ignore it, I would rather ignore it.

    Which correction should be made to this sentence?
    A. change <u>Sanford's</u> to <u>sanford's</u>
    B. replace <u>than</u> with <u>then</u>
    C. remove the comma
    D. replace the comma with a semicolon

49. Blowing at more than 70 miles per hour, <u>trees were knocked down and cars were tossed around.</u>

    Which is the best way to write the underlined portion of the sentence? If the original is the best way, choose option (A).
    A. trees were knocked down and cars were tossed around
    B. trees were knocked down, and cars were tossed around
    C. the wind knocked down trees and tossed around cars
    D. the wind knocked down trees, and tossed around cars

50. Which sentence best shows cause and effect order?

    A. The players warmed up, practiced, and prepared, so they won the big game.
    B. Some players warmed up and practiced, but others only prepared for the big game.
    C. The players warmed up. Likewise, they practiced for the big game.
    D. Some players warmed up, practiced, prepared, and went to the big game.

Writing, Part II

This part of the Posttest is designed to find out how well you write.

Essay Directions:

Look at the box on the following page. In the box is your assigned topic.

Write a short essay on the assigned topic. Keep track of how long it takes you to complete your essay. You should take only 45 minutes to write your essay.

Keep in mind as you write that your essay should have the following:

- A well-focused main idea
- Clear progression of ideas and helpful transitions
- Specific development of ideas that are clearly connected to the main idea
- Control of usage, sentence structure, word choice, punctuation, and spelling

Writing

TOPIC

A century ago, the average human life span was 50 years. Now some scientists believe that children born today could live to be 110 years old. Would you like to live to be 110 years old?

In your essay, tell whether you would want to live to age 110 or beyond. Explain the positive and negative factors of living so long. Use your personal observations, experiences, and knowledge.

Part II is a test to determine how well you can use written language to explain your ideas.

In preparing your essay, you should take the following steps:

- Read the **DIRECTIONS** and the **TOPIC** carefully.

- Plan your essay before you write. Use scratch paper to make any notes and write down any important ideas.

- After you finish writing your essay, reread what you have written and make any changes that will improve your essay.

- Make sure your essay is long enough to develop the topic adequately.

Evaluation guidelines are on page 292.

Answer Key

1. **C.** To form the plural of a base word that ends in *y*, drop the *y* and add *ies*.

2. **D.** This is a compound sentence joined by the conjunction *but*. A comma is needed before the conjunction.

3. **B.** *Senator* is used as the title of a specific person, so it should be capitalized.

4. **C.** *Whose* shows possession. The meaning in this sentence is *who is*, so the correct word is the contraction *who's*.

5. **C.** This sentence contains a comma splice. To correct it, separate the two independent clauses into two sentences.

6. **B.** The letters CDC are an abbreviation for the organization called the Centers for Disease Control and Prevention and should be capitalized.

7. **D.** When the parts of a compound subject are singular and separated by *or*, the verb should also be singular.

8. **A.** In this sentence, *felt* is used as a linking verb, so the adjective form, *angry*, should be used.

9. **D.** The helping verb *have* tells you to use the past participle. The correct past participle of the irregular verb *go* is *gone*.

10. **C.** *Their* is plural, so it cannot refer to the singular noun *runner*.

11. **B.** *Not only* and *but also* go together to form a conjunction. There is no comma used when you use *not only* and *but also* together. *Not only . . . and* is always incorrect.

12. **A.** The information in sentence 1 must come after the information in sentence 2 to make sense in the paragraph.

13. **D.** *Partnering with several conservation groups* is a dangling modifier. It needs to modify a noun or a pronoun. In this case, it modifies *we*.

14. **B.** Sentence 4 tells the main idea for all of the other sentences in the paragraph, which is about the plans the company is making to help conserve the environment.

15. **D.** A sentence about the nutritional value of fish versus red meat does not belong in a paragraph about cleaning up a river so it will support aquatic life.

16. **B.** B tells the main idea for all of the other sentences in the paragraph, which is about internal changes the company is making to conserve the environment.

17. **B.** Since sentence 10 gives more information about air conditioning, it should follow sentence 13. Sentence 10 should be at the end of paragraph B.

18. **D.** Sentence 15 is a sentence fragment. Combining it with sentence 14 corrects the fragment by turning it into a dependent clause.

19. **D.** Both paragraph C and D have the same main idea so they should be one paragraph. They are both part of the memo's conclusion.

20. **A.** Sentence 2 states the main idea that all the other sentences in the paragraph give details about; therefore, it should be the first sentence in the paragraph.

21. **C.** C is a topic sentence for the paragraph. It introduces the paragraph by stating the main idea that all the other sentences in the paragraph give details about.

22. **C.** The first verb, *are looking*, is present tense, so the sentence is present tense. The second verb also needs to be present tense.

23. **D.** Paragraph C tells how to apply for a job. D is a topic sentence that gives the main idea for the paragraph.

24. **B.** Sentence 14 tells what you should do right after you read the job descriptions so it should follow sentence 11.

25. **B.** Sentence 16 begins a new main idea. The preceding sentences tell how to get an application and apply online. Sentence 16 and the following sentences tell how to apply if you do not want to apply online.

26. **D.** This sentence should not be in the paragraph. It does not tell about the main idea or how to apply for a job. What other companies do is irrelevant.

27. **C.** *Are* is a verb. The word needed here is *our*, which is a possessive adjective that describes the following noun.

28. **D.** The subject of this sentence is the plural noun *articles*, which requires a plural verb.

29. **B.** *We* is a subject pronoun. In this sentence the pronoun is the object of the preposition *from*, so the object pronoun *us* is needed.

30. **B.** In this sentence, the subject pronoun *I* is used incorrectly. The object pronoun *me* is needed to follow the preposition *to*.

Answer Key

31. A. The appositive phrase is "An organized planner." It is set off with a comma, so choice A is correct.

32. D. The canceling of the credit card occurred in the past before another action, so it should be in the past perfect tense, *had canceled.*

33. B. *Having recovered from a bad cold* describes *Kathy.* It should be placed next to the noun it describes.

34. C. Contraptions is an informal, or slang word, so it does not fit with the formal tone of the rest of the paragraph.

35. B. The announcement occurred before another past action; therefore, it should be described in the past perfect tense.

36. C. The underlined words are repetitive. C removes the repetition without changing the meaning.

37. D. The conjunction *because* suggests an incorrect cause-effect relationship between the two clauses. *Although* correctly expresses a contrast between the two parts of the sentence. The introductory dependent clause must be followed by a comma.

38. C. The coworkers enjoyed the fettuccine in the past because the past tense verb *brought* is used in the sentence. Therefore, the past tense verb *enjoyed* must also be used.

39. B. Sentence 4 supports the main idea in paragraph A. It is not about how to make fettuccine. Sentence 4 should be the concluding sentence of paragraph A.

40. A. Sentence 7 begins a new idea so it should begin a new paragraph. One paragraph should tell about the ingredients. A new paragraph should begin with the directions for cooking the pasta.

41. A. Sentence 12 tells what you do after the butter is melted. To make sense sequentially, it has to follow sentence 14, which tells when you add the butter.

42. C. C makes the sentence have a parallel structure because it uses the imperative form of all three verbs (*beat, pour, stir*).

43. D. Sentence 17 should not be included in the paragraph because the paragraph is not about whether salt is healthy. It is about a recipe with salt as one of the ingredients.

44. A. A is a good topic sentence for this paragraph because it tells what all the other sentences are about.

45. C. Sentence 18 should move to the end of paragraph C because it is a conclusion sentence for the paragraph. It does not make sense at the beginning of the paragraph.

46. D. It is not clear to whom *he* refers, nor is it clear who was sorry or whether it was said in person or in the letter. D makes it clear that *he* refers to the owner and that the apology was in the letter.

47. B. An introductory dependent clause should be followed by a comma to separate it from the main clause.

48. D. This is a compound sentence without a conjunction joining the two independent clauses. If there is no conjunction, you use a semicolon and not a comma to join the two independent clauses.

49. C. *Blowing at more than 70 miles per hour* is a dangling participle. To fix it, you need to add something to the sentence for it to modify. In this case, the participle can modify the noun *wind.* No comma should separate the two parts of the compound predicate.

50. A. The word "so" indicates a cause-and-effect order. Choices B and C are in comparison-contrast order. Choice D is a list of events.

Part 1: Evaluation Chart

Check Your Understanding

On the following chart, circle the number of any question you answered incorrectly. Next to each group of question numbers, you will see the pages you can review to learn how to answer the questions correctly. Pay particular attention to reviewing skill areas in which you missed half or more of the questions.

Skill Area	Item Number	Review Pages
Sentences	18	16–23
Nouns and pronouns	1, 4, 29, 30	24–37
Verbs and verb tenses	9, 22, 32, 35, 38	44–59
Subject-verb agreement	7, 10, 28	60–69
Adjectives and adverbs	8	76–85
Modifying phrases	31	86–91
Capitalization	3, 6	98–107
Punctuation	47, 48	108–117
Spelling	27	118–129
Combine ideas in sentences	2, 5, 11, 33, 37	136–145
Write effective sentences	13, 42, 46, 49	146–155
Style and diction	36	156–165
Paragraph structure and topic sentences	12, 14, 15, 16, 17, 19, 20, 21, 23, 25, 26, 39, 40, 43, 44	172–179
Tone and diction	34	180–185
Order of importance and time order	24, 41, 45	186–195
Cause-and-effect order and compare-and-contrast order	50	196–205

Writing

Part II Evaluation Guidelines

If possible, give your instructor your essay to evaluate. You will find his or her objective opinion helpful in deciding whether you are ready to begin preparing for a writing test. If this is not possible, have another student evaluate your essay. If you cannot find another student to help you, review your essay yourself. If you do this, it is usually better to let your essay sit for a few days before you evaluate it. This way you will have similar views as someone reading your essay for the first time. No matter which way you review your work, use the checklist on the next page to guide you.

After you have evaluated your essay using the checklist, look at the number you checked for each question. Pay attention to the questions where you checked a 2 or a 1—these scores indicate that you need some extra practice in certain writing skills. Studying the following sections will help you to raise your score:

1. If you had trouble answering the question that is asked in the writing prompt, pay attention to pages 172–179.

2. If you had trouble organizing your ideas, pay attention to Chapter 6.

3. If you had trouble supporting your main idea with details or examples, pay attention to pages 172–179.

4. If you had trouble writing words and sentences correctly and varying sentence structure and word choice, pay attention to Chapters 1–5.

If possible, talk to your instructor, another student, or a friend about your writing. Together you will be able to identify your current writing strengths as well as any weaknesses. Based on this combined evaluation, review the sections in this book that will help you most to improve your writing.

ESSAY SCORING CHECKLIST

A. Does your essay address the question in the writing prompt with a clear main idea and stay on topic?

☐ **1.** No, my essay does not answer the question, has a weak main idea, and does not stay on topic.

☐ **2.** My essay has a clear main idea that addresses the question, but it also includes some points that are not directly related to the main idea.

☐ **3.** Yes, my essay has a clear main idea that addresses the question, and all subtopics connect to the main idea.

☐ **4.** Yes, my essay has a strong main idea that addresses the question, and subtopics that reveal thoughtful connections to the main idea.

B. Are the ideas in your essay well organized, with enough subtopics and transitions?

☐ **1.** No, the ideas in my essay are not in any order, and there are no subtopics or transitions.

☐ **2.** My essay shows some planning, but it does not contain enough subtopics and transitions.

☐ **3.** Yes, the ideas in my essay are logically connected with more than one subtopic and a few transitions.

☐ **4.** Yes, my essay is well organized with multiple subtopics and effective transitions.

C. Do the paragraphs in your essay contain details that support the main idea, and are connections between details and main idea stated clearly?

☐ **1.** No, many of the paragraphs in my essay contain details that don't support the main idea, or many of the paragraphs don't have any details at all.

☐ **2.** Many of the paragraphs contain sufficient supporting details, but the connections between details and main idea are not stated.

☐ **3.** Yes, the paragraphs in my essay contain relevant and concrete details, and the connections between details and main idea are stated but simple.

☐ **4.** Yes, the paragraphs in my essay contain excellent relevant details, and the connections between details and main idea are fully explained.

D. Do the sentences in your essay display variety in word choice and structure as well as correct usage, punctuation, and spelling?

☐ **1.** No, the sentences in my essay are not worded correctly or varied in structure, and most of them contain errors in usage, punctuation, and spelling.

☐ **2.** The sentences in my essay contain appropriate but vague words, basic sentence structure, some errors in punctuation and spelling, and many errors in usage.

☐ **3.** Yes, the sentences in my essay vary somewhat in structure, include appropriate and specific words, and contain only a few small errors in usage, punctuation, and spelling.

☐ **4.** Yes, the sentences in my essay display excellent word choice, great variety in structure, and almost no errors in usage.

Answer Key

CHAPTER 1 Sentence Basics

Lesson 1.1

Think about Writing, page 19
1. The team's <u>manager</u> <u>should win</u> an award.
2. <u>Everyone</u> <u>has ordered</u> something different to eat.
3. <u>Andrej</u> <u>searched</u> his pockets for his car keys.
4. <u>Mr. and Mrs. Hastings</u> <u>complained</u> about the defective lamp.
5. The old run-down <u>bus</u> <u>pulled</u> slowly out of the station.

Think about Writing, page 20
1. S   6. F
2. S   7. F
3. F   8. S
4. S   9. F
5. S   10. S

Think about Writing, page 21
1. Brian slowly got to his feet ____.____
2. Be careful with that lawn mower ____!____
3. Smoke is coming from the roof ____!____
4. Where did you find the book ____?____
5. Stop jumping on the bed ____!____
6. The train stops here every 15 minutes ____.____
7. Have you seen my radio ____?____
8. Ms. Luna left here at least 20 minutes ago ____.____
9. What a nightmare ____!____
10. Can you see her yet ____?____

Vocabulary Review, page 22
1. D.
2. A.
3. B.
4. E.
5. C.

Skill Review, page 22
1. F
2. S
3. S
4. F
5. F
6. S

Comparison and Contrast Chart: Sentences 1, 2, and 5 belong in the column labeled "Alike." Sentences 3 and 4 belong in the column labeled "Different."

Skill Practice, page 23
1. B. This sentence is asking a question. It should end with a question mark.
2. C. This sentence is a command. It expresses alarm or urgency and should end in an exclamation point.
3. A. This sentence is asking a question. It should end with a question mark.
4. B. Adding the phrase *Laws were passed* expresses a complete thought. None of the other options fix the fragment.
5. C. This group of words is missing a predicate. Adding the words *became jammed* fixes the fragment.
6. D. This group of words is missing a subject. The subject *wolves* fixes the fragment.

Writing Practice, page 23
Answers will vary. Make sure you follow the prompt and use a conjunction to join the two sentences.

Sample Response
Bart swims in short races that require a great deal of speed, but Brad swims in long-distance events where endurance is most important.

Lesson 1.2

Think about Writing, page 27
1. Last week he and Fernando installed new software on the department's computers.
2. The manager wants to begin regular meetings between himself and us.
3. Correct
4. When I opened the book, I noticed that its binding needs to be repaired.

Answer Key

(Lesson 1.2 cont.)

Think about Writing, page 30
Answers will vary.

Sample Answers:
Althea loves her dog Baron more than anything. Baron has a lot of energy and loves to run and play. Whenever Althea has time, she takes Baron to the park. If Althea doesn't take Baron out often enough, he gets bored and misbehaves. Baron has chewed Althea's shoes and nibbled on the corners of her old couch. Last week, Althea found a photo of her grandchildren torn to shreds. When Althea went to scold Baron, she found him curled up and napping on her bed. One look at Baron's sweet wrinkled face melted Althea's heart. She couldn't stay mad at Baron.

Think about Writing, page 32
1. whomever
2. Who
3. whoever
4. that
5. which

Vocabulary Review, page 32
1. C.
2. F.
3. A.
4. B.
5. D.
6. G.
7. E.

Skill Review, pages 33–34
1. **D.** *Mother's* is singular possessive, showing the mother's ownership (through attendance) of the college. It is not plural (*mothers*) nor is it a plural possessive (*mothers'*).
2. **B.** *Patriotism* cannot be experienced through the five human senses, while the other three answer choices can be seen or touched.
3. **C.** *Criteria* is an irregular plural; it does not take the suffix *–s* or *–es* or remain unchanged.
4. **A.** *Students'* is a plural possessive noun, showing the students' ownership of the excuse. It is not plural (*students*) nor is it singular possessive (*student's*).
5. **D.** The sentence requires a subject pronoun (*They*), not an objective pronoun (*them; us*) or a possessive pronoun (*her*).

6. **A.** The sentence requires an objective pronoun (*me*), not a subject pronoun (*he; I*) or a possessive pronoun (*theirs*).
7. **C.** The sentence requires a singular, third-person possessive pronoun (*his* or *her*), not a second-person possessive (*your*) or a third-person plural (*their*). *Its* does not refer to a person.
8. **D.** Keep the person consistent (*you*); do not change to third-person (*him, them, her*).
9. Answers will vary. Sample answer: Remove the bike from the van and fix the bike.
10. Answers will vary. Sample answer: Although Professor Barnes was smart, she did not make use of her intelligence.
11. **B.** Use a subject pronoun (*Who*); not an object pronoun (*whom; whomever*) nor a possessive pronoun (*whose*).
12. **D.** Use *that* for a restrictive clause that refers to an object; use *which* for a nonrestrictive clause; use *who* and *whom* when referring to people.

Skill Practice, page 35
1. My brother and I were bitten by mosquitoes, which appeared during the fireworks show.
2. She and Mary Beth reached their sales goals last month.
3. No one is going to like what Ms. Chang has to tell him or her about the new production schedule.
4. Gregory e-mailed Suzette's office yesterday, but Suzette didn't respond.
5. Sergio wants you and me to go to the training session with him.

Writing Practice, page 36
Answers will vary. You should have included at least two examples each of abstract, irregular plural, and possessive nouns spelled correctly. All pronoun usage should show or be edited to show correct case, agreement, and clarity.

Sample Response
They are going to have a lot of questions when I tell them about my new plan to improve my musical talent. I took your survey, and it seems I meet all the criteria for improvement. I'm lucky that I didn't inherit my mother's tone-deafness. My father's skill is something my sisters and I have admired since we were children.

Answer Key

Chapter 1 Review, pages 38–40

1. **D.** The original is a fragment. Option (D) creates a complete sentence by adding a subject.

2. **C.** The original is a fragment because it lacks a subject. *Himself* is the correct reflexive pronoun.

3. **C.** The original is a fragment because it does not express a complete thought. Option (C) provides a subject, *John*, and a predicate, *stayed home*.

4. **B.** The original is a fragment. The correction adds a simple subject, *fire*, and a predicate, *kept them warm*. (In the original, *fire* is an object.)

5. **D.** *Bookshelf* is made plural by changing the *f* to a *v* and adding *es*.

6. **D.** *Had jumped over a wall* is a fragment. Adding the subject pronoun *They* to the fragment makes it a complete sentence.

7. **D.** *It's* means "it is" or "it has." The possessive pronoun *its* is needed.

8. **D.** The pronoun follows a preposition, *with*, and therefore should be an object pronoun.

9. **B.** It's not clear who *she* refers to, so replacing *she* with *Carla* clears up the confusion. The second sentence is an exclamation, so it needs to end with an exclamation point.

10. **D.** This is an exclamatory sentence and needs to end with an exclamation point.

11. **C.** *Who* is correct because it is a subject pronoun that goes with the verb *ate*. *Whom* is an object pronoun.

12. **D.** Part of this sentence is understood. Read it as "he shoots better than she shoots." *She* is correct because it is a subject pronoun; *her* is an object pronoun.

13. **A.** *Us* is an object pronoun. Here the pronoun is the subject, so use *we*.

14. **C.** The original is a fragment because it does not express a complete thought. Option (C) provides a predicate, *was cold*.

15. The paragraph should follow the prompt and use nouns and pronouns correctly.

Sample Paragraph

My friend and I both work out at the gym, but our activities are like day and night. I like being in the water, so I take all of the water aerobics classes and also swim laps, but she dislikes the water so she never gets near the pool. Instead, she takes the kick boxing and cycling classes. We do, however, take yoga and Zumba classes together. We agree that we are fortunate our gym has such a variety of activities to please the two of us.

Answer Key

CHAPTER 2 Verbs

Lesson 2.1

Think about Writing, page 45
Answers will vary. Sample answers:
1. Sidney <u>must come</u> to the table now.
2. My aunt <u>is living</u> in Canada.
3. Veronica <u>laughed</u> at the corny joke.
4. I <u>was</u> energized after my workout.
5. Meg and I <u>run</u> five miles every morning.

Think about Writing, page 48
1. called; <u>yesterday</u>
2. waits; <u>every afternoon</u>
3. moved; <u>two years ago</u>
4. enjoy; <u>always</u>
5. will work; <u>next week</u>
6. happened; <u>last night</u>
7. demand or are demanding; <u>Today's</u>
8. will end; <u>next Tuesday</u>
9. owns; <u>now</u>
10. talked; <u>yesterday</u>

Think about Writing, page 52
1. Brian <u>threw</u> out the runner trying to steal second.
2. The rain <u>freezes</u> as soon as it hits the pavement.
3. Please <u>give</u> this package to the delivery person.
4. I didn't know what she <u>meant</u> when she said she was skating home.
5. Jill's children <u>clung</u> tightly to her when she left home.
6. Dilip is the most helpful real estate agent I have ever <u>dealt</u> with.
7. Ms. Tso <u>swore</u> to the judge that she was telling the truth.

Think about Writing, page 54
1. will begin; *In two more weeks* tells you that this will happen in the future.
2. tastes; The present tense is used for action that is always true.
3. had taken; The past perfect form is correct because this action took place before another action.
4. will have swum; The future perfect shows that the action will be completed before another future action. By the time they finish the race, the action of swimming 20 miles will be completed.
5. have said; The present perfect is used to show an action that has taken place in the past and is still true in the present.

Think about Writing, page 55
1. complete
2. were
3. be drunk
4. were
5. pay

Think about Writing, page 56
1. My grandparents deserted the old house.
2. Large shrubs hide the doorway.
3. That fallen tree jammed the cellar door shut.
4. The wrecking crew will tear down the old house.

Think about Writing, page 57
1. rode, rides
2. had bought, discovered
3. began, was
4. will finish or will have finished, begins
5. was sweating, returned
6. hope, gave
7. has memorized, will open
8. reach, had tried
9. will have run, wake
10. had bitten, ran

Vocabulary Review, page 58
1. Down: common
2. Across: majority
3. Down: regular
4. Across: link
5. Across: verb

Skill Review, page 58
1. before; in the past
2. when; in the future
3. on; in the past
4. yesterday; in the past

Skill Practice, page 59
1. C. John was at the track before Javier crossed the finish line. Therefore, the verb *arrives* should be in the past perfect tense to show that this action occurred before the action of Javier's crossing the finish line.
2. C. When a verb ends with *ch*, an *es* instead of an *s* is added to form the simple present tense. *Reachs* should be *reaches*.
3. B. *Swear* is an irregular verb. The correct spelling of the past participle is *sworn*, not *swore*.

Answer Key

(Lesson 2.1 cont.)

4. **B.** This statement takes the subjunctive form of the verb *connect* because it expresses urgency. The subjunctive form does not add an *s* to the base form.

5. **C.** The verb *exchange* should be in the past tense, so the correct form is *exchanged*.

6. **C.** *After Ted gets his tax return* is in the future tense, so the verb *bought* should be changed to *will buy*.

Writing Practice, page 59
Answers will vary. Make sure you use verbs like the following: travel, traveled, will travel; see, saw, have seen, will see; enjoy, enjoyed, was enjoying, have visited.

Sample Paragraph
I love to go to the Finger Lakes in New York. I have been there every year since I was a child. My family always rents the same house on a lake. We like to kayak and to hike. One year we also toured some gorges.

Lesson 2.2

Think about Writing, page 62
1. Those <u>fish</u> (has, <u>have</u>) been jumping since we got here.
2. Our <u>problem</u> (<u>is</u>, are) getting the tent set up.
3. <u>We</u> in the jury (<u>believe</u>, believes) he is innocent.
4. My <u>muscles</u> (<u>ache</u>, aches) from all the exercise.
5. The security <u>guards</u> at the store (<u>want</u>, wants) a raise.
6. <u>I</u> (<u>come</u>, comes) to all my son's baseball games.
7. The <u>order</u> (include, <u>includes</u>) paper clips, folders, and tape.

Think about Writing, page 63
1. (<u>were</u>, was)
2. (<u>appear</u>, appears)
3. (are, <u>is</u>)
4. (plan, <u>plans</u>)
5. (has, <u>have</u>)
6. (give, <u>gives</u>)
7. (is, <u>are</u>)
8. (<u>complain</u>, complains)

Think about Writing, page 65
1. (<u>stand</u>, stands)
2. (is, <u>are</u>)
3. (waits, <u>wait</u>)
4. (stretch, <u>stretches</u>)
5. (<u>walk</u>, walks)
6. (is, <u>are</u>)
7. (grow, <u>grows</u>)
8. (<u>do</u>, <u>does</u>)

Think about Writing, page 66
1. (<u>argue</u>, argues)
2. (is, <u>are</u>)
3. (<u>need</u>, needs)
4. (<u>seems</u>, seem)
5. (<u>require</u>, requires)
6. (appear, <u>appears</u>)
7. (<u>love</u>, loves)
8. (<u>are</u>, is)
9. (<u>make</u>, makes)
10. (<u>like</u>, likes)
11. (appear, <u>appears</u>)
12. (plan, <u>plans</u>)
13. (arrive, arrives)

Vocabulary Review, page 68
1. ascertain
2. modify
3. sequence
4. confusion
5. distinguish

Skill Review, page 68
1. the doctor's appointment and the piano lesson
2. The doctor's appointment happened on Monday, and the piano lesson was on Wednesday. Monday comes before Wednesday, so the doctor's appointment happened first.
3. Soccer practice will happen tomorrow.
4. In the tree are two tiny kittens.
5. Around her neck was a strand of pearls.

Skills Practice, page 69
1. **C.** *Neither* is a pronoun that is always singular. It takes the singular verb *wants*.
2. **A.** Ignore the interrupter. The verb *jump* should be changed to its singular form to agree with *Rosa*.
3. **B.** *Tickets* is the subject of the sentence, not *here*. The verb must agree with this plural noun.
4. **C.** Ignore the interrupter. The singular verb *runs* agrees with the singular noun *Jan*.

Writing Practice, page 69
Answers will vary. Make sure you follow the prompt and describe the events in the correct sequence. Use the correct subject-verb agreement and correct verb tenses.

Sample Paragraph
Last September I saw some of the amazing natural wonders of our American Southwest. I flew from my home in Virginia to Las Vegas. At the airport, I rented a car. The next day I hiked at Red Rock Canyon. The following day I took a boat ride on Lake Mead and strolled on the walkway that crosses the Hoover Dam.

(Lesson 2.2 cont.)

On the third day, I drove on some scenic mountain roads to Bryce Canyon, where I enjoyed two exciting days hiking through the hoodoos. From there I wound my way down more mountain roads to Zion National Park. I packed a lot into the next forty-eight hours—riding on the tour bus, hiking, and participating in ranger campfire programs. Finally, I drove back to the airport in Las Vegas and then flew home. I would gladly take the trip again, but next time, I'll stay even longer.

Chapter 2 Review, pages 70–72

1. **A.** *Who* is a pronoun that refers to *guard. Guard* is a singular noun, so the verb must be *walks.*

2. **C.** The subject of *are welcome* is the pronoun *everyone. Everyone* is a singular pronoun, so the verb should be *is.*

3. **C.** Use the past perfect tense to show that the action of the sale ending happened before Lucinda got to the store.

4. **D.** Ignore the clause *whom I do not know* and check the agreement between *somebody* and *send. Somebody* is a singular pronoun and takes a singular verb.

5. **B.** The word *while* tells you that both events happened at the same time. Therefore, the verbs should show the same tense.

6. **B.** This sentence is in the subjunctive mood because it creates a sense of urgency. Therefore, the verb *sign* should not end with *s.*

7. **B.** Ignore the interrupting phrase *along with her two little brothers.* The verb agrees with the simple subject *Sonia,* which is singular.

8. **B.** Two events occur at different times. Martha and Kim never seeing such a large roller coaster occurs before the amusement park opened. Therefore, the amusement park opening occurs in the simple past tense to show that it occurred in the past but more recently than the other event.

9. **D.** The correct past participle of *hide* is *hidden.*

10. **C.** *Eyeglasses* is a plural noun, so it takes the plural verb form *slip.*

11. **B.** The first sentence is inverted. Its subject is *carpenters,* which is plural.

12. **D.** Two events occur at different times in the past. The opening of presents occurred after cake was eaten, so the simple past tense is used.

13. **A.** The word *clothes* is always a plural noun, so it takes the plural verb *are.*

14. **A.** Ignore the interrupting phrase *along with my youngest sister.* The verb agrees with the subject *brothers,* which is plural.

15. **D.** The verb agrees with the subject *size,* which is singular.

16. The paragraph should follow the prompt and use verb tenses and subject-verb agreement correctly.

Sample Paragraphs

When I was about five years old, I picked up my dad's harmonica for the first time and began to play. He told me later that he recognized my talent immediately, so he bought a harmonica for me. He taught me the basics, and we played for our own enjoyment as well as family functions. Eventually I built up my harmonica collection so I could master playing in different keys. Now I own 10 harmonicas!

My friends and family must like my playing, because they constantly ask me to bring my harmonicas to parties, barbecues, and such. I willingly oblige, as I sure enjoy playing. I've also started playing twice a month at a local nursing home. My new friends there are quite appreciative of my music. I plan to continue playing there, and I may also start giving free lessons to children at the youth center.

Answer Key

CHAPTER 3 Modifiers

Lesson 3.1

Think about Writing, page 77
1. adverb, *arrived*
2. adjective, *dinner*
3. adjective, *children*
4. adverb, *moved*

Think about Writing, page 78
1. rapidly
2. easily
3. extreme
4. carefully
5. badly

Think about Writing, page 79
1. dark
2. sad
3. quickly
4. carefully

Think about Writing, page 81
1. cheapest
2. neater or more neatly
3. happier
4. more serious

Think about Writing, page 83
1. those
2. had scarcely
3. bitter
4. an
5. any
6. anywhere

Vocabulary Review, page 84
1. modify
2. adverb
3. exception
4. adjective
5. negative
6. visualize

Skill Review, page 84
1. (1) One of nature's <u>worst</u> storms moved <u>slowly</u> toward the <u>unprotected</u> land. (2) <u>Worried</u> people were preparing for this hurricane. (3) It would hurl <u>powerful</u> winds and <u>mountainous</u> waves at them. (4) <u>Already</u>, <u>gigantic</u> waves were beating <u>savagely</u> <u>against</u> that shore. (5) One town was <u>nearly empty</u>. (6) <u>Wisely</u>, its people had run toward <u>higher</u> land <u>far</u> <u>away</u> from the <u>dangerous</u> sea.
2. Answers will vary. Sample answers: *brave, bravely, noble, fearless, selfless, courageously, wise.*

Skill Practice, page 85
1. **B.** *Careful* is an adjective that is being used to modify the verb *drove*. The adverb is *carefully*.
2. **B.** When comparing two things, add *er*, not *est*.
3. **D.** *Didn't hardly* is a double negative.
4. **D.** The manager is trying to hire the best people of all those available. The comparison, therefore, is among more than two.

Writing Practice, page 85
The paragraph should follow the prompt and use adjectives and adverbs to create a vivid and compelling description.

Sample Paragraph
A few years ago, Hurricane Isabel paid a visit to the area where I live. I felt my anxiety growing as I nervously glanced at the ominous clouds overhead and listened to the dire warnings and predictions of the weather forecasters. I had been living through hurricanes for most of my life, but this one was the worst I ever experienced. The wind howled relentlessly for hours. The rain pounded on the roof and quickly flooded the already soaked ground. The crashing thunder and jagged streaks of lightening only added to my stress and fear. The storm finally moved on, but the worst was far from over. Our neighborhood was without electricity for two solid weeks. I am glad the name Isabel has been retired, as I would not want to live through another storm like that one.

Lesson 3.2

Think about Writing, page 87
1. At the end of the road, adjective, modifies sign. It tells where. During the storm, adverb, modifies blown and tells when.
2. During the storm, adverb, modifies hid and tells when. Under the bed, adjective, modifies dog and tells where.
3. Off the trees, adverb, modifies blew and tells where.

Think about Writing, page 88
1. bus   Louis saw the bus <u>at the corner</u>.
2. Shen   <u>Opening the door</u>, Shen looked outside.
3. smell   The smell <u>of barbecued chicken</u> made Shawna hungry.
4. runner   The exhausted runner, <u>seeing the finish line</u>, speeded up.
5. sorry   Julie was sorry <u>to lose the watch</u>.
6. books   Jacob left his books <u>at the library</u>.
7. Ms. Cardenas   <u>Already soaked to the skin</u>, Ms. Cardenas opened her umbrella.
8. soon   The basketball game ended soon <u>after sunset</u>.
9. arrived   The police car arrived at the accident scene <u>in a hurry</u>.
10. manager   <u>Hoping to get more customers</u>, the store manager lowered prices.

(Lesson 3.2 cont.)

11. crossed   Mrs. Cosmos crossed <u>over the Canadian border</u>.

12. Lenore   <u>Sitting between her parents</u>, Lenore felt quite happy.

Think about Writing, page 89

1. Yuri Gagarin, the first human in space, was from the Soviet Union.

2. Ham, a chimpanzee, tested the US spacecraft.

3. Alan Shepard, the first American in space, wrote a book about the early space program.

4. Shepard went into space in Redstone 3, a tiny spacecraft.

5. Shepard, an astronaut and test pilot, went to the moon many years later.

Vocabulary Review, page 90

1. The group of words *hoping to win*, is an example of a <u>phrase</u>.

2. The dog owner is happy to live <u>adjacent</u> to a beautiful park.

3. His answer was <u>ambiguous</u>, so I am not sure if he is coming to the party.

Skill Review, page 90

1. Pang loves to play baseball. <u>He practices every chance he gets. On Saturday mornings, he's the first one up and ready to go hit some balls.</u>

2. Zihna just completed her third marathon. She has always been an active person. <u>She ran, and won, her first race when she was only eight years old!</u>

3. Lian cried and cried. <u>When Dad tried to give her a bottle, she just turned her head away and rubbed her eyes. She didn't even want to play with her favorite toy.</u> Dad knew it was time to put the baby to bed.

4. Walter likes to plan ahead. <u>Every Sunday, he picks out the clothes he will wear during the week. He also plans what he will eat for breakfast, lunch, and dinner each day.</u>

Answers will vary. Sample answer:

5. The dog sits on his favorite pillow.

6. His shoes were wet after walking home in the rain.

7. Eating their ice-cream cones, they walked home together.

8. Liz, a chef in training, cooked for hours.

Skill Practice, page 91

1. **B.** A comma should be used to separate an introductory phrase from the rest of the sentence.

2. **D.** Except for introductory phrases and renaming phrases, phrases are not usually separated from the sentence by commas.

3. **A.** This sentence is correct as written.

4. **B.** An introductory phrase should be set off by a comma.

Writing Practice, page 91

Answers will vary. Make sure you follow the prompt and use prepositional phrases, verb phrases, and appositives.

Sample Paragraph

Dear Mr. Johnson:

   Please consider me for the position of cook at your restaurant. I was an Army cook and head cook at two restaurants. I graduated with honors from the Downtown Culinary School. Mr. Wells, my pastry instructor, said my pies were the best she ever tasted. I would consider it an honor to bring my talents to your restaurant.

   Sincerely,

   Jeffrey Knight

Chapter 3 Review, pages 92–94

1. **D.** *The produce manager* is a renaming phrase. It should be set off with a comma.

2. **A.** *Can't hardly* is a double negative.

3. **A.** *Them* is always a pronoun. It can never be used to point out a noun.

4. **C.** *An* is used before words that begin with a vowel sound rather than *A*. *A* is used before words that begin with consonant sounds.

5. **C.** *That* means "there," so saying "that there" is like saying "there there."

6. **A.** *Looks* is sometimes a linking verb, sometimes an action verb. Here it is used as an action verb. *Nervously* modifies *looks*, telling how the letter carrier looks at the dog. *Nervous* is an adjective.

7. **A.** This sentence is correct as written.

8. **C.** *I have ever read* is the clue that this book is being compared to all other books. *Funnier* compares only two things.

9. **B.** *Well*, not *good*, is used to describe health.

10. **C.** The word *more* should not be used with an adjective to which the ending *er* has been added.

11. **D.** *Easy* is an adjective. In this sentence it is used to modify the verb *sets*, so an adverb, *easily*, is needed.

12. **C.** *Isn't hardly* is a double negative.

13. **D.** *Loud* modifies the verb *screamed*, so the adverb, *loudly*, is needed.

Answer Key

(Chapter 3 Review cont.)

14. **D.** *Those* means "there," so *there* is not needed in this sentence.

15. **B.** The word *more* should not be used with an adjective to which the ending *er* has been added.

16. **A.** *My teacher* is a renaming phrase. It should be set off with commas.

17. **B.** The word *most* should not be used with an adjective to which the ending *est* has been added.

18. The paragraph should follow the prompt and include clear descriptions with images that readers can picture easily.

Sample Paragraph

Most people might pass right by If Books Could Kill, a store selling beat-up old books, but I walk right in. I love to collect books, but my favorites are detective novels from the 1950s and 60s. I carefully sort through stacks and boxes of yellowed books, hoping to find a good story. I might find a good book that's been around so long that the cover is falling off and the brittle pages are coming out. Sometimes I find a book that's been carefully preserved with no bends or tears. That's an exciting find.

CHAPTER 4 Mechanics

Lesson 4.1

Think about Writing, page 100

1. Geraldo takes the train to work every morning.
2. He is lucky because he lives on East Street, which is a short walk to the station.
3. Currently, he is reading a biography about President John Adams called *John Adams Speaks for Freedom*.
4. Geraldo may also use the time to respond to e-mails or text messages on his smartphone.

Think about Writing, page 101
Answers will vary.

Sample Answer:

My vacation begins next Friday, October 3. I plan to travel to California, where I will visit my sister Lori. I am looking forward to the visit because I haven't seen my sister or my nephews Evan and Caden in several years.

My sister lives near Los Angeles. We plan to take the boys to Disneyland. The boys are in good enough shape to walk around all day because they play baseball. However, I'm worried about whether I will be able to keep up! Hopefully, the Blue Bayou will be open for some air conditioning and refreshments.

UCLA, where I attended college, is nearby, too. I hope to have time to stop and visit with Professor Merry Palowski, who taught my favorite classes in American literature. I can show the boys the Charles E. Young Research Library, where I spent many hours studying.

Think about Writing, page 102

1. east
2. President
3. unless
4. Southeast
5. Biology

Vocabulary Review, page 102

1. D.
2. C.
3. A.
4. B.

Skill Review, pages 103–104

1. **A.** Capitalize the first word in a sentence, but do not capitalize seasons (*spring*), common adjectives (*large*), or common nouns (*city*).
2. **A.** Capitalize the first word in a sentence, but do not capitalize common nouns, such as *restaurant*, *family*, or *garlic*.
3. **A.** Capitalize the first word in a sentence, but do not capitalize directions (*south*; *northeast*) or common nouns (*coast*).
4. **C.** Capitalize first word, last word, and important words in titles, but do not capitalize verbs (*memorized*) or common nouns (*poem*; *music festival*).
5. **D.** Capitalize the first word, last word, and important words in titles, but do not capitalize articles (*the*) or coordinating conjunctions (*and*).
6. **B.** Capitalize proper nouns (*Garcia*) and titles that come before names (*Doctor*).
7. **D.** Capitalize proper nouns (*Tanaka's Dry Cleaning*), but do not capitalize common nouns (*place*; *clothes*) or verbs (*clean*).
8. **A.** Capitalize proper nouns (*Empire State Building*), but do not capitalize adjectives (*tallest*) or common nouns (*building*; *city*).
9. **A.** Capitalize proper nouns (*Madison Street*), but do not capitalize adjectives (*grand*; *oak*) or common nouns (*avenue*).
10. Answers will vary. Sample answer: We visited Santa Fe, which is located in the Southwest.
11. Answers will vary. Sample answer: Because we were having spaghetti, I bought some Italian bread to eat with dinner.
12. Answers will vary. Sample answer: While visiting Washington, DC, the Kowalski family toured the White House.

Skill Practice, page 105

1. Winton's father works for the Department of Justice. *Father* is not a proper noun as it's used here; *Department of Justice* is the name of a specific department.
2. I am taking a biology class and History 101. *Biology class* is not a proper noun; *History 101* is the name of a specific class and therefore a proper noun.
3. Did you see the movie *The Return of the King*? The preposition *of* and the article *the* should not be capitalized in a title.

Answer Key

(Lesson 4.1 cont.)

4. Kathy Chung, Ph.D., is a spokesperson for the American Diabetes Association. *Ph.D.* is an abbreviation for Doctor of Philosophy; *American Diabetes Association* is the name of a specific organization and therefore a proper noun.

Writing Practice, page 106

Answers will vary. Make sure you have included at least three examples each of titles and proper nouns or pronouns. Capitalization should be correct in all cases.

Sample answer:

I visited Busch Stadium, which is located in St. Louis, Missouri. I went to see a baseball game played by my favorite team, the Cardinals. The game was great. The first pitch was thrown out by Professor Smith, a famous mathematician. Then Mayor Rodrigez made a special appearance to raise money for charity. Dr. Jones, the founder of the charity, joined him in the speech. The pitcher threw a no hitter, and the Cardinals won. Before I left, I bought plenty of souvenirs with the mascot, Fred Bird, on them.

Lesson 4.2 Punctuation

Think about Writing, page 110

1. Caitlin, look out for that bus!
2. Correct
3. It was, in fact, the best cheesecake Ms. Littleshield ever had.
4. Why don't you ever wear your yellow sweater, Malik?
5. Yolanda, the woman who got me this job, has now quit.

Think about Writing, page 112

Answers will vary.

Sample answer:

Dear Great-uncle Quincy,

I am excited about seeing you when you come for a visit next week. We will pick you up at Kennedy Airport on Saturday, March 15, at 7 p.m. Please be sure to bring a bathing suit, towel, and sunscreen. Could you also please bring the latest family photos? I cannot wait to see you!

Love,
Cantrice

Vocabulary Review, page 114

1. D.
2. E.
3. C.
4. A.
5. B.
6. F.

Skill Review, page 114–115

1. C. The quotation is a question, so a question mark belongs within the final quotation mark; a period ends the sentence.
2. A. When combining two independent clauses with a conjunctive adverb, it is correct to place a semicolon before the conjunctive adverb and a comma after it.
3. B. When a list follows a complete thought, use a colon to introduce the list.
4. D. When a comma is used to connect independent clauses, add a conjunction such as *and* after the comma.
5. B. The question captures Kalindi's exact words, so it should be framed in quotation marks. A comma separates a quotation from the rest of the sentence.
6. D. *They're* is a contraction for *they are*; an apostrophe takes the place of the missing letter *a*.
7. A. It is correct to join two independent clauses with a semicolon.
8. B. Use a comma to separate a quotation from the rest of a sentence.
9. D. Extra, nonessential information, such as a game score, can be framed in parentheses.
10. C. Use an ellipsis to show that part of a quotation has been omitted.
11. C. Dashes may be used in place of commas for emphasis.
12. C. An indirect question ends with a period, not a question mark or semicolon.

(Lesson 4.2 cont.)

Skill Practice, page 116

Marcela checked the schedule one last time. The train was due to arrive at 6:45; she had fifteen minutes more to wait in the bitter cold. It would be worth it in spite of the fact that she forgot her gloves at home. She could still hear her mother's voice urgently calling down the hall, "Don't forget your gloves!" Marcela refused to dwell on her forgetfulness; instead, she imagined the look she would see on her friends' faces when she stepped off the train. Ten years was a long time. Would they recognize each other? Marcela was certain that memories of their years together at Middletown High School would make it feel as if they were together just yesterday.

Writing Practice, page 117

Answers will vary. Check that you have edited your letter to show correct usage of apostrophes, commas, end marks, colons, semicolons, quotation marks, ellipses, dashes, and parentheses.

Sample Letter

Dear Sir or Madam:

I am writing to apply for the position of customer service associate. I am seeking a full-time position in your main office. I am a highly driven worker who does well in a team setting. I am motivated to succeed in a business setting, and I learn new skills quickly. My past employers are willing to provide references that show my willingness to take on new challenges and meet goals. I look forward to talking about this with you further.

Sincerely,

Kaleb Jackson

Lesson 4.3

Think about Writing, page 121

Part A

1. brake
2. know
3. here
4. whether
5. passed
6. right
7. week
8. through
9. coarse
10. choose

Part B

The founders of the United States didn't <u>know</u> whether they <u>would</u> succeed in winning independence from Great Britain, but they <u>knew</u> they had to try. <u>Their</u> goal was freedom. This country was founded on the <u>principle</u> of equality for all. The founders <u>passed</u> on to us <u>their</u> belief in democracy. The Constitution guarantees our <u>right</u> to free speech. That means everyone is allowed to say whatever he or she thinks, <u>whether</u> anyone else wants to <u>hear</u> it or not.

Think about Writing, page 126

Answers will vary. Sample answers:

1. You could consult a specialized dictionary for biological terms, or look in a print or online encyclopedia article about the insect.

2. You could use your composing software spell check feature and also consult a print dictionary. You could also ask someone to proofread for you.

3. You could consult a print dictionary and ask someone to proofread for you.

4. You could consult the old directory and ask someone at the company who knows the employees to proofread for you.

Vocabulary Review, page 127

1. E.
2. D.
3. F.
4. C.
5. A.
6. B.

Skill Review, page 127

1. I play <u>basketball</u> every Saturday morning. Basketball: a game that involves throwing a ball into a hoop

2. She served a <u>homemade</u> apple pie for dessert. Homemade: made at home

3. The kids played with their new <u>dollhouse</u> for hours. Dollhouse: a house made for dolls.

4. holly/home   homage
5. thud/tick   thunder
6. cry/cup   culture
7. blow/board   blueberry
8. cotton/cover   cousin

Answer Key

Skill Practice, page 128

1. **B.** The preposition *through* is correct in this sentence.

2. **D.** The possessive pronoun *your* is correct in this sentence.

3. **C.** The possessive pronoun *whose* is correct in this sentence.

4. **B.** The word *family* refers to one family. Therefore, the possessive requires *'s*.

5. **D.** *Wood* is a homophone for the correct word, the helping verb *would*.

6. **D.** *Whether* is a homophone for the correct word, *weather*.

7. **C.** The contraction *There's* is correct in this sentence.

Writing Practice, page 129
Answers will vary. Make sure you follow the prompt and follow correct spelling rules.

Sample Paragraph
If all writers spelled words however they wanted, written communication would be quite confusing. For example, if someone writes an article about an animal, and spells the animal's name *heir* or *hair* instead of *hare*, the readers won't understand the content of the article. In the workplace, production would probably go down. Orders would get mixed up if the correct spelling of numbers is not used. Imagine what would happen if a worker ordered too reams of paper or ate dozen pens! We all need to rely on consistent, correct spelling.

Chapter 4 Review, pages 130–131

1. **D.** Doctors refers to a general group of people. It is not used as a title for specific people, so it should not be capitalized.

2. **C.** *It's* is a contraction meaning "it is." In this sentence, the possessive *its* is needed.

3. **D.** The last word in this sentence means *also*. It is not a number.

4. **B.** Use a colon when a complete thought is used to introduce a list.

5. **D.** Use a semicolon to join independent clauses in a compound sentence when a conjunction is not used.

6. **C.** *In fact* is used as an interrupting phrase. It should be set off with commas.

7. **B.** The two parts of this quotation make one complete sentence. *Will* should not be capitalized because it continues the sentence.

8. **B.** A dependent clause that comes at the end of a sentence is not set off with a comma.

9. **B.** *Uncle* is not used here to replace a name, so it should not be capitalized.

10. **C.** Use an apostrophe to show that the *o* in *not* is the missing letter in this contraction.

11. **A.** A comma should not be used to separate the month from the date.

12. Answers will vary. Check that you have edited your letter to show correct usage of capitalization, punctuation, and spelling.

Sample Letter
Dear Joe,

I'm sorry you had to miss Keli's party last Saturday. The party was in the pavilion at Jacob's Park. Tommy, Omar, Winona, and Su Jin all attended.

We all missed you. The first thing Keli did was ask about you. She said, "Is Joe coming?"

"No," I said, "don't you remember he had to work today?"

I hope you'll be able to make it next time.

Sincerely,

Jonas

Answer Key

CHAPTER 5 Sentence Structure

Lesson 5.1

Think about Writing, page 139
1. Ann starts a new job soon, but she hasn't told her present boss.
2. There are no good movies in town; however, a great rock band is playing.
3. My house is a mess; I never seem to have time to clean it.
4. The plane's wings were covered with ice; as a result, the departure was delayed.

Think about Writing, page 142
1. <u>After</u> backing into the garage, Sarah loaded the truck.
2. Melissa wants to go to the zoo <u>unless</u> the weather turns cold.
3. <u>As soon as</u> I tell Santwana I saw a spider, she will want to leave.
4. <u>Even though</u> that dog has a loud bark, it's really very friendly.
5. The doctor says the wound will heal <u>if</u> I keep it bandaged.
6. I have to finish this project <u>whether</u> I like it or not.

Vocabulary Review, page 143
1. C.
2. D.
3. B.
4. A.

Skill Review, page 143
1. Because the sky darkened, I knew it was about to rain.
2. This sentence is correct as written.
3. I do not like coffee, but I enjoy drinking tea.
4. My brother does not like the cold, yet he helped me build a snow fort.
5. Ms. Ruiz does not have a lawn mower, and she doesn't want one.
6. This sentence is correct as written.

Skill Practice, pages 144–145
1. **B.** A semicolon is used instead of a conjunction to connect the two clauses.
2. **A.** *While* shows that the two events—reading a magazine and eating lunch—happen at the same time. *Until* also relates the ideas by time, but it does not make sense.
3. **A.** *But* shows a contrast between the two ideas—healthy plants and wilted plants.
4. **D.** *Unless* shows a condition: one thing will happen if something else happens.
5. **B.** *While* shows a time relationship between the ideas.
6. **C.** *Because* introduces the reason why he won't pay his bills on time.
7. **C.** A semicolon should be used before the conjunctive adverb *however*.
8. **D.** The first clause is a dependent clause. Because it comes before the independent clause, it is followed by a comma.
9. **A.** *So* connects the cause, *We are out of milk*, to its effect, *I will go to the store to buy some.*
10. **D.** *Therefore* shows a result.

Writing Practice, page 145
Answers will vary. Make sure you follow the prompt and use at least one dependent clause that uses a conjunction to show time, as well as several compound and complex sentences.

Sample Paragraph
Last summer I successfully organized a neighborhood clean-up day. First, I formed a committee with several neighbors. We set the date for the clean-up and then everyone volunteered for the tasks on the list I had created. Our enthusiasm was contagious; almost everyone in the neighborhood participated. We removed debris from the walking path, which had become quite filled with litter. The garden center and hardware store donated materials, so we were able to build beautiful planters at the entrance to the neighborhood. After we were finished, we admired our work, and I agreed to head the project again next year.

Answer Key

Lesson 5.2

Think about Writing, page 148
1. before going on vacation

   Your bill should be paid before you go on vacation.
2. Hanging on the wall

   Javier stared at the beautiful painting hanging on the wall.
3. beginning on Main Street

   The parade, beginning on Main Street, included clowns, elephants, and bands.

Think about Writing, page 149
1. I spent the weekend working in the yard, painting a door, and fixing a cracked window.
2. Regina said she would fix supper, set the table, and clean up afterward.
3. That candidate is energetic, concerned, and honest.
4. When Taro got home, he found mud on the carpet, scratch marks on the furniture, and broken glass on the floor.
5. The workshop leader explained how to speak clearly, appear skilled, and ask for a raise.

Think about Writing, page 152
1. would get
2. C
3. had locked
4. could
5. were

Think about Writing, page 153
Answers will vary. Sample answers:
1. Cathy told her son to clean his closet and his room since <u>they were</u> a mess.
2. The walls were bright green and the carpeting pale gray, <u>a combination</u> we thought was really ugly.
3. People are actually living without heat and hot water, and <u>this situation</u> must be changed.
4. <u>The police department</u> says that crime is increasing in our city.

Vocabulary Review, page 154

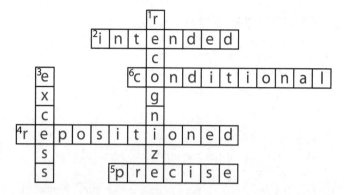

Skill Review, page 154
1. Acacia always dreamed of riding a horse across a large field.
2. C
3. Yesterday's news surprised and saddened us all.

Skill Practice, page 155
1. **B.** The snow occurred during the night, before the sun came out. The simple past shows that the sun came out after the snow fell.
2. **C.** This is a conditional statement. The first verb, *had gone*, is the past perfect. It must be paired with a verb such as *would have* along with a past participle.
3. **C.** In the original sentence, the pronoun *she* could refer to either *Isabel* or *her daughter*.
4. **D.** The story is not about a haunted house on the train. *On the train* is a misplaced modifier and should come at the beginning of the sentence.
5. **A.** This sentence is correct as written.
6. **C.** Changing the first use of the pronoun *he* to *Boris* makes the sentence much clearer.

Writing Practice, page 155
Answers will vary. Make sure you follow the prompt and clearly state your ideas.

Sample Story

The first time I read one of my writing pieces aloud in class I was nervous, because I did not have much confidence in my ability as a writer. My teacher and classmates were attentive listeners. They gave me helpful feedback on the content of my piece and my delivery style. I applied their suggestions, and the second time went much better.

Answer Key

Lesson 5.3

Think about Writing, page 159
1. The temperature should get to eighty degrees.
2. I often forget people's names.
3. First list the necessary ingredients.
4. I don't write letters because I never have enough time.

Think about Writing, page 163
1. Lee told us that Greg should <u>have</u> received the package by now.
2. <u>As</u> I've said before, most people never know how well off they are.
3. Sarah divided the remaining cake <u>among</u> the three of us.
4. Phan will certainly be <u>at</u> the game Saturday to see her brother play.
5. When she got up <u>off</u> the ground the last time, Yoko gave up skating.
6. Tina's got a sharper memory than any <u>other</u> person I know.
7. The actors in that movie were worse than <u>those in</u> the movie I saw last week.
8. Sid said he knew someone who would try <u>to</u> get us tickets.

Vocabulary Review, page 164
1. Luisa wondered if she would <u>encounter</u> her old boyfriend at the reunion.
2. Silvio is always in a rush, so I have learned to be <u>concise</u> when I speak with him.
3. That author has a <u>style</u> of writing that I enjoy reading.
4. I avoid using <u>idioms</u> because their meanings are often misunderstood.
5. The guest speaker's <u>diction</u> was perfect. Every word grabbed the audience's attention.

Skill Review, page 164
Answers will vary. Sample answers:
1. Going to the movies is as entertaining as watching television.
2. Jabrille's clothes got drenched when he went out in the rain without an umbrella.
3. That shiny red apple looks tasty.
4. The actor was petrified that she would forget her lines.
5. Violent winds ripped the large tree out of the ground.
6. When I dropped the dish, it smashed into hundreds of tiny pieces.

Skill Practice, page 165
1. **A.** The original sentence is repetitive. This sentence has the same meaning but is less repetitive.
2. **B.** This sentence is written in the active voice and is less wordy than the original.
3. **C.** The original compares a speech and *second* that does not make sense. The writer meant to compare the first candidate's speech with the second candidate's speech. *Candidate's speech* needs to follow *second*.
4. **B.** The preposition *from* should be used after the word *borrow*.
5. **D.** *Between* is used to refer to only two things. In this sentence, four children are being referred to, so *among* is the correct preposition for this sentence.

Writing Practice, page 165
Answers will vary. Make sure you follow the prompt and use formal style and correct diction.

Sample Essay
As an adult, I have lived in both Monterey, California, and Philadelphia, Pennsylvania. Each place has its own unique character. I prefer the weather in Monterey, with its year-round mild temperatures. Monterey is a small town compared to Philadelphia, but because it is a tourist destination, there is a lot of traffic congestion, similar in some ways to downtown Philadelphia. The views along the Monterey coastline are breathtaking, but a stroll along the Schuylkill River Trail is also a pleasant experience.

Answer Key

Chapter 5 Review, pages 166–1681

1. **B.** *Would of* is incorrect diction. *Would have* is correct.

2. **A.** *If* tells readers that if the first idea is true, then the second will be true, too, which doesn't make sense. *Unless* shows that if you do one thing, then the other won't happen, which does make sense.

3. **C.** The original sentence lacks parallel structure.

4. **D.** The original sentence contains two nonparallel elements.

5. **C.** *Like* is incorrectly used with a subject-verb combination: Mr. Murray said.

6. **D.** *Even though* is a conjunction showing contrast. Here the writer is telling why the Caribbean climate is considered tropical.

7. **C.** The original sentence leaves it unclear whether the dog belongs to John or to his brother.

8. **A.** *In spite of the fact that* begins a dependent clause and should be preceded with a comma.

9. **B.** The original sentence has two repetitive ideas: *the future time before us* and *world leaders around the globe.*

10. **D.** The sentence contains an *if* clause with *were,* so the correct form for the main clause is *would* plus the base form *be.*

11. **D.** *At last* and *finally* are repetitive. Also, the sentence is wordy because it is in the passive voice.

12. **D.** The original sentence contains a misplaced modifier. It says the auto dealership was on sale.

13. **B.** The transition word *Because* explains why Ted and Sonia left the country.

14. **C.** Use *between*, not *among*, when referring to two people or things.

15. **D.** The original sentence lacks parallel structure.

16. Answers will vary. Make sure you follow the prompt and correct capitalization, spelling, and punctuation.

Sample Memo

To: Ms. Jenkins

From: Syed Hasan

Re: Paper Supplies

The accounting department is constantly running out of the special forms that we use to invoice clients who purchase our computers. In the past, we could not order more than two boxes of forms at a time because we had no room to store them. I have recently noticed that the third and fourth-floor storage closets have several empty shelves. I propose that we move all the items into one closet and use the empty closet to store accounting forms and other paper supplies.

Answer Key

CHAPTER 6 Text Structure

Lesson 6.1

Think about Writing, page 174

1. ineffective; Sentences 4–6 do not support the man idea.
2. effective
3. ineffective; Sentences 4–6 do not support the main idea.

Think about Writing, page 177
Answers will vary. Sample answers:

1. Our department has developed a plan to increase profits through improved customer service.
2. Andrea decorated her new apartment elegantly and inexpensively.
3. As a volunteer, you can contribute to the library in a variety of ways.

Vocabulary Review, page 178
1. effective
2. topic sentence
3. supporting sentence
4. main idea
5. paragraph
6. concluding sentence

Skill Review, page 178
1. 1.
2. 7.

The summary of the passage will vary. Sample answer:
Wild animals are increasingly showing up in urban areas. Animal control officers have come up with a way to manage the issue without harming the animals.

Skill Practice, page 179

1. **B.** This sentence effectively summarizes the main idea of the paragraph. Sentence A is too general, and sentence C is too specific. While sentence D is a true statement, it is not a point of the paragraph.
2. **C.** This sentence effectively summarizes the main idea of the paragraph. The characters are ones you might find in a science fiction novel; they are noteworthy more for their strangeness rather than for their "wide range." Items A and B are not supported by the paragraph
3. **A.** This sentence effectively summarizes the main idea of the paragraph. Items B and C are supporting details, and item D is not even mentioned in the paragraph.

Writing Practice, page 179
Answers will vary. Make sure you write two paragraphs. Put your topic sentence first in the first paragraph. Put your topic sentence in the middle or at the end of the second paragraph.

Sample Paragraphs
I have always spent a lot of time at the public library. From the time I got my first library card when I was seven years old, I enjoyed browsing the tall stacks of books and selecting some to bring home to read.

Now that the library has computers, it's convenient to go there to do research and check my e-mail. I like to check out audio books to listen to in the car, and I often get DVDs to watch at home while I use the treadmill. I plan to continue spending as much time as possible at the library.

Lesson 6.2

Think about Writing, page 183

1. Remove sentence 4. The tone is too casual and impolite (even hostile) for this formal letter to a government agency.
2. Remove sentence 3. The tone is too serious for this light e-mail. The content and diction would be more appropriate in a formal essay or article.
3. Remove sentence 5. The slang and general word choices are too casual for this informational paragraph.
4. Remove sentence 3. The slang is too modern for the time period; the language is also not formal enough for the paragraph.

Vocabulary Review, page 184
1. tone
2. appropriate
3. informal
4. author's purpose
5. formal

Skill Review, page 184
1. to inform or explain
2. to persuade
3. to entertain

Answer Key

Skill Practice, page 185

1. **C.** Some students might associate nervous hand motions with a speaker looking foolish and choose option B; however, the real problem is that sentence 5 contains the informal use of the word *all* and the informal word *stupid*, which don't match the formal tone of the article.

2. **B.** Sentence 16 contains slang, which is inappropriate for this serious article.

Writing Practice, page 185

Answers will vary. Make sure you paraphrase, or use your own words to summarize the passage.

Sample Paraphrase

If you change your usual habits, you will be able to save water and money on your water bill at the same time. Don't leave the water running when you work at the sink. Instead, put water in a basin and wash dishes in it. Just run the water to rinse them. You can also buy a shower head that regulates the amount of water flow.

Lesson 6.3

Think about Writing, page 188

Answers will vary. Ideas could include *paint the walls, buy new furniture, eliminate clutter, add more lighting.*

Think about Writing, page 192

1. 2, 4, 3, 5, 1
2. 5, 2, 1, 4, 3
3. 2, 5, 4, 1, 3
4. 3, 5, 1, 2, 4
5. 2, 5, 4, 3, 1

Vocabulary Review, page 193

1. order of importance
2. time order
3. elaborate
4. cluster map

Skill Review, pages 193–194

1. first, second, most important
2. order of importance
3. time order
4. time order
5. Order of sentences with sample transitions: 1, 3 (First), 2 (Next), 4 (Now), 6, 5
6. Answers will vary.
7. Answers will vary.

Skill Practice, page 195

1. **D.** Option D is the best topic sentence for this paragraph because it focuses on preparing interview questions and implies that good candidates have been chosen. Options A and C are each only partially correct because they do not mention the questions. Option B is totally incorrect.

2. **B.** Sentence 12 should begin paragraph D, which focuses on the interview and is the final section of the article. Sentence 12 is a good topic sentence for the paragraph.

Writing Practice, page 195

Answers will vary. Make sure that your organizational structure matches the topic of your writing. Your transitions should help the reader understand your writing.

Sample Paragraph

I have always wanted to hike the Grand Canyon. First, I would gather all the food, hiking gear, and camping equipment I would need. Then I would travel to Arizona. Once I was there, I would hire a guide and hike down the canyon.

Lesson 6.4

Think about Writing, page 199

1. A, C, D; Electric cars are not a cause of air pollution.
2. Answers will vary. Causes could include *producing excellent work, saving the company money.* Effects could include *making a higher salary, getting more responsibilities.*

Think about Writing, page 202

Answers will vary. Sample answers:

1.

Care: Dogs: daily walks, brush fur, feed twice per day

Care: Cats: scoop litter, comb weekly, feed twice per day

Behavior: Dogs: playful, can be trained to do tricks, need walks or other exercise, play with toys

Behavior: Cats: playful when young, difficult to train, need some exercise, play with toys

2.

Qualities: Ocean: vast, salt water, lots of animal life

Qualities: Pond: small, usually freshwater, some animal life

Appearance: Ocean: color varies depending on location, shore is usually sandy or rocky

Appearance: Pond: color varies depending on location, shore is usually muddy or grassy

(Lesson 6.4 cont.)

Think about Writing, page 203
Answers will vary. Sample answers:

Career Choice 1: waitress

Career Choice 2: salesperson

How they are alike: deal with public, try to convince people to spend money on items, have to maintain an upbeat attitude, wear professional clothes or uniform

How they are different:

Skills needed:

waitress: knowledge of menu and food, ability to stay on feet for hours, ability to handle multiple tables and requests

salesperson: knowledge of product, knowledge of sales techniques, math skills for calculating discounts or totals

Educational Background:

waitress: none specific, can study hotel and restaurant management

salesperson: high school or college degree, can study sales and marketing

Potential job availability:

waitress: high

salesperson: high if willing to travel

Possible Salary:

waitress: hourly rate plus tips

salesperson: hourly rate plus commission

Potential for advancement:

waitress: head waiter or restaurant manager

salesperson: head salesperson or move to a job managing other salespeople

Summary

Waitress and salesperson are jobs that may not seem similar, but they have a lot in common. Both jobs require employees to be polite, friendly, and upbeat. Both succeed when they can convince customers to buy additional items. In a restaurant, a waitress may try to sell additional drinks, desserts, or appetizers. A salesperson will try to sell customers more expensive packages or add additional items to the purchase.

Both careers have pay directly related to their sales and performance. Most waitresses earn tips based on a percentage of the diner's check, while most salespeople earn a commission that is a percentage of their sales figures.

Many waitress jobs do not require specific schooling. Some sales jobs do require a degree in sales and marketing. The need for employees in both jobs is usually high, and both have room for advancement.

Vocabulary Review, page 204
1. C.
2. E.
3. A.
4. F.
5. D.
6. B.

Skill Review, page 204
Answers will vary. Sample answers:

1.

Cause: traffic jam

Effects: late for work, get into a bad mood from sitting in traffic

2.

Activity 1: playing guitar

play existing songs

create music

Activity 2: painting

create fine art

paint new pictures

Both:

skill improves over time

artistic

creative

Skill Practice, pages 205
1. **B.** Option B is the best topic sentence for this paragraph because it introduces the topic of paragraph C—ways in which the new workweek is similar to and different from the old. Option A is too specific as only sentence 14 covers similarities. Option C is also too specific because only sentence 17 talks about the Monday through Thursday schedule. While true, option D is not the point of the paragraph.

2. **B.** The transition *As a result* helps make the cause-effect relationship clear. None of the other options expresses this relationship.

Writing Practice, page 205
Answers will vary. Make sure your paragraphs show comparison and contrast and use transitions.

Sample Paragraph

Han Solo and Luke Skywalker are two characters from *Star Wars*. Luke is a Jedi in training, while Han is a ship captain and a smuggler. At the beginning of the film, Luke is young and naive. Han, however, is experienced and worldly. Both characters join the fight against the evil empire, and both characters care about Princess Leia.

Answer Key

Chapter 6 Review, pages 206–213

1. **D.** Sentence 4 is too casual and offensive to belong in this objective, informational article.

2. **C.** Sentence 9 is about planning, so it belongs in paragraph B, which has planning as its main idea.

3. **C.** Paragraph D is trying to cover two subjects: organizing and staffing. It would be more effective to start a new paragraph with the first sentence about staffing.

4. **A.** This makes a good topic sentence for paragraph E, because all of the sentences in the paragraph discuss directing.

5. **D.** Sentence 20 has nothing to do with the topic of the paragraph or even of the article as a whole. It's about a different kind of coaching, so it does not belong in paragraph E.

6. **D.** Sentence 23 wraps up paragraph F, so it should go at the end of the paragraph.

7. **D.** Sentence 5 is irrelevant. The paragraph is about Anna's history, not about the present.

8. **D.** Sentence 12 is too slangy and modern to belong in this historical, informational article.

9. **C.** It makes sense to tell why the king summoned Anna right after telling that he summoned her. Also, there is nothing in sentence 18 for "That might sound easy" to refer to.

10. **A.** This sentence belongs in the paragraph that talks about what the king wants. It connects so closely to sentence 20 in content that it must be in the same paragraph.

11. **C.** All of the other choices relate to the topic of the paragraph, but only choice C states its main idea.

12. **C.** The books and movie about Anna are a different subject from Anna's actual experience, so they belong in a separate paragraph.

13. **B.** The sentence following the topic sentence states the most important reason.

14. **A.** The word *when* indicates the effect of the sun sending flares of particles into space and also tells the time this effect occurs.

15. **C.** The word *causing* fits best in the context of the sentence.

16. **D.** The cause and effect are given in the sentence. The word *when* indicates the time sequence for the cause and effect.

17. **A.** *On the other hand* shows a contrast between the two cooks' efforts.

18. **D.** *But* shows the contrast between the two blogs.

19. **C.** Sentence 4 is too formal in tone to match the rest of the paragraph.

20. **A.** The most important reason should come immediately after the topic sentence.

21. **C.** Sentence 5 describes something that happens at home and should follow the other sentences about home activities.

22. **D.** Choice D is the only choice with a formal tone.

23. **D.** Choice D makes a good topic sentence because all of the sentences in the paragraph discuss ways to fit exercise into a daily routine.

24. **A.** Choice A is the only choice that has a formal tone.

25. **A.** Sentence 6 is the topic sentence for the paragraph, so it should be at the beginning.

26. **A.** Choice A is the next logical step in the process.

27. **B.** The author's purpose is to persuade, indicated by the use of the word *should*.

28. **B.** Choice B explains the effect of the mall opening and transitions to the rest of the paragraph.

29. **B.** Choice B indicates the contrast between the two types of trees.

30. **C.** Your essay should follow the prompt and use transitions to help the reader understand how the ideas are related.

Sample Essay

The streets in my neighborhood are full of potholes. We had an especially rainy fall followed by a cold, snowy winter. Weather conditions like that always damage our streets. Usually, the county begins repairs as soon as the springtime weather arrives. However, this year the budget for street repairs has been cut, so only the streets with the most severe damage will be fixed. My neighborhood does not meet the county's criteria for severe damage. I think this is a mistake. If the potholes on the streets are not fixed, they will get worse. Then the repair bill for the county will be even higher. Also, spring is the time when people begin selling their houses. If the streets are in disrepair, the neighborhood will not look attractive and the housing prices will go down. Potholes are also a safety hazard for walkers, kids on bicycles, cars, and parents pushing strollers. I hope our county supervisors reconsider and fix all of the potholes.

Essay Writing Practice

Text Structure, pages 214–215
Answers will vary. Here are some points to consider.

- Make sure that you have stated the main idea of your essay in the first paragraph.

- If you use order of importance to structure your text, rank your ideas. Use the order of either most important to least important or least important to most important. Check to make sure you are consistent with your ranking. Making a cluster map during your prewriting will be helpful in keeping your ideas organized.

- If you use time order to structure your text, tell the events in the order in which they occurred. Use transitions such as first, next, finally, at the same time, and afterward. Creating a time line or chart during your prewriting will be helpful in determining the correct sequence of events.

- If you use a cause-and-effect structure, determine whether you want to start with the effect and then explain the cause, or start with the cause and explain the effect. If an event has either multiple causes or effects, make sure to list all of them. Creating a cause-and-effect diagram during your prewriting will be helpful in determining the correct organization.

- If you use a comparison and contrast structure, organize your ideas in either a whole-to-whole pattern or a point-by-point pattern. Creating a Venn diagram during your prewriting will be helpful in determining the similarities and differences.

- Edit your essay. As you proofread your essay, make sure that you have used a tone throughout that is appropriate for your subject, purpose, and audience.

Answer Key

CHAPTER 7 The Writing Process

Lesson 7.1

Think about Writing, page 220

Answers will vary. Sample answers:

1. My best vacation: trip to Costa Rica, went ziplining, stayed in a treehouse, saw lots of different kinds of animals

2. My oldest friendship: met in first grade, joined scouts together, moved to different cities, but still talk every week

3. What I'll be doing five years from today: living in a new city, traveling to another country, successful in a new job

4. An exciting sports event: 2004 World Series, come from behind to sweep the series, curse of the Bambino broken

5. Someone I admire: the mayor, committed to improving education, came from my neighborhood

6. My favorite restaurant: opened in 2008, serves tapas and Spanish food, fun atmosphere

7. A dream come true: going to Paris, traveling up the Eiffel tower, eating baguettes and cheese along the river

Think about Writing, page 221

Answers will vary. Sample answer:

My oldest friendship

1 met in first grade

2 joined scouts together

4 moved to different cities, but still talk every week

3 never keep secrets from one another

Vocabulary Review, page 222

1. process
2. brainstorming
3. prewriting
4. generate

Skill Review, page 222

Topic: Why Thanksgiving is my favorite holiday

___(X)___ roasting the perfect turkey

_____ preparations

___(X)___ the history of Thanksgiving

_____ family traditions

___(X)___ different traditions around the world

Topics and list of ideas will vary.

Sample answer:

Why the leash law is a good idea.

1. Many people are afraid of dogs and feel safer if the dog is under control.

2. Even the best dogs might get excited and run into the street.

3. Dogs can get easily startled by loud noises and run off.

4. Dogs are naturally curious and might get into things they shouldn't.

5. It is easier for owners to discourage dogs from making messes where they shouldn't when the dog is on a leash.

Skill Practice, page 223

1.

My First Job

___(1)___ 16 years old

___(2)___ needed money

___(4)___ first day on job

___(X)___ my first grade teacher

___(5)___ length of employment

___(3)___ interview for job

___(6)___ what I learned

___(X)___ computers have taken over many jobs

2.

Sample answers:

I: I will always remember my first job.

A. 16 years old

B. first day on job

C. what I learned

D. I learned a lot and will never make that mistake again!

Lesson 7.2

Think about Writing, page 225

Answers will vary. Check that the introduction includes a topic and main idea.

Think about Writing, page 226

Answers will vary. Check that each big idea begins a new paragraph.

Think about Writing, page 227

Answers will vary. Check that the conclusion does not include any new information.

(Lesson 7.2 cont.)

Vocabulary Review, page 228

1. stages
2. rough draft
3. incorporate

Skill Review, page 228

1. The second paragraph should begin with *The first cut affects trash pickup.*
2. The third paragraph should begin with *The school budget will also be affected by budget cuts.*
3. The fourth paragraph should begin with *Finally, library hours will be scaled back.*

Skill Practice, page 229

Answers will vary. Introduction should include a topic and main idea. Sample introduction:

Do you like standing in line just to find out that the last ticket for a movie has been sold? What about paying five dollars or more just for popcorn? And how do you feel about people talking or using their phones during the movie? It's the worst. When you rent movies, you don't have to put up with any of these annoyances. You can enjoy a movie right in you own home with your own snacks. Renting is a far better way to watch movies than going to the movie theater because it's quieter, you can set your own schedule, and it's more cost effective.

Lesson 7.3

Think about Writing, page 231

Answers will vary. Make sure your ideas are clearly stated and that you words choices are appropriate and interesting.

Think about Writing, page 232

Answers will vary. Check that you have corrected errors in spelling, grammar, capitalization, and punctuation.

Vocabulary Review, page 233

1. B.
2. A.
3. C.

Skill Review, page 234

1. C. When writing about how to carry out a procedure, instructions should appear in time order.
2. B. When writing about your opinion, it makes sense to support your opinion with details in order of importance from least to most important.

3. D. Cause-and-effect organization works well when writing about something that caused something else to happen.

Answers will vary. Check that the concluding paragraph wraps up the points made in the body of the paragraph.

Sample Conclusion

After school programs are important for students. We would be doing students a disservice if they were cut. Students would have too much unsupervised time and miss out on valuable interactions and activities. Let your town legislators know that you want to keep the programs.

Skill Practice, page 235

Answers will vary.

Sample answer:

Are you feeling stressed? Does it seem like there's not enough time in the day to accomplish everything you need to do? Do you find yourself running out of patience? It is important to find time every day to unwind, de-stress, and relax. This is good not only for your physical body, but for your mind as well. There are lots of different ways to slow down and relax.

One way to accomplish this is to meditate. If you can find just 30 minutes a day to meditate, you will start to notice a difference in many areas of your life. That's not a lot of time. Some people are intimidated by the idea of meditation. Don't be. Meditation is simply finding a quiet place to sit, close your eyes, and let your mind let go of all the stresses in your life. It takes practice. Many people say they can't stop thinking about everything else they need to do and feel antsy sitting still when there's so much to get done. If this happens to you, remind yourself that you're worth 30 minutes a day and that taking the time to meditate will help you get more done during the rest of the day.

Many people find it helpful to practice yoga. There are many forms of yoga, so you need to find the form that suits you. You can learn yoga by taking classes or by renting yoga DVDs. The latter option allows you to learn yoga in your own home.

Whatever method you choose, it is important to find time to de-stress every day. Meditation and yoga are just two options. Go for a walk, ride a bike, or take a cooking class. The key is to find something you enjoy that helps you relax.

Answer Key

Essay Writing Practice

The Writing Process, pages 236–237
Answers will vary. Here are some points to consider.
Make sure to follow the steps of the writing process in the correct order as you develop your essay.

Prewriting
- Brainstorm a list of possible topics to write about. Make the list as comprehensive as you can. Then go back and eliminate any topics that are too broad or too narrow.
- Decide on the audience for your essay. It can be younger people, peers, officials, or friends.
- Determine the purpose of your essay. Are you going to inform, entertain, or persuade your readers?
- Organize your ideas. Choose the organizational structure you want to use. You may want to refer back to Chapter 6 for a review of patterns of organization.

Writing
- Create the first version, which is your rough draft. Get your ideas down on paper.
- Start with an introductory paragraph that tells the topic and states your main idea. Add one or two interesting details that will make your readers want to read more.
- Use one paragraph for each idea in the body of your essay. Again, make sure to include interesting facts and details.
- End the essay with a concluding paragraph. Summarize your information, but don't add anything new.

Revising and Editing
- Check to make sure your organizational structure is consistent. Make any necessary changes.
- Read your essay again and see if you want to use any different words or ideas. Add or remove details as necessary to clarify your ideas.
- Edit for spelling, grammar, and punctuation. The spell check feature on some word processing programs may have some inaccuracies. Use a dictionary to double check any words you are unsure of.
- Create your final draft.

CHAPTER 8 Text Types and Purposes

Lesson 8.1

Think about Writing, page 242
Answers will vary. Sample answers:

I. Introduction
Rhetorical question regarding school uniforms

II. Claim
Public school students should be required to wear school uniforms.

III. Reasons and Evidence
A. Uniforms lower the cost of clothing for students.
statistics contrasting average costs of school clothing with uniforms
B. Uniforms protect low income students from bullying.
quotation from middle school student
C. Uniforms keep distractions from learning to a minimum.
quotation from teacher about causes of conduct problems

Think about Writing, page 243
Answers will vary. Sample answers:

IV. Counterclaims
A. Uniforms limit self-expression.
  a. quotation from teacher
  b. response: Students can express themselves with accessories or in other ways.
B. Uniforms are cheaply made.
  c. facts about materials and production of uniforms
  d. response: Students quickly grow out of their uniforms, and for most students, they last for a school year.
C. Uniforms do not fit everyone well.
  e. quotation from psychologist who specializes in body image issues
  f. response: Everyone has to deal with the same uniform issues, and some of them do come in different styles.

Think about Writing, page 244
Answers will vary. Sample answers:

V. Conclusion
A. *Restatement of claim:* American public schools should move to adopt uniform policies for students.

B. *Summary:* because school hallways should lead students to classrooms where they can develop their minds; they should not serve as fashion runways; evidence: low cost of uniforms, protection from bullying, minimizing distractions
C. *Final Insight:* quotation from someone who supports school uniforms

Vocabulary Review, page 246
1. D.
2. C.
3. B.
4. F.
5. A.
6. E.

Skill Review, pages 246–247
1. C. A rhetorical question is one of the recommended introduction strategies. The other strategies include action, reaction, or a quotation; the remaining answer choices do not provide examples of any of these strategies.
2. B. The writer says that uniforms lower the cost of student clothing. Statistics contrasting the cost of traditional clothing with uniforms would support this reason. The description and the quotation would not provide cost information. The photographs would provide individual prices, but not overall averages per student, per family.
3. A. Government websites are generally reliable sources. Teen magazines feature pop culture, rather than articles by subject matter experts. A letter to the editor and a parenting blog can be written by anyone and likely show bias.
4. D. The writer says that uniforms keep distractions from learning to a minimum. A teacher could give first-hand information regarding typical causes for conduct problems at a school. The anecdote and the statistic may be related to the claim, but they do not support this reason. A fact about school learning objectives alone is not sufficient; the writer needs to explain how these learning objectives may be affected by distractions or discipline problems related to student clothing.
5. D. A school principal is a good source of data regarding learning and discipline. A *.com* website is likely intended to sell something, not provide scholarly research. A YouTube video and a Web forum can be created by anyone, expert or not.

Answer Key

Skill Practice, page 248–249
Answers will vary, but your argument should mimic the structure and style of the sample essay. Check to make sure you have included an effective introduction, a claim, reasons and evidence, counterclaims, and a conclusion.

Lesson 8.2

Think about Writing, page 252
Answers will vary. Sample KWL chart:

K	W	L
• They probably already know some basic cooking skills, since they asked me for a recipe.	• They want to get my chicken nachos recipe and need for me to explain how I make it.	• They will learn how to make chicken nachos for themselves.

Think about Writing, page 254
Answers will vary. Sample Sequence graphic organizer:

Introduction: "Raoul's Chicken Nachos are the tastiest snack I've ever had!" —Tony Smith
Topic Sentence: This recipe is easy and delicious, and you can use the meat filling in a number of ways.

Step 1: Preheat oven to 350 degrees F. Place 3 Tbsp. vegetable oil in a large skillet and set it over medium heat.

Step 2: Stir 2 crushed cloves garlic and 6 sliced green onions in the vegetable oil until tender.

Step 3: Mix in 2 shredded cooked chicken breasts and salt and pepper to taste, and toss until well coated with oil. Stir in 1 cup of salsa.

Step 4: Arrange half a 12-ounce package of tortilla chips on a baking sheet. Spoon the chicken mix over the chips.

Step 5: Top with an 8-ounce package grated Monterey Jack cheese and ½ large tomato, diced. Bake in oven 10 minutes and serve.

(Lesson 8.2 cont.)

Think about Writing, page 255
Answers will vary. Sample answer:

Another solution (*Problem-and-Solution*) is to organize course materials. Students who earn poor grades are often the ones whose folders have papers spilling from them. If (*Cause-and-Effect*) a student is unable to find his or her things, then (*Cause-and-Effect*) it is difficult to study or complete assignments. First, (*Sequence*) get a three-ring binder and a set of dividers. Create a section for each course. Then (*Sequence*) as the instructor gives assignments and notes, date them and place them in the appropriate section in chronological order. This system enables a student to find what he or she needs quickly and efficiently.

Think about Writing, page 256
Answers will vary. Sample answer:

Restate the topic: Raoul's chicken nachos is a great party dish, and the filling is also good in tacos and quesadillas. *Summarize main idea and important details:* This easy chicken dish can be used for several purposes. Be sure to cook the chicken breasts and chop the garlic and green onions in advance for quick assembly.
Final insight: (Connection to Reader:) I hope you enjoy making these!

Vocabulary Review, page 257
1. C.
2. E.
3. A.
4. B.
5. D.

Skill Review, pages 258–259
1. Answers will vary. Sample answer: Action is used to introduce the topic. The writer describes a student who opens a report card and does not know if the grades will be good or bad.
2. Answers will vary. Sample answer: I would use an example, such as a quoted item from a test. Then, I would model how to identify the purpose of the test question and explain how identifying the purpose helps a student respond.
3. **B.** Books and handouts from school may be referred to as *materials*, but not *objects*, *stuff*, or *gadgets*.
4. **D.** *But* shows contrast. *Because* shows cause and effect, and *many* and *do* are not transition words.

Skill Practice, page 260
1. Answers will vary. Sample answer: *Anecdote:* Don't yank your best friend out of a meeting just because your screen is frozen again! *Quotation:* As my friend Salita would say, "A frozen computer is a problem you can control." *Fact:* Just remember the three buttons to push to force a program to close. *Connection to reader:* Now you know you don't have to stare helplessly at a spinning wheel when your computer freezes.
2. Answers will vary. Sample answer: More organization would be helpful for me in the area of grocery shopping, because I don't plan ahead. As a result, I tend to spend too much money at the store. I could be more organized by writing a shopping list as well as clipping coupons. However, I would have to do this before I left the house in the morning.
3. **A.** Venn diagram—Compare and Contrast
   B. Series of boxes with arrows—Sequence
   C. Two boxes with an arrow—Problem and Solution
   D. Two boxes with an arrow—Cause and Effect

Writing Practice, page 261
Answers will vary. Make sure you have followed the structure set out in the lesson. Your text should introduce the topic, state the topic and the information to come, develop the topic in several body paragraphs with clearly organized ideas, and conclude by restating the topic, summarizing the main ideas and details, and giving the reader a final insight. Be sure that you have proofread your work. Also make sure that you have used varied transitions, precise language, and headings or graphs, where appropriate.

Lesson 8.3

Think about Writing, page 264
Answers will vary. Sample answer:

Exposition
Narrative Point of View: First person
Primary Character/Protagonist: me as a young child (round)
Important Secondary Character(s)/Antagonist(s): the usher who wouldn't let me go to my seat (flat), my parents (round)
Context (setting and conflict): The setting is a minor league baseball field, and the action takes place in the stands. The person checking tickets wouldn't believe me that I had a ticket for a seat in his area.

Answer Key

Think about Writing, page 266

Answers will vary. Sample answer:

Dialogue: Marisa: "My mom just never listens to me."

Pacing: slow when Marisa is complaining and crying; fast when Marisa and her mother are on the phone

Transitional Words and Phrases: "After I came home," "Then she said," "When I was with my friends"

Precise Language: "slumped" instead of "sat;" "whimpered" instead of "cried"

Description and Sensory Language: tears rolling down her cheek, muffled protests coming from the phone

Vocabulary Review, page 267

1. D.
2. E.
3. A.
4. C.
5. B.

Skill Review, pages 268–269

1. A. The narrator, who uses first-person, not third-person, pronouns, participates in the story, but she is not objective. She calls her uncle "crazy," for example.

2. A. Rachel is the main character on whose actions readers focus. Mom, Uncle Cos, and the siblings support Rachel.

3. C. Readers can visualize the image *"writing my name in the dirt with a stick"* and *"my eye sensed movement."* These images do not appeal to the senses of smell, taste, or sound.

4. D. The word *spooked* describes the cattle's reaction to a coyote. *Something* and *near* are vague words. While cattle is more precise than *animals*, for example, it is not as specific and colorful as *spooked*.

5. A. The phrase "After two nights" tells when in time the event occurs in relation to the previous events. The other sentence parts do not include time transitions.

6. D. The tenth paragraph provides the final reflection. Paragraph one provides the context. Paragraph three and six provides the rising action.

Skill Practice, page 270–271

Answers will vary. Make sure you have followed the structure set out in the lesson. Your text should define the narrative point of view, introduce the characters, and establish a setting. Your events should be organized logically with transitions to help the reader understand the sequence. Your characters should be developed through description and dialogue; the reader should be able to picture the characters or understand why the characters do the things they do.

Writing Practice

Text Types and Purposes, pages 272–273

Answers will vary. Here are some points to consider.

Argument

- Open by clearly stating your claim. For example: *Overuse of automation has caused the customer service support for medical billing to deteriorate.*

- Your paragraphs should support your claim with reasons and credible evidence. For example, to support a claim about overuse of automation, you might discuss the amount of time that is wasted trying to reach a customer service support representative and a report documenting mistakes caused by automated data entry.

- Edit your argument. As you proofread the argument, be sure to use appropriate transitions such as *then*, *next*, or *later* to indicate a shift in time.

Informative or Explanatory Text

- Make sure that you have stated the main idea of your informative or explanatory text by the end of your first paragraph.

- Make your language precise, and use vocabulary appropriate to your topic. Consider the difference between *Use the wrench to undo the lug nuts* and *Use the lug wrench to loosen the lug nuts, but do not remove them.*

- Edit your informative or explanatory text. As you proofread the text, be sure to use appropriate transitions such as *then*, *next*, or *later* to indicate a shift in time.

(Writing Practice cont.)

Narrative Text

- Make sure your first sentence grabs the reader. Strategies to consider are plunging readers into the middle of an exciting scene (*The bases were loaded with two outs, and the crowd was screaming my name*) or asking a question to which many readers can relate (*Did you ever find you'd drifted apart from a friend over a lie?*).

- The sequence of events in the middle of the narrative should be logical. Make sure there are no unexplained gaps in time.

- Edit your narrative. As you proofread the text, be sure to use appropriate transitions such as *then*, *next*, or *later* to indicate a shift in time.

Glossary

A

abbreviation (uh bree vee AY shuhn) a shortened form of a word or name

abstract noun (AB strakt noun) a noun that names an idea or an emotion

action (AK shuhn) a strategy for structuring an argument used to describe an event

action verb (AK shuhn vurb) a verb that tells what the subject of a sentence does

active verb (AK tiv vurb) a verb that shows the subject doing the action

active voice (AK tiv voiss) the way a verb is used to show that the subject does the action

adjacent (uh JAY sent) next to

adjective (A kik tiv) a word that modifies, or describes, a noun or pronoun

adverb (AD verb) a word that modifies, or describes, a verb, an adjective, or another adverb

affix (A fiks) a word part that is added to the beginning or end of a base word

alter (AWL tur) to change something

ambiguous (am BIG yoo uhss) unclear

anecdote (A nik doht) a short story about real people or events

antagonist (an TAG uh nist) the character who stands in the way of the protagonist's goal

antecedent (an tuh SEE duhnt) the noun or pronoun that a pronoun refers to

apostrophe (uh POSS truh fee) a kind of punctuation used to show possession or to form contractions

appositive (uh POZ uh tiv) a modifying phrase that gives more information about a noun; it is made up of a noun and other words that modify that noun (renaming phrase)

appropriate (uh PROH pree uht) in writing, language that fits the purpose and audience

article (R tik kul) a special adjective used with a noun

ascertain (A ser tayn) to make sure

author's purpose (AW thurz PUR puhss) the reason a piece of writing is written, which may be to enterain, persuade, or inform readers

B

base form (bayss form) the most basic form of a verb; the form you begin with for all verb tenses

bias (BAHY us) favoritism toward one point of view

body (BOD ee) the main part of a piece of writing that gives the details and facts about the main idea

brainstorming (BRAYN storm ing) a way of getting ideas to write about in which the writer lists every idea that comes to mind

C

capitalization (kap uh tuh luh ZAY shuhn) the use of capital, or uppercase, letters

cardinal direction (KAR duh nuhl duh REK shuhn) one of the four main compass points: north, south, east, or west

cause (kawz) the reason that something happens

cause-and-effect order (kawz-and-uh FEKT OR dur) a way of organizing information that tells how one event made another event happen

character (KA rik tuhr) a person or animal who takes part in the events of a story

chronological (KRON uh loj i kuhl) in time order

citation (sahy TEY shuhn) a reference to a source document

claim (kleym) a statement of the writer's opinon

clause (klawz) a group of words that contains a subject and a verb

climax (KLAHY maks) the turning point of the story

cluster map (KLUHS ter map) a web graphic organizer that helps organize ideas

cohesive (koh HEE siv) clear

colon (KOH luhn) a kind of punctuation used to introduce items in a list

combine (kuhm BINE) to join together

comma splice (KOM uh spleyess) a sentence consisting of two clauses joined incorrectly by a comma without a conjunction

command (kuh MAND) a type of sentence that states an order or request and ends with a period

common (KAH muhn) regularly used

common noun (KAH muhn noun) a type of noun that names a whole group or general type of person, place, thing, or idea; common nouns are not capitalized

common verb (KAH muhn vurb) a regularly used verb

compare (kuhm PAIR) to examine two or more things to see how they are alike

comparison (kuhm PAR i suhn) the act of showing how two or more things are alike

comparison-and-contrast order (kuhm PAIR i suhn-and-KAHN trast OR dur) a way of organizing information to show how one thing or idea is similar to or different from another thing or idea

complex sentence (KAHM pleks SEN tuhnss) a sentence that contains one independent, or main, clause and one or more dependent clauses

composition (kahm puh ZISH uhn) a piece of writing such as an essay

compound sentence (KAHM pound SEN tuhnss) a sentence that contains two or more connected independent clauses or simple sentences

compound subject (KAHM pound SUHB jikt) a subject of a sentence that is made up of more than one part; the parts are connected with words such as *and* or *or*

compound word (KAHM pound wurd) a word made up of two smaller words

concise (kuhn SISSE) saying what needs to be said using as few words as possible

concluding sentence (kuhn KLOOD ing SEN tuhnss) the closing sentence of a paragraph that restates the main point, connects to the next paragraph, or ends in a lively way

conclusion (kuhn KLOO shuhn) the last part of a piece of writing that summarizes or bring the writing to an end

concrete noun (KON KREET noun) a noun that is experienced through one or more of the five senses

conditional (kuhn DISH uh nuhl) a clause that begins with the word *if*

conflict (KON flikt) a problem the primary character faces with another character, nature, or fate

confusion (kuhn FYOO shuhn) a mix-up

conjunction (kuhn JUHNGK shuhn) a type of word that links parts of a sentence by showing how the parts are related

conjunctive adverb (kuhn JUHNGK tiv AD verb) an adverb or adverb phrase that works like a conjunction

context (KON tekst) the surrounding words or sentences that help explain the meaning of a particular word or expression

context clues (KON tekst klooz) the words surrounding an unfamiliar word that can sometimes provide hints about the word's meaning

contraction (kuhn TRAK shuhn) a shortened form of two words with some letters left out; an apostrophe is used in place of the missing letters

contrast (kuhn TRAST) to examine two or more things to see how they are different

convention (kuhn VEN shuhn) a way in which language is written or spoken that is regarded as being correct

convey (kuhn VAY) to communicate something

counter claim (KOUN ter kleym) an opposing view

credible (KRED uh buhl) deserving of belief or trust

D

dangling modifier (DANG guhl ing MOD uh fye ur) a modifying phrase or clause that does not modify any word in the sentence

database (DEY tuh beys) an online listing of reliable, published reference materials

declarative sentence (di KLAR uh tiv SEN tuhns) a type of sentence that makes a statement

dependent clause (di PEN duhnt klawz) a group of words that contains a subject and a predicate but does not express a complete thought

descriptions (dih SKRIP shuhns) observations of items, people, or events

determine (di TUR min) to decide

dialogue (DAYH uh lawg) the speech of the characters in a story

diction (DIK shuhn) word choices and usage

distinguish (diss TING gwish) to recognize

E

economical (ek uh NOM uh kuhl) getting the most meaning with the fewest words

editing (ED it ing) correcting mistakes in grammar, punctuation, capitalization, and spelling

effect (i FEKT) what happens as a result of something

effective (i FEK tiv) successful

elaborate (i LAB uh rate) to explain more fully

emphasize (EM fuh size) to stress or call attention to

encounter (en KOUN tur) to come across

examine (eg ZAM uhn) to look closely at something

exception (ek SEP shuhn) a situation in which the usual rule does not apply

excess (EK sess) too much

exclamatory sentence (EKS klam uh TOR e SEN tuhns) a type of sentence that expresses excitement

exposition (ek spuh ZISH uhn) the beginning of a narrative plot where the writer introduces the characters and establishes a context for the story

F

fact (fakt) information that can be proven

falling action (FAWL ing AK shuhn) the events that lead toward an end to the conflict

first-person narrator (furst PUR suhn NAR ey ter) a participant in and the person who tells the events described in a story

flat character (flat KA rik tuhr) a character who remains the same over the course of a story

formal English (FOR muhl Eng LISH) businesslike language

fragment (FRAG muhnt) an incomplete sentence

future perfect tense (FYOO chur PUR fikt tenss) a verb form that shows an action that will be completed by a specific time in the future

G

gender (JEN dur) the quality of being male or female

generalization (jen ur uhl luh ZEY shuhn) a rule that applies to most words in English

generate (JEN uh RATE) to produce, or come up with, something

graphic (graf ik) a chart, graph, diagram, photograph, or other visual representation

H

helping verb (HELP ing verb) a verb that is used with other verb forms to form different tenses

homophones (HOHM uh fonez) words that sound the same but are different in meaning and sometimes in spelling

I

identify (eye DEN tuh fye) to name

idiom (ID ee uhm) a special group of words whose meaning cannot be understood just by knowing the meaning of the individual words; together, the words have developed a special meaning

imperative sentence (im PAR uh tiv SEN tuhns) a type of sentence that states a command

implement (IM pluh ment) to put into use

incorporate (in KOR puh rate) to include; in writing, to include details and facts that explain the main idea

independent clause (in di PEN duhnt klawz) a part of a sentence that contains a subject and a predicate and expresses a complete thought

infinitive (in FIN uh tiv) a verb form that begins with the word *to*

informal English (in FOR muhl Eng LISH) casual conversation

intended (in TEN did) meant for

interpret (in TUR prit) to explain or figure out the meaning of something

interrogative sentence (in ter OG uh tiv SEN tuhns) a type of sentence that asks a question

interrupting phrase (in ter RUHPT ing fraze) a group of words in a sentence that comes between the simple subject and the verb

introduction (in truh DUHK shuhn) the first part of a piece of writing that tells what the topic and main idea are

inverted (in VUR tid) reversed

inverted sentence (in VUR tid SEN tuhnss) a sentence in which the usual subject-verb word order is reversed so that the verb comes before the subject

irregular verb (i REG yuh luhr verb) a verb that does not form its past and past participle forms in a regular, or predictable, way

irrelevant (i REL uh vuhnt) not important; off the subject

L

limited third-person narrator (LIM i tid thurd PUR suhn NAR ey ter) a teller of a story who focuses on the thoughts, feelings, and actions of one character

link (lingk) to connect

linking verb (LINGK ing verb) a verb that tells what the subject of a sentence *is* or that links the subject with a word or words that describe it

logical (LOJ i kuhl) makes sense

M

main idea (mayn eye DEE uh) the most important point that a paragraph discusses or develops

majority (muh JOR uh tee) more than half of a total

misplaced modifier (MISS playssd MOD uh fye er) a describing word or phrase whose meaning is unclear because it is out of place in a sentence

modal auxiliary verb (MOHD uhl awg ZIL yuh ree vurb) A verb that expresses several meanings, such as ability or opinion.

modify (MOD uh fye) to change or to describe

multiple (MUHL tuh puhl) several

N

narrator (NAR ray tur) the person telling the story

negative (NEG uh tiv) meaning *no* or *not*

nonrestrictive clause (non ri STRIK tiv klawz) a clause that has commas and contains information that is not essential to the meaning of the sentence

noun (noun) a word that names a person, place, thing, or idea

O

object pronoun (OB jikt PROH noun) a type of pronoun that is the object of a verb or preposition

objective first-person narrator (uhb JEK tiv furst PUR suhn NAR ey ter) a teller of a story who participates in events, but tries to report the events without exercising judgment

occupation (ak kyuh PAY shuhn) a job

omniscient (om NISH uhnt) all-knowing

opinion (uh PIN yuhn) a belief

order of importance (OR dur uhv im PORT uhnss) a way of organizing writing that ranks details from most important to least important or vice versa

organizing (OR guh nize ing) the step in the writing process in which a writer puts his or her ideas in order

P

pacing (PEYS ing) the speed of action

paragraph (PA ruh graf) a group of sentences that works together to communicate one idea

parallel structure (PA ruh lel STRUHK chur) a correct form of sentence structure in which all elements of a compound sentence that are alike have the same form

paraphrase (PA ruh fraze) to use your own words to restate something

passive verb (PASS iv verb) a verb that shows the subject being acted upon

passive voice (PASS iv voiss) the way a verb is used to show that an action is done to the subject

past perfect tense (past PUR fikt tenss) a verb form that tells that an action was completed in the past before another event or before a certain time in the past

perfect tense (PUR fikt tenss) a verb form that tells that an action has been completed before a certain time or that will be continuing until a certain time

pertinent (PUR tuh nuhnt) important or on the subject

phrase (fraze) a group of words that contains either a noun (or pronoun) or a verb but not both

plot (plot) the sequence of events in a narrative

plural noun (PLOOR uhl noun) a noun that names more than one person, place, thing, or idea

point-by-point pattern (point-beye-point PAT urn) a way of organizing comparison-and-contrast writing by telling about one point, or feature, of one item and then comparing and contrasting the same feature of a second item; after that, another feature is compared for two items, and so on

point of view (point uhv vyoo) the perspective from which the story is told

possession (puh ZESH uhn) the act or state of owning something

possessives (puh ZESS ivz) nouns that show that a thing is possessed, or owned, by another person, place, or thing

possessive pronoun (puh ZESS iv PROH noun) a type of pronoun that replaces a noun that shows ownership

precedes (pree SEEDZ) comes before

precise (pri SAYHS) exact or specific

predicate (PRED i kit) the part of a sentence that contains a verb telling what the subject is or what it does

predict (pri DIKT) to guess what will happen in advance

prefix (PREE fiks) a word part that is added to the beginning of a base word

preposition (prep uh ZISH uhn) a word that shows the relation of a noun with another part of the sentence

prepositional phrase (prep uh ZISH uh nuhl fraze) a word group that begins with a preposition and ends with a noun or pronoun

present perfect tense (PREZ uhnt PUR fikt tenss) a verb form that tells that an action was started in the past and is continuing in the present or that it has just been completed

prewriting (pree RITE ing) the first step in the writing process, during which ideas are formed, developed, and organized

primary character (PRAHY mer ee KA rik tuhr) the main or most important character in a story

process (PRAH sess) a series of actions for doing something

pronoun (PROH noun) a word that replaces and refers to a noun

proper noun (PROP ur noun) a type of noun that names a specific person, place, thing, or idea; proper nouns are always capitalized

protagonist (proh TAG uh nist) the primary charaacter whose actions the story follows

punctuation (puhngk choo AY shuhn) marks, such as periods, commas, and quotation marks, used in sentences

Q

question (KWESS chuhn) a type of sentence that asks something and ends with a question mark

quotation (kwoh TAY shuhn) the exact words that somebody has said

R

reaction (REE ack SHUN) a strategy to structure an argument used to analyze thoughts

recognize (RE kuhg nize) to identify someone or thing

reference (REF uh ruhnss) the connection to the antecedent of a pronoun

reflect (ri FLEKT) think directly about the significance of an event

regular verb (REG yuh lure vurb) a verb that forms its past and past participle forms in a regular, or predictable, way

relative pronoun (REL uh tiv PROH noun) a pronoun that introduces a relative clause; who, that, which, and whose are relative pronouns

relevant (REL uh vuhnt) having importance; being on the subject

renaming phrase (ree NAYM ing fraze) a modifying phrase that gives more information about a noun; it is made up of a noun and other words that modify that noun (appositive)

reposition (ri puh ZISH uhn) to put something in a different position

resolution (rez uh LOO shuhn) the solution to the problem

restrictive clause (ri STRIK tiv klawz) a clause that does not have commas and contains information that is essential to the meaning of a sentence

revise (ri VIZE) to change writing in order to correct or improve it

rhetorical question (ri TAWR i kuhl KWES chuhn) a statement phrased in the form of a question; it does not require an answer

rising action (RAHY zing AK shuhn) the events that make the primary character's conflict more challenging or compelling and builds to the climax

rough draft (ruhf DRAFT) the first draft of a piece of writing in which ideas are put into sentences and paragraphs for the first time

round character (round KA rik tuhr) a character who changes over the course of the story

run-on sentence (ruhn-on SEN tuhnss) a compound sentence that is incorrectly joined so that the ideas run together

S

secondary character (SEK uhn der ee KA rik tuhr) a character who supports the primary character

semicolon (SEM i koh luhn) a kind of punctuation used in forming compound sentences and in separating items in a series that contains commas

sensory language (SEN suh ree LANG gwij) language that appeals to at least one of the five senses

sentence (SEN tuhnss) a group of words that contains a subject and a predicate and that expresses a complete thought

sequence (SEE kwuhnss) the order in which events happen

setting (SET ing) the time and place of the action in a story

simple future tense (SIM puhl FYOO chur tenss) a verb tense that shows an action that will occur in the future

simple past tense (SIM puhl past tenss) a verb form that shows actions that occurred at a specific time in the past

simple present tense (SIM puhl PREZ uhnt tenss) a verb form that tells what is happening or is true at the present time, that shows actions that are performed regularly, or that tells what is always true

simple sentence (SIM puhl SEN tuhnss) the most basic, or simple, form of the complete sentence; it has one subject and one predicate and expresses a complete thought

simple subject (SIM puhl SUHB jikt) the most basic part of the subject of a sentence; it is what or whom the sentence is about but does not include any descriptive words that are part of the complete subject

singular noun (SING gyuh lur noun) a noun that names only one person, place, thing, or idea

stages (STAY jiz) steps in a process

standard English (STAN derd Eng LISH) form of spoken and written English language recognized as correct and acceptable

statement (STATE muhnt) a type of sentence that gives information and ends with a period

statistics (stuh TIS tiks) number-based facts

style (stile) how words and sentences are used to express meaning

subject (SUHB jikt) the part of a sentence that tells whom or what a sentence is about

subject pronoun (SUHB jikt PROH noun) a type of pronoun that takes the place of a noun that is used as the subject of a sentence

subjective first-person narrator (SUB jek tiv furst PUR suhn NAR ey ter) a participant in and teller of a story who shows bias

subjunctive mood (SUHB juhnk tiv mood) a verb form that expresses a command, a wish, or a condition that is contrary to fact

suffix (SHUF iks) a word part that is added to the end of a base word

summarize (SUHM ur ize) to express the main ideas of a passage in your own words

support (suh port) to help prove

support conclusions (suh PORT kuhn KLOO shuhns) to provide evidence to back up your conclusion

supporting sentences (suh PORT ing SEN tuhn sez) sentences in a paragraph that add details to back up the main idea

T

tense (tense) the time of the action

third-person narrator (thurd PUR suhn NAR ey ter) a teller of a story who does not participate in events and uses third-person pronouns, such as they, she, or his

time order (time or dur) a way of organizing writing according to the order in which events happen

tone (tohn) the language used by a writer to make his or her point

topic sentence (top ik SEN tuhnss) the sentence in a paragraph that tells what the rest of the paragraph is about

transition (tran ZISH uhn) connecting word or phrase that gives the reader a clue about the order of events or how the events are connected

V

verb (vurb) the most important part of a predicate; tells what the subject is or does

verb phrase (vurb fraze) a group of words that begins with a verb and acts as a modifier

verb sequence (vurb SEE kwuhnss) the order and tense of verbs in a sentence; the verbs must work together to tell correctly when the different actions happened

visualize (VIZH oo uh lize) to create mental pictures

W

whole-to-whole pattern (hole-too-hole PAT urn) a way of organizing comparison-and-contrast writing by first telling all about one item and then telling how another item is alike and different from the first one

Index

V

W